THE TRUTH OF THINGS

THE TRUTH OF THINGS

Liberal Arts and the Recovery of Reality

MARION MONTGOMERY

SPENCE PUBLISHING COMPANY • DALLAS

1999

Published in the United States by
Spence Publishing Company
111 Cole Street
Dallas, Texas 75207

Library of Congress Cataloging-in-Publication Data

Montgomery, Marion
    The truth of things : liberal arts and the recovery of reality / Marion
    Montgomery
        p. cm.
    Includes bibliographical references and index.
    ISBN 1-9653208-7-1 (hard)
    1. Education, Higher—United States—Philosophy.   2. Education,
Humanistic.   I. Title.
LA227.4.M66   1999
378'.01'0973—dc21   98-49943

Printed in the United States of America

The purpose of the study of philosophy
is not to learn what others have thought,
but to learn how the truth of things stands.

St. Thomas Aquinas

Contents

Preface

PLATO, AFTER THE EXECUTION OF SOCRATES in 399 BC, went into exile, returning to Athens after some years to found his Academy. One might say that this proves one good effect of our first arresting teacher evaluation, though as Socrates remarks after his condemnation, such good ends were not intentional on the part of those students testifying against him at his trial. Of those who condemned Socrates, Plato has Socrates say "They have done me no harm, although they did not mean to do me any good." For a moment at least, following his condemnation, they might feel relieved. These are the Athenians whom Socrates names as specialists—poets and politicians, craftsmen and rhetoricians (as Socrates names them by profession in the *Apology*). No longer threatened, since Socrates is sentenced to death, they may return to the usual tenor of their days, that clear and present danger having been removed. Socrates, in the final haunting public statement which concludes the *Apology*, says, "We go our ways—I to die, and you to live. Which is better God only knows."

And so a fortunate accident in the history of Western civilization—this first student evaluation brought to terminal resolution by hemlock. But Plato, at the moment a rich young dandy, must have been shocked by the enclosing world's reality. He sees then as unde-

ix

niable his Athens in a rapid decay. From our late perspective, we might put it that Athens was on one of those slippery slopes on which we are caught again and again in our history when we become captive to an idea out of reality. All about Plato, democracy proved in radical fermentation, a souring from which Athens never recovered. And that young patrician, with his youthful dreams of perhaps becoming a writer of plays, flees Athens, leaves home. He becomes a philosopher peripatetic, a *starets* of intellect, or perhaps more properly, an intellectual Odysseus.

A decade later, Plato returns home. Judging by the issue of his return, especially as reflected in the philosophical drama he leaves us, he must have been enabled by then to know the place for the first time. He could at last better understand the relation of his possible academy to the always volatile *polis*. And he must have been the more haunted by the memory of his old mentor now dead and largely gone out of the Athenian mind in the lapse of a decade. The wisdom in Socrates's remembered words moved a wiser Plato to set about recapturing, to the benefit of his new Academy, that permanent wisdom. The Academy established, its reputation becomes pervasive in Western intellectual history, centering in the patrician-turned-poet's recovery of that resolute, genial teacher now dead, an old wise man who left no publications on his *vita*.

The first among his students, Plato thus dramatized Socrates in timeless monuments to intellect, the dialogues. And in that local wash of ideas upon present events, Plato began to draw students, including his own student of students—Aristotle—the Stagirite who migrated south out of Macedonia to the rumored Academy. And we? We are still attempting to come to terms with this Greek triumvirate—the scholar Aristotle issuing out of the garrulous old man Socrates, Aristotle's intellectual grandfather, through that affluent and talented young gentleman philosopher and would-be dramatist, Plato. Socrates, Plato, Aristotle: they in turn are teachers of giants in those old days from Alexander the Great to St. Augustine and St. Thomas Aquinas and down to us.

And so the intricate after effects of that first student evaluation, the famous trial of Socrates, in which he is charged with examining the nature of truth too closely and so corrupting Athenian youth. In his own defense, he enunciates his first concern for the intellect: that it "care about the greatest improvement of the soul." The statistical results of that public evaluation, incidentally, were well-suited to administrative decision. Some 280 of those to whom Socrates presents himself as teacher at his trial find him guilty as charged. Another 221 would have forgiven his teaching as not responsible for corrupting Athenian youth, presumably judging that an Alcibiades hardly needed a teacher to discover moral corruption. It will be Plato's evaluation, of course, that speaks to the virtues of Socrates as teacher.

Socrates ridicules a subsidiary charge against him, namely that he not only taught but took money for his teaching. He needed only to point to his impoverished state in defense. Xanthippe, his wife, may well have had a legitimate grievance against Socrates for not taking money, leaving their children to be raised in the increasing family poverty. (Not much is heard of Socrates's three sons in the aftermath of that famous trial and execution.) As for Socrates's own judgment of the "punishment" justly due him when he is declared guilty, he is required by the formal procedure of the trial to propose it for his jury's consideration. "What would be a reward suitable to a poor man who is your benefactor, and who desires leisure that he may instruct you? There can be no reward so fitting as maintenance in the Prytaneum [Athens's "city hall"]." In our terms, he proposes a permanent chair in philosophy at state expense. That is his proposal, against his accuser Meletus, who demands the death penalty on the poet's behalf.

Out of such confused beginnings, out of personal experiences of the world of humankind at home and abroad, Plato returns home to establish his Academy ten years after Socrates's death. And in doing so, he influences forever Western (and much of Eastern) pursuits of order in nature and in society made in the name of education. He establishes the Academy on a fundamental premise: knowledge, properly pursued and governed by the truth intellect encounters, anticipates a growth of the intellectual person toward understanding, and sets him on the road toward intellectual perfection through the hope of wisdom. As he has his mentor Socrates say at his trial, at the price

of his life, "The unexamined life is not worth living." That principle
has been the traditional justification of the academy in the West ever
since, though a principle now eroded almost beyond recovery. The
prospect of its final solution—its finally dissolving in a final leaching
out of intellect from the academy—seems imminent at our century's
end, in danger of being accomplished by a pragmatism struck in, as it
were; pragmatism perverted requires that the person's life be left
unexamined, lest the sovereignty of the individual in his pursuit of
self-love be compromised.

This species of pragmatism is currently exercised through intellectual sophistry—Socrates's old and most bitter enemies, the Sophists, being still with us. Through a pragmatism made respectable to
the *polis* in the late nineteenth century, the "American mind" became
increasingly its own specialization, an honorable perfection of means
thus perverted to an end by intellect itself. Thus prudence, the governor of pragmatism, was usurped. That transformation is evidenced
to us particularly in the variety of professionalisms to which the academy has become primarily devoted. The distortion lies in the assumption that specialization is the primary end, whereby we may be
declared "educated"—another word for which, increasingly, is "em-
ployable." Such an elevation of an honorable, but secondary, dimension of "higher education" has been made possible and makes itself
possible as end, because the generality of our social body has become
enthralled by technological revolutions which promise more and more
of less and less. We see the acceleration of this distortion of intellectual responsibility in the interval from the invention of the steam
engine and its promises of transformation of nature down to our own
invention of electronic devices promising a transcendence of reality
through virtual reality, that last escape possible to self-love drawn
into spiritual despair.

And so we find ourselves a long way from Plato, though his name,
or a phrase credited to him or Socrates, may appear on a random
cornice of a decaying building on some university campus. Such in-
scriptions are largely lost in this new academy, the multiversity of
recent notoriety, where told (in its literal sense) but unknown thou-
sands pursue higher education tailored to "individual" need or desire.

Up to the Renaissance, and then lingering thereafter until the accelerated dissolving in our century, the common concern for knowledge by the intellectual community still anticipated knowledge as leading to understanding, and thence mayhap to wisdom, the old Platonic ideal. That concern was oriented to the discrete *person*—not to the "individual" and his specialized needs.

In the *person*—as opposed to the abstract individual defined gnostically and abstractly by his peculiar needs and unexamined desires—there had once been supposed an inherent love of or desire for the relative perfection of his particular gifts as person. Education, then, might make possible the limited perfection of the person's peculiar gifts as an intellectual soul incarnate, requiring a piety *toward* and a piety in the person which did not assume that his dignity as person was determined by the terminal degree earned as an instrument of power. The orders of education, in the traditional view, do not register the worth of a person to community according to the level of his membership in community, though it recognized, and did not blink in its recognition, that (as St. Paul says) through the grace given us as person, we have gifts differing one from another. The point was self-evident to intellectual souls incarnate before and after Paul—by Plato, Aristotle, Augustine, Aquinas; by both ancient and recent stewards of intellect. But such stewards most recently have had difficulty in maintaining their stewardship in service to intellect as the common gift to a humanity differing in degree, certainly as they might attempt stewardship from within the academy itself. Theirs is a vision increasingly foreign to the latest pragmatic concerns, the latest utilitarian emphasis upon education as itself the highest good to the "individual" and to "society."

And so these essays that follow are from one such steward, who supposes himself to be such at least. As such I am convinced of a prophetic responsibility: namely, to recall us to known but forgotten or programatically rejected understandings of education. I would speak to such a concern, on behalf of that abiding "academician," the "lover of wisdom," the true "philosopher," who proves timeless in history, and so who will and must recover those virtues suited to the academy as devoted to "higher education" in the interest of community in time. Of course, as the point is put in one of these pieces, to love wisdom is not thereby to be made wise, as if our beginning were our end. Rather, to love wisdom is to desire and to labor toward the gift of wisdom. To love wisdom is to remove obstacles to wisdom, through whatever perfection is possible to those discrete gifts of intellect peculiar to each person—to each according to his gifts. That was, and continues to be, the fascination of that continuing witness of Socrates, who as intellectual creature (without academic degree) proves exemplum of the intellectual person as *homo viator*—the person as philosopher, the lover of wisdom pursuing to his last breath, with both wonder and awe, the truth of things. Or so Plato remembers Socrates dying on his prison cot in the *Phaedo*. How excruciating to his young followers, his reporting the details of the hemlock's effect on his body in death's gradual dissociation of sensibilities, the separation of thought and feeling. In this light we may at least glimpse wisdom in its effect upon the person Socrates, calm yet still arduous in his pursuit of his perfection as this particular person thus particularly gifted. He had even attempted poetry in those last days, lest he had misunderstood the injunction of his familiar spirit that he must "make music," concluding that the poets in Athens were free of his death bed competition, since his gifts were not the poet's, but the philosopher's as musician.

And so are we all *particularly* gifted, though not *exceptionally* gifted as Socrates was both. Particular gifts, then, were not seen by Socrates as an end in themselves, as they were to his antagonists, the Sophists. Without this understanding of the proper address toward the seeking of knowledge, the academician becomes at best a technician, as if technology itself were the god to be served. As an exemplum to the academic person, then, Socrates proves at his greatest himself the best of all students.

Such is a distinction these essays intend to recover, a distinction which should properly be nurtured by the academy, though in our moment the academy distorts such a distinction in the variety of vested interests struggling for dominance. In the recovery of this distinction lies the possibility of an ordinate pious-address to specialization itself as both desirable and honorable, but not ultimate to the well-

being of the person, nor ultimate to community. Thus even "academic" specialization might be recovered as desirable, but desirable
as a means to a higher end in service to the body of community, not
merely servicing the appetitive order of individuals collectively called
society, but in service to the community as a body of members. In
that term *society* the nature of *community,* as is the nature of *person*
through the reductive term *individual,* has been lost.

As for the confusing reality of the academy in our moment, within
it there continues the deliberate (though sometimes merely accidental or thoughtless) deconstruction of both person and community.
Such is the effect of the distortion of the traditional understanding
of the liberal arts. The deconstruction has occurred in order to redi-
rect liberal arts disciplines, peculiar to an ancient curriculum, to serve
the practical convenience of the academician or the department or
the school in its pursuit of specialization. What has ensued is the
conflict of disparate ideologies in contention for power over the fal-
tering academic body. So disparate are these ideologies, indeed, as to
lead to civil wars, though each faction will in some moment of heated
battle declare its cause that of the "rights of the individual" or of the
"common good," as opposed to its responsibilities to the person and
the common nurture of persons in community.

If we look at the academy at the close of our century, we find
there are no longer "two cultures," arts and sciences, aligned separately and in opposition, their battle lines extending out of the academy into society. That was Sir C. P. Snow's mid-century argument
and lament, in his once-famous *Two Cultures,* the circumstances of
intellectual confrontation by the "arts" on one side and the "sciences"
on the other having grown out of nineteenth century dislocations.
We, as Flannery O'Connor's provincial Modernist isolated on a back-
country farm might say, are more advanced than the scientist-novel-
ist, Snow. For we now have multiple cultures, as many as there are
sovereign individuals committed to the paramount rights of the "self."
That integer the "individual" is more and more coming to itself in a
dark wood as an isolated, alienated, frustrated, and increasingly furi-
ous "consciousness" in reaction to all save itself, however wily it may
at times become in idealizing self-love with borrowed clichés from

that older intellectual tradition stretching back to Plato. What is
happening is that the thing called *individual* discovers itself a lost
person—the condition necessary to the effects we now witness on those
intellectual reservations called the academy, whereon there proceeds
as yet unchecked the barbarization of intellectual integrity.

Intellectual barbarism envelops persons for the moment in the
conspicuous spectacles of crisis in the political and social dimensions
of our lives as a people, and the confusion is particularly evident within
the academy as it pretends to serve us from its privileged position.
Its fundamental doctrine, suited to manipulations by self-love in pursuit of the conveniences of power, is a presumption about the nature
of intellect itself, radically at odds with the traditional orthodoxy of
Western Christendom. Intellect, this doctrine holds, is autonomous.
And that principle accepted, one is justified in an angelism presumed
both means and end to self-rescue. What Dante called perverted
love, love turned in upon the self, replaces that openness of charity
through which existence and the Cause of existence can be celebrated.
The substitute doctrine has gained ascendancy since the Renaissance,
at last permeating Western people and their institutions at every level.
And so the final chapter in this volume approaches critically that
new religion, Modernism, with some attention to its recent history.
But a word in advance here may help prepare the reader.

In that new religion of Modernism, authority is made to depend
upon the power accumulated by a particular fortunate or gifted intellect responding to the moment's contingencies—whether he be (to
put the point at once playfully and seriously) an instructor before
freshmen, a chaired professor, a dean, a senator, or at an extremity of
the new priesthood, a Hitler or a Stalin. What is crucial is the relativity accompanying power, which when the relativity itself becomes
the guiding metaphysical vision can but result in abusive internecine
destructions of community. The reality of relative power becomes
central in determining the actions of the particular person coinci-
dent with the struggle for power. And that is a contradiction, since it
recognizes a reality separate from the intentionalizing of power.

This is to say that the Modernist doctrine of autonomy of intellect cannot acknowledge any given, such as its own relative power,

since the survival of autonomous intellect through will cannot acknowledge a givenness. Such an acknowledgment would require of
intellect itself that it confront the mystery of givenness. There must
to the contrary be first, last, and always an affirmation by the intend-
ing autonomous intellect of a self-credit. The principle popularized
and seductive of naive intellects, most particularly the idealistic young,
is a slogan now met everywhere: *You can be whatever you want to be.*
That is a denial of gifts, and a denial very central to Modernism's
most celebrated philosophy, Existentialism, now formally out of favor in the academy, even in departments of philosophy, though yet
pervasive in the intellectual community, whether in the sciences or
the arts. Existentialism is *formally* out of favor, since any philosophy
formalized and adopted as patterning action becomes thereby a focal
point of rigorous interrogation, requiring only one Socrates or Plato
or Aristotle to expose its flaws.

Such rigorous interrogation within an approving auspices of the
academy at once implies and gradually recovers principles governed
by truth, regardless of any pervasive intellectual relativism. But without such a pervasive relativism, that intellectual chaos characteristic
of the academy at our century's end becomes critically vulnerable.
Indeed, it is such endangerment that gives rise to the academy's support of the "politically correct" as a protection of intellectual Chaos.
Existentialism in its Modernist dress is that of a species of relativism
which is the second most ancient spiritual commitment. The first is
that openness which the love of wisdom would recover to community, that openness of awe and wonder before the truth, which might
well be termed a consent to reality proper to love. The second oldest
is self-love, for which ancient intellectual tradition Jean-Paul Sartre
proved for a time an effective spokesman. We recall that Milton in
his great epic *Paradise Lost* dramatizes this philosophical relativism,
almost endangering his poem as his agent of self-love almost steals
the poem from him, for the temptation to self-love lies in Satan's *non
serviam.*

If Modernism trembles even now on the point of conquest, it
does so through some species of "democratic" consent to relativism.
(Ours is not the only species of "democracy," as the Soviet and Nazi

citizens might have said to us in the 1930s.) This is to say that Modernism can have its way opened to power only through the consent of the popular spirit. And that spirit has proved amenable as it becomes mesmerized by any of several versions of utopian Edens as projected imminent through collective power, predicted therefore by projection in five- or fifty-year plans by any current lord or lords of power. As for the mesmerizing means necessary to popular consent, material conveniences oriented to appetitive ends have proved widely effective in this century, whose slogan is an ancient one turned upside down: once wisdom held that man does not live by bread alone; now bread becomes the rallying standard. (How inevitable the slang term for money, *bread*, though the user of the term seldom has in mind actual milk for the infant or grain for its mother.)

And so man, persuaded that the essence of his nature is that of appetitive animal, disguises such a raw reductionism of humanity through sophisticated justifications of the appetitive as ultimate, borrowing in doing so words and concepts from the older tradition it has perverted. The skillfully rhetorical advocate for the "common good," in manipulating what Richard Weaver calls "god-terms," has his way with a common consent, our century particularly littered with the destructions consequent upon such consent. At century's end, however, we encounter one effect upon that common consent not anticipated by Modernism, whose spokesmen currently sound the alarm. The citizenry has become cynical. In evidence, a report by the Committee for the Study of the American Electorate, which finds that in the 1996 Presidential election, despite an increase of registered voters by seven million over the 1992 election, voter turnout declined in every state of the union as compared to that already low turnout in 1992.

That the citizenry has become cynical may be a sign of hope. That is, cynicism may be seen as a symptom of spiritual agitation, and as such promising of some restoration. In cynicism, then, there may begin an awakening to the spiritual destruction of persons in consequence of the person's having been reduced to an integer—the "individual"—in that new Gnostic intent to collective power which is bent upon reconstituting both nature and society through its new "metaphysics." The *meta* of this *physics* becomes the angelistic self as lord of the limits of reality, that angelistic self therefore the only acceptable god to Modernism. In a new disguise of totalitarian intent by such a self, the term "democracy" is transformed from its ancient Greek address to a desirable polity, the possible polity engaged by Socrates, Plato, Aristotle.

In its place, we have an adaptation of the Nietzschean myth of autonomous intellect as the only acceptable "democracy" of the self. The activist slogan becomes "Every individual a Super-individual." We need only listen carefully to political arguments here and abroad to recognize this as true, since every "individual" must by law be declared to have a right to "be" whatever that individual wishes to be. The danger, and the hope, in our recognition of this truth by the "popular spirit" would be despair, out of its arrest on a sentimental faith in the individual's appetitive desires as ultimate. Hence we suggest that the cynicism growing within Modernist establishment of the outer parameters of human existence might issue in an eruption of those false parameters in recovered hope.

This Modernist religion and its strategies, concentrated upon intellect as materialistically imminent (through biophysics in its rapid advances in genetic specialization), now occupies the academy. But it has done so for many years. As we suggested, however, it can do so only with the consent of "society" at large, which it purports to serve first and last. At the moment, though with that growing cynicism that wakes intellect in the diverse "public" to a skepticism as a growing threat to the Modernist presumptions, the academy still enjoys society's consent. That is, it enjoys the material support necessary to its survival—a givenness to be transformed by its religion of service to community. The givenness of consent and the givenness of taxed income to higher education is transubstantiated to a largesse beyond reckoning, according to elaborated catalogues and public relations brochures. That such a mystery occurs needs only the evidence of peer testimony among specialized intellects, advertised by those public relations departments of universities that require several George Orwells to reveal absurdities.

The wind has shifted, however, and from a new quarter blows a

temperate but increasingly hot climate upon academic reservations—
the cynicism we suggest as a growing breeze of hope. And so these
essays are at once a primary indictment of the academic world of the
moment, and a secondary indictment of the fragmenting, decaying
community which has so vagrantly consented to and supported the
academy which has proved almost its mortal enemy. But beyond those
concerns is deeper, more positive concern for the abiding reality, which
I believe will speak to the student, old or young—the student discovering himself akin intellectually to Socrates. He will find himself in
a line of descent, a continuing community of intellect, which maintains that the person is intellectual soul incarnate. As such, responsible for the perfection of his gifts as person possible only in a pursuit of wisdom, he may even in these most desperate straits of intellect pursue understanding, which recovers to him the hope of wisdom.

TWO OF THESE ESSAYS first appeared in *Modern Age*: "The Segregation That is Needed," v:1 (Winter 1960) and "Wanted: A Better Reason as Guide," xxxii:1 (Winter 1988). "The Fallacy of Practicality"
appeared in the *Arlington Quarterly*, 1:3 (Spring 1968). "The Journey
Toward Wisdom" in a shorter version was the Henry A. Bundschu
Visiting Scholar Lecture at Rockhurst College in November 1991.

THE TRUTH OF THINGS

Introduction

THE FIRST THREE OF THESE PIECES were written as essays; the
next three as invited lectures; the final piece was in response
to an invitation to write a definition of "Modernism" for an
encyclopedia but too extensive for that use. They are diverse as well
in that the first two were written long ago, while I was just beginning
my teaching career—a beginning which lasted for many years. (A
friend described me at that period as "the oldest PFC east of the Mississippi River.") I wrote the first, "The Segregation That Is Needed,"
just as the question of race was becoming a social, political, and educational concern across the country. The piece was published in 1960
but written in the late 1950s. A part of my intent there was to fore-
warn that a merely legal solution to such a problem, and such problems attendant upon the question of race, would exacerbate the
problem if limited to a technical concern for legal justice. An adequate solution, I contended, must rest on principles determined by
the realities of our nature as specific, created persons.

That would mean we must recover those principles—valid because determined by reality itself in all its particularities—by confronting those existential realities anew. Thus we might regain
confidence in our own experience. And I had no doubt that our experience would echo again and again the experiences of others, not

3

only in the present moment, but anciently and in the future. For that is the secret of "tradition," "Modernist" caricatures of traditionalism notwithstanding: the experience of a discrete intellectual soul in its moment of history finds an echo of its experience in the thoughtful testimony of those souls preceding it in history. But it is not simply a sequential history, tradition thus narrowly supposed, that produces the verity to be held. It is the truth of existence itself in all its complexities reflected in the immediate experience of others. That is the subtlety in a sound "traditionalism" easily overlooked or distorted.

The reality is that distinct gifts attach to the specific person precisely because he is *specific*. And rather than necessarily bespeaking an inequality among persons which would justify revolt against reality itself, the *specificity* of gift is to be valued, honored, respected by a common piety, a piety required of our relation to existence itself. Piety, then, is the proper deportment of intellect in its consent to the actual limits of the specific gifts of being as discovered within the complexity we call reality. Those gifts of being make a thing to be the thing it is and no other in relation to, and only in relation to, their limits. Now, if this be a valid principle derived from the experiences of reality itself by the intellectual soul, it is a serious violation to deny the particularities of each singular creature. The most immediate violation is of the very "self" in which denial of limit is centered. To pretend to an *equality* of gift in discrete intellectual creatures, as opposed to advancing a contextual social equity of "opportunity" toward the realization of discrete potentialities, is to transgress against the reality of personhood. That such transgression is common is a central complaint I raise early and late, noting in doing so that the transgressors confuse (whether deliberately or in ignorance) the contextual social equity, which is rightly proper, with a substantive equality declared specific in discrete persons. The pretense is that by the mere declaration of an intrinsic equality of gifts in persons an *essential* identity among persons is thereby effected. One sees at once how convenient such a confusion of thought is to political or ideological expediency. What is to be lamented as consequent to such manipulative expediency we too seldom see: the victim of such transgressions of reality again and again is the person in whose name the transgression is committed—transgressions of our personhood always committed in the name of justice. Indeed, such has been the effect of the strategy that we slowly come to be suspicious of anyone who cries a new program in the name of "justice."

I believed at the time of these early essays, as I believe now—though I think I understand my belief more fully now—that it is through gifts differing one from another that we are the particular person we are. But the very gifts which make us particular also define finitudes in us. Without the limit of gifts, we would not be at all. It is the limit of our being this *particular* person that circumscribes us, making us thereby different one from another. What is crucial in this view is that we recognize that difference as here understood is not determinate of our moral worth as persons. The moral dimension emerges through intellectual action. We do right or wrong according to whether we respond *to* or *against* reality itself, according to whether we govern actions by a will that consents to the truth of things, or resist the truth of things by willful self-love.

The refusal to make such a distinction clouds our understanding of justice and leads us to take abstractions of reality as absolutes. It is this sort of transgression of reality that plagues us as a community of souls in our attempts to order community socially or politically or educationally. One indication of the impasse we have reached from our failure to make fundamental distinctions is the present civil war conducted against industrialism's abuses of creation. The laissez-faire uses of creation having lost orientation in responsible stewardship, the "environment" unquestionably suffers, though we are not always clear in our naming of that suffering thing. Those who intuitively object to encroaching disorders rally persons who are most variously disaffected to "environmental" causes that more often than not lack an ordinate grounding in complex reality. Thus the vague doctrine called "environmentalism" lacks that old grounding in reality that could locate the disorder in the individual soul, and so require moral responsibility in the name of that soul, rather than in the name of an amorphous "environment." In that older vision of the orders of existence within which the soul flourishes or decays, the responsible office of stewardship related discrete persons to creation as stewards of creation. For stewardship recognizes and sets as central to the circumstances of human existence in nature man's peculiar position. Man differs from all other creatures within the orders of being itself, in respect to which difference the doctrine of stewardship affirms his responsibility for the well-being of the whole of creation. It is a responsibility *consequent* to his peculiar nature. *Stewardship*, then, is a more specific and concrete terming of the proper relationship of man to creation than that magic term extracted from the complexities of being and sterilized by abstractionism, "environmentalism."

We have abandoned that old perspective in favor of reducing all the orders of being to an equality, to an identity, whereby man is yet distinct from other creatures, but only as a destructive aggressor.* Thus his responsibility for his conduct toward creation by virtue of his intellectual gift dissipates, till intellect itself is denied an ascendant actuality as a positive good in creation. We would rather be a pair of ragged claws than man thinking. Thus man is, in a sense, decreed bestial in this vagueness of thought, precisely because he is an intellectual creature. All else is "natural," is *angelic* as it were, because perfectly "natural" when freed of man's intellectual intrusions upon it. What happens when this species of thought, associated with environmentalism as a movement, encounters rapacious laissez-faire transgressions of existential creatures is a continuing battle which might well be named by Matthew Arnold's once famous lines:

---

*   On this Fourth of July (1991), I received a catalogue from an environmentalist mail order business which presents a parody of the Declaration of Independence, though it intends no parody but rather a transcendental version as the formative doctrine of environmentalism. Declaring that "all creatures and their offspring in perpetuity are endowed equally with certain inalienable rights" (summed up in the phrase "Safe Environment" in the document), it details a concern to "promote Conservation of Resources" and "embrace Renewable Energy Technologies," and so on. To these concerns we are invited to "mutually pledge . . . our commitment to promote conscious and conservative use of energy." We should declare that "to these goals we dedicate our lives."

we are here as on a darkling plain
Swept with confused alarms of struggle and flight,
Where ignorant armies clash by night.

I

On the centenary of Leo XIII's *Rerum novarum*, which engaged the secular materialism sweeping East and West a hundred years ago, John Paul II issued his encyclical *Centesimus annus*, calling points of order in the continuing struggle by recalling reality as the determinant of order. But meanwhile the civil war continues, and its locus of ideological engagement has become the academy in this concluding decade of our century. With the academy's facilities for abstractionism, technological instruments of an impressive variety operated by impressive intellects specialized almost to the extinction of intellect, the orders of creation are progressively reduced to identities. Whether in respect to atoms or individuals, intellect by means of the machine becomes arbiter of order. Specific intellects, contrary to the operative principle of identity executed instrumentally, operate as agents of order among identities which were once seen as distinct existent things. That such a commanding of power over being is thoroughly illusional when taken as vision allows destructions in the true orders of being. That is the inevitable effect in this moment, and nowhere is that destruction more evident than in the reduction of persons to integers in the mechanism called "society."

Nor is that reductionism anywhere more evident as intellect's *modus operandi* than in the academy. Hence an irony of great magnitude: the collapse of the academy. For the academy, properly the steward of intellectual order, having failed in its stewardship, has fed the general community false doctrine. The effect redounds upon the academy. Thus at the political level of our life as a community, we have become habituated to deny the discrete gifts of particularity to each person in the name of "individuality." The distorted principle we suppose to be self-evident. We assure our young that *anyone* can be a surgeon or concert pianist, or even president of the whole country. We put it: "*Anyone* can be whatever *they* want to be!" The unsuitable verbalization, at the expense of grammar and clarity, is an effect on the surface of a fear of "discrimination." For to say "whatever *he* wants to be" is discriminatory. But the obfuscation is out of false concepts more than being merely a surface failure in the use of signs, of words at the level of grammar. The failure of the academy to see this difference between the disease itself and the symptoms of disease largely explains the failure of those "remedial courses" that now inundate undergraduate education. It becomes depressing to see a new truth about higher education: curricula are built either on the necessities of remedial courses or on ideological programs. And when the remedial courses become dominated by ideological concerns, any sanity to any curriculum is hopelessly destroyed.

One need only listen to commencement addresses by name speakers to hear variations on this false shibboleth, which leads the young into cruel realities if they are not still young enough to recognize its falseness. For when such a young person's disoriented desire encounters reality, he will not have had a sufficient preparation to discriminate: to know whether the "system" denies his dream (and there are always manipulators at hand to assure him this is indeed the full truth), or whether his own gifts, whether his own "nature," limits his desire, or whether the tensional causes between established "system" and personal limit require a more careful sorting out. He becomes too often, not a rebel without a cause, but a frustrated soul denied that elementary knowledge of reality which would allow him to discriminate among causes. For he has been encouraged to believe himself his own cause, often by confused patrons with good intent but bad judgment. Thus his unexamined desire is elevated as a power sufficient to effect its object as a rightful possession. However vaguely he "feels" that he would like to be pianist or surgeon or the like, he has a "right" to be such. In his failure, he will "feel" that he has been denied a "natural" right, rather than that he has been denied the dignity possible through his gifts perfected in themselves, which perfection may fall far short of his being a surgeon or a pianist.

The letter divorced from reality through such shibboleths as those used to confuse our young is an empty letter, a vacuum of a letter pretending to be an ideal formulation, whose "transcendent" anchor turns out to be at best his own vague desire. What is thus presumed by a reductionist faith in such empty formulae is that desire itself is sufficient to summon substantive reality. By *willing* the desired thing—so it is supposed—the "calling" desired will be effected. There is comic ridicule, easy to our words, when we hear an evangelist advance himself as "self-called," though he insist he is called personally by God to act for our salvation. But we generally fail to see the same operation in our secular conduct, whereby we assume that our identity as person is the effect of our own self-calling: that is the principle when we declare that an individual can be whatever he wishes to be. Where intellect supposes the will a sufficient agent to transform any reality, the rigid letter of the law by a common consent becomes the instrument with which to manipulate reality. Such instrumentality, created by abstractionism, has always proved expedient in keeping certain manipulative persons in offices of power, whether high or low offices—in the family, in the community, in the seats of government or institutions. But perhaps never before has such abuse through abstractionism been so widely practiced among mankind as in our century. It is this expediency which has contributed more and more to the academy's collapse. The bitter irony of the academy's role in our fragmenting disorientation as community, its expedient consent to false words, is that it is the academy's special charge to stand against *unreality* as a governing principle to intellectual actions. Put positively, it is the academy's responsibility to see that words are suited to the complexity of reality, not divorced from reality in order to build dream visions incapable of realization and so disintegrative of the community, however much declared integrative.

We shall not be concerned directly with the political dimension of the academy's manipulations of the truth of things, but rather with the intellectual consent of academicians to falsifications of reality, the high treason of intellect to itself. For it is that consent that establishes false principles as ideals to justify intellect to itself as its own cause. We have said that such consent to violation of the truth of things, including the truth of discrete persons, declares an equality among persons as *substantively* fundamental. Even so, the practical necessities to the operation of the academy gives the lie to this principle: namely the abstraction from person of that modernist creature, the *individual*. Individual, then, becomes an integer in the calculus designed to manipulate society. But reality denies the academy's pretense to this intellectual imposition of substantive existence by the agency of its own abstractions. Academies, famous or unknown, have found it increasingly necessary to establish remedial programs in the elementary grammars of science, mathematics, and language. The necessity is in part because of the failures of secondary schools to train in such grammars, but observe how quickly the necessity becomes an end. Soon "higher education" is at least relieved, if it is not boastfully proud, of its graduates who are barely literate persons with an AB or BS degree.

II

Always reality reasserts itself, to the confusion of those holding false principles. They must then shout those false principles louder and louder against the inexorable, if slow-chapped, pressures of reality. Now the denial of reality through false principles is a species of spiritual revolt, not merely an intellectual error, and as such it is bound to estrange intellect more and more from reality, precisely because it is a spiritual revolt. Intellectual error tends to be self-correcting, but the root cause of spiritual revolt is some version of *non serviam*, which is exacerbative. Upon that willed self-removal, intellect may be commanded to build. A willed intent of decreed equality among all things is desire transformed into being—that is, *supposed* substantive by will itself as the agent cause of existence. But such supposed manipulations of existence by the finite intellectual creature will be at last recognized for what they are: a willful intent to an equality, not *among* all mankind, but an equality between the transgressing, intentional gnostic soul and God. That is the theme we encounter often in our great art, expressed succinctly in *Paradise Lost*. Milton has his Satan say the motto of this modernist principle. He has a "mind not to be chang'd by Place or Time," the necessary condition of detachment from reality executed by an intellectual will to detachment. And so he declares the operative principle of intellectual action out of that detachment:

> *The mind is its own place and of itself*
> *Can make a heaven of hell, a hell of heaven.*

I would call this action of willful intent against the reality of existence *formalized sacrilege* against being itself, a revolt more fundamental than merely against "Place or Time." For the contention of this satanic principle is with God, not with time or place. The issue is which has power to create being *ex nihilo*. The satanic principle is determined to be, though finite intellect, the cause of being itself. That is, after all, the fundamental ground determining the dependence of particular created creatures, in this instance Satan himself, upon the primal cause of existential reality, God Himself. And it is not a ground established primarily by any time or any place. The "ground" is in the will of a free agent. And only by denial does it seem possible to that free agent to overcome its own finitude. That is the fundamental temptation to intellect. This perspective upon finite, human intentionality to its own autonomy reveals the action in man himself as participating in the diabolic, an arresting charge against modernism which must be made. I was once less comfortable with such arresting charges, as I was with such terms as *formalized sacrilege* or *diabolic action* and with judgments of intellectual perversity. Of course, I seem not to have lacked judgmental intent in those early days as these early essays reveal, though perhaps I was judgmental more in the sense of that term as it might be applied to Jeremiah.

It is also true that I was less persuaded in those days that in the end "all manner of thing shall be well," which is to say that perhaps a fuller understanding of the causes of our disorder allows me hope as never before. In an Old Testament climate of circumstance, one may recognize the hovering doom without a sufficient fullness of understanding to justify any hope. In a sense, jeremiads may be a true version of circumstance, whose accuracy within the limits of time and place endanger the prophet through the very detachment necessary to him for the version of the truth he pronounces. From that realization, I am more comfortable with judgmental terms, because I acknowledge the risk. In part I am more comfortable because I have seen over the intervening years the distortions of our personhood through the abstractionism practiced to *private* expedient ends, rather than to *personal* ends. That is to say that, as a Jeremiah, I am concerned for the recovery of reality, the recovery of the personal dimension of our existential nature. Abstractionism practiced in the interest of *individual* autonomy, characterized by Satan's words from *Paradise Lost*, while in essence a revolt against the cause of all being, is in its immediate effect destructive of the *personhood* of the intellectual creature in revolt. He is caught up and separated from reality by the illusion that abstraction is self-derived power, justifying a form suited to intellect's willed substantiation of existential reality.

Such reflection appears abstract in itself, no doubt, and the argument requires measuring by actuality—by our experience of our own existence in the world. Thus we reflect: in our concern for policy as a community consent, whether in relation to church or state or academy, how often do we hear such terms as *person* and *community* used with a resonance suggesting that the terms are anchored in reality itself? The operative terms, indeed, tend rather to be *individual* and *group* or *segment*, terms colored by our habit of abstraction to which statistical evidence so easily adheres. For *individual* carries suggestions, as we said, of the person as *integer* in a larger mechanism we must make "run," namely the state or the institution. And *group* or *segment* is suggestive of assembled parts of that mechanism which must be balanced in relation to each other so that the mechanism will run. It is important, then, that *person* as a term be understood as designating a reality more complex than its reduction to integer. For *person* speaks toward the discrete, *specific* (in its root sense as in *species*), created entity.*

By these circumscribing terms, we attempt to name a creature

---

* Concerning the complex relation of *person* to *community*, see my extended exploration, "The Quest for Community Ground: A Scholastic Foray," *Liberal Arts and Community: The Feeding of the Larger Body*.

singular unto itself, but also member in a larger whole. It is by its nature singular, but by the creative action of its Creator it is also included in the larger body of creation. It is not established in its singularity by its own willed autonomy, though intellect is sufficiently subtle within the limits of its finitude to present an appearance of such self-willed autonomous singularity. The extensive comedy of social manners through history, particularly in respect to the categories of autonomous deportment such as dress codes or sexual aberrations divorced from principles of discrete being within the body of existential reality, speaks the intellect's proclivity to *sign* its autonomy as if sign were its causal instrument. The first instance is that of Adam and Eve—the *ad hoc* response to nakedness with the fig leaf. But always, such activity, intent on autonomy, is forced to recognize that it *depends* on being—depends upon that which exists prior to its action. Fig leaves are prior to the recognition of nakedness. That is why such activities as those in the old garden are so often comic. When explored with a fullness of understanding through art, as in Dante's *Divine Comedy*, the comic ends not in tragedy as it well might, but in comedy in Dante's sense of the term— that is, in a return of intellect to its proper relation to existential reality, a recovery of the self in the truth of self. In our term, that is a recovery of *personhood*.

In this light, let us consider: it is this specific creature *as specific* that we intend to recognize in an ancient communal sacrament. Through that recognition the specific person is made member of the body of community. I mean the sacrament of baptism. Assembled before God, a gathering of persons name the new, specific person as specific. By that communal sacrament the person is recognized as well as new member in the larger body. He is proclaimed *before* God and *to* God with a given, not a surname, in a communal act of consent to his personhood. The distinction between *given* and *surname* has become obscured, and daily becomes further lost. First we abandoned the sacramental rite of baptism itself. Subsequently, our modernist revolt against the realities of our own being exacerbate that loss. For in that revolt, we intend our existence as separate from and independently unbeholden to, nature or family or community or

God. And we would do so through the act of naming ourselves. Such is one effect of Nominalism, at the most local level, far removed from the old high battle between the partisans of St. Thomas and those of William of Occam.

Given the general triumph of the modernist revolt which denies personhood in the name of individuality, it becomes crucial to remember our true occupation as intellectual creatures, in relation to the limits of that occupation. Our common occupation as created intellectual creatures, differentiated in disparate callings, is our action of naming, however disparate our actions caused by disparate gifts. It is primarily through our acts of *naming* that we are *makers*: In this action of naming we participate "creatively" with the Uncreated Cause of all things, who is the Cause even of our own gifts as namers, as makers. Such is our "calling" as specific creature. Now that "calling" requires to its fullness a response: "Here, Lord, am I." Such is the sign in our making, though the action is most various as manifested through sign. The response of an intellectual creature to his calling, then, is his action in making, whether we mean his making of a poem or a garden or an automobile, of a dwelling or an estate or a draft of a constitution or of a law. Whatever we *do* as response in our quest for our proper calling is the consequential naming of ourselves in relation to our potentialities. The circumscription of the "I" that we are by its discrete gifts defines the limits of our potentiality. That response, circumscribed by gift then, cannot escape that circumscription by its Nominalist revolt. Not *I am I by the grace of God*, says that revolt, but *I am I by the grace of my own self-intent to be independent of all existence; I am this I which I name.*

But the action whereby we name the person in baptism is an action peculiar to persons as distinct both from such autonomous revolt and from all other creatures in the inclusive body of creation. And it is through the gift held in common by persons, namely our discursive intellects, a gift subject to willful abuse. And so it is by naming, but by naming truly (that is, in relation to reality beyond the person as cause) that the person arrives proximately (though never fully) to a consent to reality in all its complexity. I say *proximately*, since the fullness of the potential of the discrete person—the absolute fulfillment of existential limit to finite existence—lies always beyond death. On this side of death, the intellectual creature moves, through knowledge out of experience, toward understanding as distinguished from knowledge. For knowledge, contrary to modernist assumptions, is a subordinate province in intellect, in which (to speak metaphorically) letters corresponding to knowledge as held by intellect are relevant necessities but not absolutes determining truth. If knowledge is concluded by intentional intellect to be the ultimate reality possessed by intellect—its realization of its full power as an existent thing—such knowledge proves always subversive of reality, most immediately the reality of the perverse intellect itself, which would suborn truth by the instrument of its own knowledge.

I shall speak in these essays of this confusion, relating it to that significant dislocation of our intellectual concerns initiated by William of Occam, namely Nominalism. This is a point Richard Weaver made fifty years ago. Nominalism, viewed historically (though it is in truth more ancient than Occam), supposes that intellect's "naming" of things is purely arbitrary, and my term *purely* is most deliberate. For the nominalist supposes his action of arbitrary naming to be thus purified by his intellectual intent, as if the given and the historically inherited by such a denial thereby absolves intellect of error in its initiating denial. Thus it disjoins naming from reality by declaring the action of naming arbitrary. The arbitrariness thereby becomes suggestive of intellect's own godhead. The principle thus pronounced becomes instrument to intellectual action of naming as the means to power over existence. But such naming serves only to further remove intellect from actual existence. Thus, by the illusion of a self-purified intentionality, accomplished by intellect's willed divorce from reality, those nagging questions of right and wrong are set aside. Questions of the nature of sin, which in historical perspective engages the question of Original Sin, are thus avoided.

That is the necessary strategy to Nominalism. And when it is successful, it declares the power of its own use of name to be that the letter of this law is absolute because of its disjuncture from reality. Thus a power seems established for the manipulations of existence, the manipulations of being. What is not at first apparent is that the absolute thus established is precisely the *tyranny* of power over being through the instrumental letter. We observe this principle in operation from subversive advertisements of consumer products to political manipulation of worthy and unworthy causes. In thought thus subverted, language itself becomes a convenience to a refined intellectual intent, an instrument denied to the general community. Names are merely a process manipulative of being, specifically man's invention *ex nihilo*. Thus there emerges the autonomous mind, self-justified as absolute. What this Nominalistic address to existence would set aside must be recovered, if "higher education" is itself to be properly recovered. The thing itself justifies the name we give it and is not justified as a thing by our giving it a name. Our naming is an act of consent to the existent thing and not an act of a substantiating justification of the thing by intellect. Such is the truth justifying the Shakespearean cliché beyond that "romantic" feeling which reduces it to cliché: a rose by any name smells as sweet, and that *smelling sweetness,* that *essence* rose, establishes the validity of any name in our common consent, but it does so *through* the name to the rose itself.

III

Of the Nominalist endangerment to intellect, more in the pieces to come. What is here of interest is the anciently understood relation of *given* to *surname.* For that understanding is crucial to our recovery of the reality of our personhood to a mutual consent that makes possible a community of intellect ordered by existence and not by intellect's disjoined perception of existence whereby it appears as a chaos upon which to practice its own substantiating pretenses through the instrument of name. What we have forgotten, in respect to the significance of surname, is that anciently it was an *additional* name, one added to the *significant* name, the *given* name. This creature is christened John, and he is the son of John, and so he is John Johnson. And his own child may well be John Johnson III. The point is that in this ordering of the names of creatures, so that community may respond to this new soul in existence, the significant name—that is, the name signifying a discrete person—is the given.

That is, the actually *John*, not son of John. That is why, in the sacramental order of baptism when the priest commands the parents to "name this child," they do not say John Johnson III. They say *John*, with that consent of faith whereby it becomes agreed between them and God as it were that this particular gift in creation, this child, will be known and loved and supported in his own deportment toward community and creation, on his own separate journey to his proper end. He will be loved as John. This does not mean, as the Nominalist would have it, that the name is either arbitrary (since he could as easily be "named" William or Alfred) or in that extreme rejection of Nominalism that the name he now bears in itself somehow carries actually his essential, actual nature. Rather, what is "signified" is the common consent within this intellectual body, a communal consent in the family natural and the family Church, that the signifying is properly centered upon reality itself, the discrete actuality now "called," in the world, John. That is why we used to value as high praise someone's saying that we are as good as our word, by which is meant that a concern for the truth of things requires of us that the names of things as we use them intend our own orientation to truth in our personhood.

What we mean when we say "I give you my word" is well understood when we know that the word given is, fundamentally, our own name, the necessary token of our passage into the community of the lovers of the truth of things. Considering the surname historically, we remember that it is a nickname as well. That is, it is a descriptive term added *to* the given name, either as an act of acceptance by the general company of souls designated by the surname (the Johnsons, the Carlisles, or the like) or as descriptive of an occupation or of a distinctive habit of being in the person in regard to his deportment to existence as a person. For he may be understood not only as John, the son of John, but as John the maker of wheels. He may be called John Wheelwright. Or he may be called "Old Hickory" or "Light Horse Harry" or "Ivan the Terrible." If such recalling of known but forgotten things, in respect to the naming of that "thing" created, the specific person, seems elementary, we need only look about us to discover that it is nevertheless largely a forgotten community consent to the person in community, in *intellectual communion.* It is one of the curious ironies at the moment, for instance, that some young women in their revolt insist on bearing their given and surname into marriage, lest they be sublimated by a spouse's surname, overlooking that in the logic of that position they are already subjugated by their "maiden" surname. The gesture, though understandable, given the chaotic state of our social disorders at the moment, distorts the fundamental reality: it is the given name (and some persons "legally" change even their given name by the letter of law) that is central to personhood. The given name is a focus of communal recognition of personal worth. Any name is always, whether given or surname, merely an "added" name in the Nominalistic view. But the reality at issue is that the name is most importantly a sign of our common consent to and valuing of the particularity of this discrete creature.

It is not, of course, that given names are not themselves influenced by history, ancient or recent, as the reading of the "Stork Calls" in a Sunday paper shows readily enough. The latest pop hero or military hero or political hero—depending upon the community climate of the moment—will have numbers of "namesakes" in the world. What is important, however, is that we have lost our sense of the importance of a relation between the fundamental intent of *giving a name,* an act of homage to the actual existence of a thing, and whatever relation that act of giving has to antecedent or peripheral realities. The antecedent or peripheral are secondary to the validity of naming, in which validity lies our concern for the essential. The child named by parental whim for the pop hero of the moment satisfies an emotional impulse in the parent at that moment, and by such acts of whim the Nominalistic distortion of reality itself will be exacerbated. We lose the primary significance, our consent to and homage to the new actual person, the infant. The parent need not be a scholastic, learned in the thought of William of Occam or Thomas Aquinas, to contribute to exacerbation or recovery. Ideas have consequences, some deleterious and some supportive of reality, whether the activator of the idea in the instant fully understands his intellectual actions.

Now, such thoughts as these point to the concerns over our

abuses of language beginning to rise in my own thought as I set out as teacher of literature, in which calling the names of things in relation to the things themselves is important indeed. In our literature, the act of giving names is dramatically significant again and again, the epithet for instance being of central importance from our earliest poetry into our present. One remembers how serious the relation of name to thing, though with comic effect, in a tensional moment when Odysseus convinces the cyclops that his own name is Noman. And we remember as well that Odysseus has the advantage of sophistications that allow him not only to survive but to survive and tell his story as if he were himself Homer, as close as we come— before Dante perhaps—to the poet as hero, the namer as hero.

As teacher in the 1950s and 1960s, I began to realize that such recognitions were not only delightful when encountered in the poetry of our heritage, but were significant to our continuing survival as a people, as persons properly oriented to the complexity of reality through our intellectual gifts. And I saw that, more and more, both the delight in such recognition and our realization of the importance of that recognition was being lost, both through intellectual carelessness and intellectual chicanery.

As for my term *segregation* in the first essay, it is to be distinguished here from the term *segregation* as a devil-word, loosely used in the interval since 1960 to effect *ad hoc* solutions to social and political problems by countering it with the god-word *integration*. In using that term then I was concerned, as I still am, that our educational institutions would suffer *disintegration* through programs based in abstractions, though the abstractions were declared sovereign cures to our social and political ills. At hand as one cause of my concern was the general crisis reflected by our panic over the Russian launching of a satellite. Meanwhile, the sometimes compassionate, but more often merely passionate concern, for equal justice before the law led to technical concerns for law, and to such an extent of concern that the law profession suddenly became the most desirable of professions, for a variety of "personal" reasons. What we now witness is John Lawyer so multiplied that only specializations in the letter of the law allows us to distinguish among them. They are the new scholastics of abstractionism. And if I may turn abstraction to account of the phenomenon, it is at least startling that 70 percent of the world's lawyers are citizens of our country. These "angels" largely given to scholastic game conjured to a numerous habitation on the tips of the letters of the law, engage us in tensional debate over strict or loose interpretation of the letter as a perching place. The letter turns out for the most part to be a subjective image of a vague desire clasped by factions of the polity. Desire itself is justified in the issue by our disoriented "feelings" about right and wrong, which feelings appear largely to be merely whim when our common sense forces us to consider them. And so we come to the "cynical" 1990s. The cynical climate of public opinion in our decade, as we consider the actual operations of our political institutions—whether executive, legislative, or judiciary—yield to us from public deportment of our representative figures, not hope, but despair.

In the 1960s, after Sputnik, there followed from that vague ambiance of thought sometimes given the impressive epithet "the will of the people," new civil rights legislation, speeded along by the spectacles of encounters uncivil and bloody in Arkansas, Mississippi, Georgia, Alabama, and so on. The best effect of those encounters was to recall just how lost we have become from the realities of our humanity—our potential for both good and evil actions. But that recovered recognition controlled only by the letter of the law has proved empty. Surely we may learn from the experiences that the letter, if not securely anchored in the realities of human existence, easily obscures or denies humanity itself through the abstractionism which has become our substitute for metaphysical vision, but which leaves us no vision but only the empty abstractions.

Who can now deny, on the risk of being as good as his word, that such legislation executed in the name of the letter—in the name of justice abstracted and so disjoined from reality—has caused sorrow to persons in instance after instance, whatever statistical evidence adduced to show that we are now considerably advanced in justice under the law? I submit an instance, a lead story in an evening paper just at hand, which might justify my call for a recovery of the proper intellectual discrimination. The headline announces that "Johnson [my name is a substitute for the young man's own surname] Passes SAT, Can Play for Grenadiers." Again, my substitute added, a nickname of an athletic team. With the exuberance of an Achilles as ringmaster at the funeral celebration for Patroclus, the reporter cries that "With the final horn about to sound" against Johnson, a media "All-American" prep player, he finally came through. On his third attempt at the SATs he scored seven hundred, thus becoming eligible as a college freshman (1991). His future Coach: "We're excited." How did he accomplish his rescue? Said Johnson: "I just buckled down for some 20 days and tutored for like 45 or 50 hours a week."

Knowing smiles are insufficient here. One recognizes how minimal an SAT score of seven hundred is, in respect to "higher education." (And I am quite aware of the controversy over the validity of SATs.) One might even be somewhat embarrassed by Johnson's "tutoring" himself for a work-day week. But one notes the important description is not of his academic possibilities. What is "relevant" is that he is very tall and has an amazing statistical record as a prep player. What is heart-rending here is that Johnson is being used against the truth of his personhood—by the media and by the school, one of the institutions of higher education, and with not only a public consent to that abuse, but with the public celebrating the abuse. That the incident is not exceptional, of course, needs no remarking, given the recent history of athletics in higher education. That such an abuse of the reality of Johnson's personhood is also not exceptional needs attending, for he is already a victim to the Nominalistic abuses of reality in respect to his existence as a person who should be properly loved, his existence as one of God's intellectual creatures. It is our loss of understanding of just what it means to be such a creature that is my old and my continuing concern.

IV

That concern, then, began to focus, in the course of my journeyman labors as teacher, upon the ascendancy of abstractionism over reality. It is abstractionism in its uses of spectacle against reality itself that is most disorienting to community. Questions now topical, questions of class or race or sex, have become more and more removed by abstraction from the actualities of persons in their relation to other persons, so that there is now abroad such a climate of distrust, each for the other, that any virtue in community seems remote. I know my own present experience, walking on my old campus. There was a time when eye met eye, smile elicited smile, a good mannerly word was spoken. It was a climate notable, spoken of beyond our own region as "Southern hospitality." But now, such has been the effect of recent antagonisms, that one risks being taken as aggressive if he display such greeting. I resolve that nevertheless I shall make those gestures of "body language," signifying a relation of person to person though most probably misunderstood. And I experience various response. There is often still a direct warm return, a sign of some hope. But too often one meets the averted eye and sometimes even a scowl such as in the old days might have made one step behind a hedge to check his attire. It is a depressing experience, but signalling something of what is now awry in "higher education."

By the 1960s I realized that abstractionism had caused a decay quite extensively evident in the intellectual community. We were left with educational problems hardly promising any reasonable or truly just address to the emerging complex of social problems that were being increasingly committed to the charge of educational institutions. At that moment we did turn attention to educational recovery, a proper turning, but made for the wrong reasons and so predoomed to failure. Sputnik had just streaked across our horizon, focusing all eyes for a brief moment with awe and disquiet. In response to that discrete spectacle, we questioned whether our celebrated know-how and can-do would be sufficient to this new challenge to those freedoms we spoke much of in relation to our domestic and foreign policy. Those "freedoms" we had come to consider largely on the level of sentimentality, on the level of feeling vaguely associated with more vaguely conceived principles, expressed more often than not as vaguely articulated virtues of community responsibilities. We had lost our proper words for things. Nevertheless, there was a sudden flurry to establish systems and programs for the recovery of things and to marshal those things against the seeming threat of Godless Communism as our epithet had it. The difficulty was, it developed, that we had pretty much lost any understanding of our term *God* as applied to the reality of His existence, so that we found ourselves using not an epithet ordered by reality but a shibboleth made opaque to our understanding of it by long neglect.

The second of these collected pieces I wrote at the beginning of the 1960s, at which point I became irreversibly committed to teaching as my calling, but also committed to teaching where I had encountered "higher education," at my own University of Georgia. Though sometimes invited to move elsewhere, I never wished to, even though I recognized more and more immediate local challenges to the principles I thought ought to govern higher education. Already, I anticipated the difficulties in those local circumstances that might well distract me from my teaching, though even then I never supposed those difficulties peculiar to the place I chose to stay. That I was right in that judgment seems to me more abundantly obvious since then. Not my academy only, but the American academy in general was already sliding toward the collapse that now seems immanent.

My concern in writing "The Fallacy of Practicality," not a very happy title, was with local history, with immediate experiences of academic and administrative disjunctions reflected in the manipulations of an already attenuated curriculum. The adjustments underway were expediencies justified by the sudden influx of students under the "G.I. Bill," of whom I was myself one. I experienced those manipulations as a student first. Then I began to see them more clearly when I became an instructor of English in the decades of the 1950s and 1960s. What I saw revealed, in discouraging ways, was that those adjustments in the name of necessity were not—even granting the necessity—undertaken out of principles of higher education in themselves valid. A solution for the moment, with little remembrance of the past nor vision of future consequences, was the policy. I discovered that what I understood to constitute a liberal arts education was quite foreign to the understanding of those in command of the institution. That was personally a discouraging experience, but I was then firmly supported by colleagues committed to liberal arts—some old teachers of mine, some my contemporaries. I did not abandon hope.

The essay's immediate occasion was not, or so I then supposed, out of my own concerns but in response to a growing despair in one of my colleagues, a despair which at the time made me uneasy because its darkness seemed possibly suicidal. He threatened to give up teaching altogether, though those close to him knew him to be an excellent and committed teacher of considerable learning and potential. I hoped my argument might encourage him to hold fast in his dark days, which now by comparison seem rather more enlightened on educational principles because those principles were still held doggedly by some of us. I gave him the essay, which was later published in an obscure journal, *The Arlington Quarterly*, in 1968. It has been read only (it now seems) by him and me and the editor of that journal. Whether because of the piece or not, my colleague did not give up teaching, though he did give up on my own school. I have had no news of him for years, but I believe he continued teaching in a smaller school in a bigger place, New York City, a far remove from Athens, Georgia. I am rather confident that he discovered much the same difficulties there as in Georgia, such is the pervasive nature of intellectual decay in our world.

In those days, he and I and two other instructors had undertaken our own "honors" course, with no support or approval from the "administration." We each selected one or two students from our regular classes and met them once or twice a week in the late afternoon—additional "work" for them and for us as understood in terms of the statistical decree of "teaching loads." Not long afterward the teaching load would be designated EFT, meaning "equivalent full time," through which a formula could be fitted to the individual teacher that reconciled his actual teaching with his "research time" and his "administrative time," the latter requiring a formal appointment to administrative work—Director of Freshman English or Director of Sophomore English or Administrative Assistant to the Department Head. But that was still in the future, as we became more efficient in handling the shrinking presence of the teacher in higher education. Meanwhile, the concern in our voluntary honors program, which carried neither E F T nor course credit for the student, was to give those students the experience of delight in intellectual pursuits, each according to his particular gifts, with the intent of revealing as well that not only delight but consequential sustenance to personhood attended such extra "work." We each selected not only one or two students, but the material we were to read, and the students bought whatever additional texts were thus required. That there were additional texts said something of the problems already apparent in the formal courses, if one grant good judgment on our part in distinguishing good, better, best among texts other than the "required" ones, to which such comparative terms were not suited.

In some respects, the informal classes were indeed informal, conducted somewhat as if in a literary salon, for we did proceed with an orderly address to poems and stories and essays. The gatherings differed from other notable literary gatherings, such as for instance those gatherings of the Fugitive poets we knew about in the 1920s at Vanderbilt University. We did not assume an ungoverned conduct for our students. Of course, neither are those famous salons in our literary history ungoverned, since there will be or will emerge one or two dominant minds in any such gathering. (One supposes no problem of order to those gatherings of the Inklings, for instance, though on occasion there may have been tensions as to who was the dominant presence.) Anyway, ours was a clear distinction between teacher and student, though there was a mutually respectful manner among us which made for delights we might think of as social, civilized encounters. That is, we were persons to each other, though persons differing not only in potential but in actual gifts. Still, we did meet in empty class rooms of a drab building on late afternoons, and there were not those attendant social amenities possible that salons usually afford. State law would allow no such.

Ours was a colloquy governed not only by recognitions of the discreetness of persons intellectually but by differences in good literature as well. Some poems, like some minds, are better than others. The experience was especially valuable to me, since through it I learned more and more how to read and how to talk about what I read, and it was this advantage that we mutually shared, instructors and students alike. One of those students, incidentally, went on to take her doctorate, writing on the appreciation of Faulkner's fiction among French critics. She continued her life teaching literature, not at some institution of fabled reputation, but at a small college in a small town. She did so with much the same enthusiasm for literature that she had shown as a freshman, as I know from her sometime visits back to the University. And years later her son appeared one day in my Honors Freshman class—for by then an honors program had been formalized, in which better students were given the sort of training I have always thought proper to all students professing themselves candidates to higher education. The son's brightness and enthusiasm continued a growing family tradition of respect for and devotion to the truth of things as rendered by well-ordered words, which had been our object to instill at the outset of our attempt to recover the virtues of liberal arts education to one institution of higher learning. The principle was to credit individual students—elect students out of the general disordered flow of the system—with the mystery of peculiar gifts individually possessed, to be nurtured within a climate of minimum expectations of their responsibility to those gifts. Institutions had by that time so entrapped themselves in the confusion of size that size itself soon justified the institution. This was the point where the new ideal became the subsequently infamous "multiversity," though at the time all sorts of high sounding justifications of size as determinate of quality were bruited about.

Bigger is better; more is bigger; bigger is more and also best, if biggest. The terms were rather flabby always, but the argument seemed to suit admirably that already destroying feeling about the person and his gifts. Each is like each, so all are like each and each like all. There must be an egalitarian comradery maintained by a feeling of good intention of all to all, vague feeling superceding true charity. And by that time, one aspect of that feeling was that since there is "virtue" in education per se, proved by material progress, it must be a *moral* virtue. And so not only must each be entitled to education but to an education at its highest reach, in the name of what is morally right. It was a right of each individual, and educational institutions were morally obligated to supply formal learning. We were well on the way to an "open university" long before that concept became officially established. That openness abandoned long ago the initially persuasive approach to universalism in higher education once attributed to Thomas Jefferson: each according to his gifts, regardless of his means. Now, we are burdened by the dislocated tenet of our faith in the absolute equality of gift—however qualified in pursuing that equality in our gestures toward intrusive realities, economic or other. The dilemma to educational institutions became that the means of education must be made commonly equal to serve gifts now declared equal. That, it was declared, is the moral responsibility of government and of institutions. To deny that operational tenet, even in the light of reality as beheld by common sense, is to commit the one unpardonable sin against humanity, as *humanity* had become an abstraction from reality itself. As for an Inquisition, very much required in such a climate of feeling from which thought is in exile—why that office is presently assumed by the self-appointed guardians of the "Politically Correct," the Guardian Angels of the academy.

There is a residual sense of the practicality of education in that dislocated common feeling, for still it is supposed that through education intellectual egalitarianism will itself become the absolute to human existence. But when I wrote my essay against such "practical" expectations of the liberal arts education as had become dominant, it served more than an attempt to encourage a colleague. I see now that it served to clarify and reassure me that I had committed my life to a worthy labor against considerable odds, in the interest of the good of community which must at last come to see things as they are, or else disintegrate as community. We must not only accept differences in gift within community, but treasure difference as the largesse of being itself. So my commitment was worthy, and it was important not only to me as a person but important to my family, (which was growing), and to the immediate community of which I was a part. The essay seems worth including here, then, not only because it attempts to speak to student or teacher about those permanent things binding the intellectual community when truly seen by intellect. It also speaks prophetically to the impossible circumstances already overwhelming the academy, whereby universities were becoming education mills justified on false moral grounds. It tried, and tries, to deflect those forces that are degenerative in their effects. We still hold those false ways, but more and more we see that more is less if we mean more students mean less education, as when number alone is the determinate principle. Still, administrators justify expansion of education "facilities" on the strength of numbers alone, though they color the argument with residual symbols used as clichés. They yet speak of *best* minds in relation to an assembled faculty, for instance.

v

What followed "The Fallacy of Practicality" was the notorious 1960s, the "radical" assault upon higher education of which I have some observations in the recent pieces, the section designated "Now." By the time that essay came to print, however, there was little attention possible to its concerns, such had been the distracting spectacles of that decade. Perhaps it may now say things worth repeating. And especially so, in relation to the recent, added pieces written since my formal retirement from my university. I was devoted to that university, as student and teacher, for forty or more years of my life, and my "early" retirement was more strategic than a necessity of the turning years. From here in Crawford I am better able to speak *toward* my own school. I do so by speaking more largely, more widely, less explicitly to it. In this present condition of my servitude to the intellectual life, I am not daily depleted by the routine of constant engagement with local idiocies that besiege intellectual truth.

What I am concerned to do in these later pieces is to address generally, not specifically, the present collapse of higher education. But what I have to say in the 1990s is already implicit in what I was saying in the 1950s and 1960s. Thus I still see the radicalism of the 1960s, insofar as it so easily enlisted young minds, as in part a response by the young against an indifference to the truth of things, the end proper to intellectual concern. My own early response was itself an intuitive revolt against what came to be called the "establishment," though my own radicalism differs fundamentally from that set loose in those days, whose peculiar destructions have only added to those destructions by the "establishment" itself. Some of those differences I speak of elsewhere in an essay whose title suggests my own position: "Richard Weaver against the Establishment." I myself reacted, not in concert with those confused forces beginning to occupy the universities (*actually* occupying them by physical violence). I reacted against the established betrayors of intellect, who built through their betrayals those "multiversities" that loom so large now in the city of man, not as new wonders of the world but more and more as towers of Babel.

If much of my concern for social and political and religious questions appears more implicit than direct in those two early essays here gathered, it may be a weakness in the pieces. But it seems to me, after thirty or forty years, that I nevertheless understood intuitively certain truths about that moment of our panic in response to Sputnik, a panic which has dissolved progressively into issues of social and political policy that set us one against another, or one faction against another, however loudly it is said at a national level of exhortation that we are one people as never before. The "thousand points of light" seem rather separated by such intervals of darkness that only a recovery of a metaphysical orientation of light to light gives much promise of a *unity* in *community*, words whose cognate kinship speaks complex realities requiring a metaphysical vision of reality. These late pieces, then, signified by the subtitle "Now," address that concern, though in them I allude to other work of my own in which the concern is more fully explored. These pieces oriented to our present circumstances ("Now") address our present estate as community in relation to old failures of the intellectual community, not simply those failures since the end of World War II. Just how long in the making those failures have been I address in the final piece, "Modernism," which in its enlarged historical view upon our present disorder suggests not only the intellectual context of present disorder in the academy but reflects my own orientation toward the causes of disorder. In this aspect, it will serve as whatever protection a reader may desire, since from it he may know where I stand in saying the things I say.

My intent in these late pieces, then, is to address the abiding circumstances to the problems of "higher education," and if that address has validity, then bringing the pieces together—the early and the late ones—may yet encourage some student or some teacher somewhere. I do not suppose that I shall have the pleasure again of looking up from a class roll, having called the name of a student long since graduated, to find that student's son or daughter before me, intentionally having chosen my class from the vast array. Old students do continue reassurances that what I have had to say about the truth of things has been on occasion sustaining to them. And so I have every confidence that some teacher and some student somewhere will be encouraged, should he read these pieces, or some of them. This is to say that perhaps I may yet encourage a rescue of firm stones out of the present rubble which is the American academy in the 1990s. I know with certainty that I am obligated to attempt such encouragement. For, to adapt T. S. Eliot to that obligation, I know that, if the academy is to be cast down, we must build it and rebuild it, first and last. That is, we must build always and continuously with stones from the rubble. With the realities held together with our always decaying intellectual mortar.

It remains now to say only that such building is a community undertaking, but that community must be more largely understood than we sometimes take it. For the community in time is not merely a community of persons here and now, surviving out of the accidents of history. Persons have a continuousness in history in one way or another. Thus my reader will recognize, either to his comfort or disquiet, that all along in my own attempts as teacher in "higher education" I have been supported and sustained by companionable minds such as T. S. Eliot and C. S. Lewis. By Eric Voegelin and Gerhart Niemeyer; by Jacques Maritain and Etienne Gilson and by Richard Weaver and Cleanth Brooks and Allan Tate and Donald Davidson. Indeed, by a multitude more numerous than I may here name or later footnote. Their support implies no *identity* of their vision and mine in detail. For ours is a common concern for the truth of how things stand in themselves, as measured by the realities of our experiences of those things. The concern is not to be *right*, but to be guided by whatever truth we come to. And that brings me to name less recent members of the company I keep, who have been presences alive and validly active now as in their own "historical" days: I mean such presences as Homer and Plato and Aristotle; Dante and St. Augustine and St. Thomas Aquinas. Again, they are a company too numerous to name, though their presence in my own words will be often evident, even though I do not summon them by name directly to my words. They too are companionable, in that their dominant concern as intellectual creatures is to understand the truth of how "things" stand, a concern which they certify as persons through their own honoring of their given names, which we in turn must honor, as we may—each according to his gifts.

PART I

THEN

I

The Segregation That Is Needed

SINCE OUR FIRST "AGONIZING REAPPRAISAL" of educational materials and methods in 1957, occasioned by the Sputnik panic, we have begun once more to slump back into pre-Sputnik complacency. There was at first an urgent flurry of talk about attracting gifted young people into the teaching profession, and we have even made federal funds available through Congress toward that end—money by act of Congress being the most ready answer to any pressing problem. There was likewise much talk of better salaries for teachers, of stronger parental support in the maintenance of discipline and work and of a new emphasis on a hard core of studies related to science. It was a happy season for hurling bricks at the ever-tempting heads of the professional educators, those feather merchants whose vested interest lies in the system of education developed and sold to the American consumer with Madison Avenue skill. For since John Dewey gave them the light in *Reconstruction in Philosophy,* they have carried it unto all the people with a fervor that has resulted in the deification (but not the definition) of Education. But what Lyell and Darwin were to many a comfortable Victorian congregation, well-adjusted to nineteenth-century pleasures, the Sputnik was to the innumerable converted and baptized worshipers of Education. They suddenly discovered that our intellectual comfort was the result of intellectual drowning rather than baptizing, that what we needed was not the muddled doctrine of "equal education for all."

I

After that initial panic, the bear's breath began to seem not so hot on our neck—rather, well . . . warm and even perhaps friendly. Nevertheless the embarrassment of the unexpected crisis left us with anger to express. We began to sound more like enraged alumni who discover at the homecoming game that their much publicized quarterback has his position through influence rather than through ability, than like a congregation whose faith in omnipotent Education had been shaken. There has been more "Kick out the coach" than "Examine the priest on points of doctrine." For we are not, despite our pretense to the contrary, a religious people, being interested in emotional peace and contentment and a workable product from our institutions.

Well then, the coach must go. The cry is not new, it has simply been louder recently. There has been constant criticism of doctrinal points held by the educators of educators. One could collect an amazing bibliography to support the statement. But the voice of interrogation has been unpersuasive, partly because it has not addressed itself to the problem of the better bear trap, a utilitarian concern which most *motional* (that is, devoted to that other undefined American god, Progress) Americans can understand. There is a persuasiveness in the argument that higher mathematics is necessary to the national welfare since only through higher mathematics will it be possible to outdo our adversaries and competitors. What chance have the ancient arguments concerning the value of mathematics for its own sake? How persuasive is it to point out that Einstein was not looking for a way to make an A-bomb when he devised formulas that made the H-bomb possible? We make the same demands upon the new coach as made upon the old. In the past we demanded in the name of Progress, not higher mathematics but business math, not the grammar and logic necessary to rational thought but business

English—while those old fuddy-duddies, the "professors" whose re-treat was generally the ivory towers of liberal arts colleges, talked angrily, then desperately, and then cynically, if at all. Oh, for a Jonathan Swift among them! But in an age capable of seeing only a literal horror of a misanthrope in the "Modest Proposal," the follow-ing quotation can only be taken as praise:

> The evolution of the prescribed education "lingo" has been an amazing development. If, in 1900, a teacher at the University had brought a hen to class for teaching purposes, while an in-novation, the hen was simply a hen. By 1910, this hen was a "problem." By 1915 the hen became a "project." Around 1920 the hen became a "unit of work." By 1925 the same hen devel-oped into an "activity." By 1930, she became the basis of an "Integrated Program." And ten, in 1936, the poor old hen had become a "frame of reference." As 1941 drew to a close, she implemented into an "Area in a Workshop." By 1942 she ap-peared to have been "calibrated as a part of orchestration of school and community activities." After the summer of 1945, she was the concomitant of "Motivated Evaluation."

Does this not bespeak Progress? If there is criticism, it is likely to be directed at the facts: for instance, any one who is advanced in henology enough to attend one of the elaborate annual conferences at my university entitled "The Chicken of Tomorrow" could imme-diately point out that the writer must be talking about several hens, not just one. Everyone knows hens do not live forty-five years.

So those professors of the ivory tower (currently expected to pro-duce something more basically necessary to our survival than a chicken of tomorrow) watched helplessly. The demigod Education, worshiped by the people, gouged intellect first with one horn in the name of high school social adjustment and then with the other in the name of an immediate monetary return on four years of college. Professors who professed abstract values proved Humpty Dumpties easily pushed from the wall, and it took the Russian Sputnik to make their argument persuasive among the voters of the nation. Social adjustment in high school and business math build no satellites; and while business English may make one adept at the creation of business jargon and Jaycee public relations speeches for Allied Can, Inc., it does not equip one to read fearful handwritings on the wall. The panic of 1957, then, was simply the outer sign of the inner weakness the educational coaches had promoted and nurtured for three generations. Alumni-itis struck in. New coach! New scholarships for potential quarterbacks! Let's get in there and support our team!

II

New coach indeed. But what characteristic ought we to look for? The ability to produce a better chicken of tomorrow or larger H-bomb? Give us that winning team! But it is a great mistake to continue the sloppy analogy between the good teacher and the good coach or practical product-finder. Nevertheless, our thinking half-habits make us act as if the analogy were absolutely sound. We want a man as coach who can discover talent, and through proper exercises develop it toward the perfection of our desires. We can muster "democratic" support for such an approach so long as there is a chance that our team will not win. From the conception of the All-American High School Boy as a junior edition of Chaucer's Miller, we turn to a conception of him as a junior Univac. Contemplating these two American dreams of manhood, one can be thankful for the force of inertia, the product of complacency among parents and vested interest among the high priests of Education. We are saved for the moment from absolute dominion of either.

　　What kind of coach do *I* want? First of all, I don't want a coach at all. I want what is just as respectable and far more efficient: the good teacher. The good teacher, I should think, is first of all one whose awareness of these two American ideals of man as left guard or Univac does not leave him desperately cynical. He must see that there is some middle course between ape and essence, though he will not be one to champion such a course with the catchall phrase of "education of the whole child." Furthermore, being aware of the two extreme conceptions of the All-American Boy, the good teacher must also be aware that his is, and will continue to be, a constant struggle with the fanatical and inconstant alumni who are in the majority—the alumni, so recently calling loudly for the coach's scalp, whom the teacher knows immediately as Junior's Mama and Papa. For Mama and Papa will in one emotional context malign him for damaging the child's immortal psyche because Junior is not graded on the curve on his history test covering names of English kings and at the next, in times of acute Sputnik-itis, condemn him for pussy-footedness when "the safety of the nation is at stake."

I think undoubtedly this good teacher I am talking about (and to) will find himself possessed of more than the ordinary degree of Original Sin; otherwise he would not be a schoolteacher in the first place. Adam had got so concerned with knowing that he ate the fruit to be equal to God in knowledge (and those of us who find such relief in putting the failure of our educational system solely on the professional educators ought to remember Adam, who didn't get to stay in Eden by blaming Eve). Ever since Adam, man has been cursed by the desire to know, and the good teacher is the person who manifests this curse most constantly. Furthermore, he is not to be set apart from that supposedly insufficient judge, the layman, as being the man with the most education degrees, longest bibliography, or most popular with the students. Neither Socrates nor Christ was popular. I would like to have the following motto cast in bronze and placed as paperweights on the desks of all board of education chairmen, presidents, deans, principals, department heads, and teachers:

THE GOOD TEACHER EMULATES SOCRATES AND CHRIST, NEITHER OF WHOM WAS POPULAR WITH THE MAJORITY OF HIS HEARERS, NOR WROTE ARTICLES OR BOOKS, NOR HELD DEGREES— HONORARY OR EARNED—FROM RECOGNIZED INSTITUTIONS OF LOWER OR HIGHER LEARNING.

The first, indispensable quality in the good teacher, displayed in myriad ways, is his desire to *transcend* rather than to *adjust to*. The teacher's ability to adjust to degrees and bibliographies as end products rather than means, his ability to adjust to his students and the community may destroy his ability to transcend: intellectual evolution becomes retrogressive.

Now the privilege of transcending the ordinary level of knowledge, as the good teacher does, is accompanied by the necessity of judging degrees of knowledge. Willy-nilly, Mama and Papa upset and angry or not, the teacher must judge. Of course he fears that his light may be darkness, but he will know when his darkness is a light unto the outer darkness that may be represented by Mama and Papa and Junior. He judges, knowing that democracy as conceived by the Greeks and adopted by our Founding Fathers has so far decayed into intellectual anarchy that Mama and Papa may consider him presumptuous, arrogant, even immoral when he exercises intellectual honesty by saying that Junior has not mastered rudimentary mathematics. Except, I must keep repeating, in that year of grace, 1957. That year Mama and Papa may still have felt the same way, but they were also moved by the desire for survival. Part of our muddle-headed thinking about Junior and his school (and we are all like Junior's Mama and Papa some of the time) lies in this: we have extended the grim and honorable old injunction to "judge not lest ye be judged" to regulate the school teacher's duty because we confound *soul judgment* and *mind judgment*, because we don't know Christ from Socrates. We take the Bill of Rights as an assurance that every man's son is equal to every other man's son in intellectual potential. Of course, when I put the statement that bluntly, it will be denied by all as an absurd piece of thinking or a deliberate distortion. The point, though, is that we act by that view and have developed our educational system in this century with this conception as fundamental to "democratic" education. This was a desirable tenet for the initiators of the new system, for to arm the people with such a conception is to provide the necessary votes to provide the necessary laws and monies to build that new system. The ambitious politician knows well that he must not take Education's name in vain—that is, he must not question the holiness or supernatural powers of that god by questioning unlimited suffrage. Suffer all the little children to come unto me for at least twelve years, and deny them not, if you want the office. Until 1957.

So no wonder that Mama and Papa resent any strict judgment of Junior's intellectual progress that might indicate he has gone as far as he should at the end of junior high. How dare you say Junior can't do as well as Banker Brown's boy in mathematics? He is *just as good* as Johnny Brown. Just as good—as if *goodness* of an individual has anything to do with his intellectual prowess. Of course, if the teacher is diplomatic, he may say that Junior *will not* do as well as Johnny Brown. This gives Papa occasion to smile knowingly, still holding inviolate Junior's potential equality of intellect while enjoying the pleasure of his being a little rascal who needs only a trip to the woodshed to set him on the road to realization, perhaps even to the presidency (while Mama wants a more *inspiring* and *sympathetic* teacher).

Now Junior already accepts the fact that Johnny Brown is better at his books than he, just as Papa has finally accepted the fact that Jack Jones can kick the football farther than Junior. But democratic anarchy leaves one without a place, and Mama and Papa are consequently in quest of status. Of course, man has always been a status-seeker, ever since the confusion commenced between the relative potential of individuals and the absolute potential of the individual: Cain slew Abel a long while back. Nevertheless, status-seeking has changed in its ends. The values which have been treasured most highly have been outvoted, foremost among them being intellectual accomplishment for its own sake. To be good, we now feel, is to have found one's safe place in the world. Environmental determinism (to which I shall speak again directly) encourages us to better ourselves by adjusting to environment, not by attempting to realize our true intrinsic worth—not by trying to transcend environment. To be saved then is to have finally arrived at the four-bedroom house with double carport. How may Education save one? Through business math and business English for the masses. And elementary psychology to keep us happy till we can get that house.

No surprise then that we establish our educational system to provide safety of adjustment to the natural and social world. Now no doubt there is still resentment on Papa's part because Junior continues to kick that football only an average of twenty-five yards, despite all the milk and steak and practice, while skinny Jack Jones kicks it fifty. (One thing the twentieth-century Papa has over his grandfather: a scientific scapegoat to replace God. He can blame Junior's relative inequality, when forced to recognize it, on his genes, and *his* on *his* father's, in a comfortable retrogression, thus freeing himself of any guilt feeling. The modern epic has been the scientific justification of genes' ways to man.) Jack has a knack with a football just as Johnny Brown has a knack with a mathematics formula, but the distinction between twenty-five yards and fifty yards on the football field is an incontrovertible fact of inequality, a gift easily tape-measurable. Disallowed is any popular scientific personality mysticism which would make it necessary for the football coach to grade Junior on the curve. Papa must accept or be ridiculed.

Papa will not only accept this inequality on the football field; as often as not he will contribute to an athletic scholarship to send Jack Jones to State U. And then, just as self-righteously, he will turn to Junior's problem in mathematics and feel that for the mathematics teacher to suggest that there is an incontrovertible distinction between Johnny's and Junior's potential is a sign that Junior has a poor teacher—one who can't get the material across. Such a teacher, usually, is said to lack that heal-all, Compassion, by which Papa and Mama mean (though they do not know that they mean it) the ability of a teacher to lie to Junior about his intellectual potential, with a kind face, of course. Junior will be considered dull if he does not get credit for the course, at least sufficient credit to allow him to go to State U to watch Jack Jones play on Saturday afternoons. A scholarship for Johnny Brown, in the event his father cannot send him to pursue mathematics? Witness:

I happened to be attending the State University of Iowa when the first successful launching of an American satellite was announced. What an orgy of self congratulation followed: one of the key members of the team that put the Explorer in orbit was none other than Professor van Allen of the Physics Department at SUI, a native son. Furthermore, the initial data from the new satellite were being broken down at that school. The press of the state flooded all news media with stories and features: van Allen as boy, as student, as teacher. The family history. Family home. Other successful members of the family. The van Allens at the White House reception for the satellite team. Then the inevitable: the suggestion was made and quickly formalized that a scholarship fund be established in van Allen's name, the proceeds from which were to be used to finance talented students interested in physics. After elaborate planning, organization, promotion, and collection by the citizens of the state of Iowa—spurred on by civic-minded leaders and government officials—a few hundred dollars were finally deposited in the van Allen fund, considerably less than a thousand. Meanwhile, anxious alumni of SUI provided funds to buy the basketball coach a new automobile. He had made a good showing that season.

This, while an unusually dramatic example, is nevertheless essentially a typical example of the way we Mamas and Papas feel about Junior and Jack Jones and Johnny Brown. And this is consequently the way we act, for—as I have already asserted—we act on feelings, not thoughts. Feeling and its act are built into the system, drilled into our teachers through professional courses in the muddlement of thinking for the sake of that empire building whose pretext for existence has been the "development of the whole child." It is one of the ironies of our situation that there is a sounder and more respected democracy at work on the high school football fields of the nation than is allowed to operate in the classroom. Who would dream of erasing the distinction between varsity and intramural teams? I do not observe that Mamas and Papas generally worry about the damage done to Junior's psyche when he doesn't make the varsity team or when he only makes the second or third string. Certainly most Juniors seem to "adjust" well enough without being allowed a turn as quarterback or left end in the big Thanksgiving Homecoming Game. When Junior exits from the stadium waving his school colors on the end of a stick, he does not give the appearance of a child suffering from an inferiority complex.

As a matter of fact, it is Junior's nature (as it was and sometimes still is Mama's and Papa's) to respect relative ability. It is only by rigid suppression of such respect, through the public relations work of those with maladjustment theories to sell, that he is finally prepared to step into his father's shoes and suppress his own son's native sense of relative values—in the name of Education and Progress and Democracy. Meanwhile, Junior doesn't feel that he is not as good on the scale of absolute value of the human being as Jack simply because Jack is first string while he is third—provided only that Junior be allowed to live with himself long enough to adjust to himself. It is considered dangerous, as it well may be, for one to get to know himself too well; the emphasis is on living with others.

It would be well for us Mamas and Papas to notice that often Junior tries hard to equal Jack on the football field. We honor competition everywhere except in the classroom.

III

I have said, and here re-emphasize: The good teacher must accept as a starting point an alumni association of parents who generally cannot make a distinction between intellectual accomplishment and moral goodness. Then he must, soundly and according to his intellectual principles, insist upon judging intellect. For herein lies his true compassion for Junior, as for Jack and Johnny. Johnny makes consistent A's because he is exceptional (in the old sense of the word), and Jack kicks the football fifty yards because he is exceptional. Is Junior as second man to be told that his twenty-five yards are really forty or his C in mathematics a B plus? If Jack Jones simply cannot do mathematics because he is exceptional (in the newest euphemism for the old-fashioned *dumb*), he should not be given the Social C. Not even when he works diligently, makes no trouble, and is needed for the Thanksgiving Homecoming Game. (Usually he isn't required to know anything about mathematics to be eligible to play, but he must have a passing grade in the subject.) If both Jack and Junior fail to master the material, they should be given the F, which despite popular superstition is not equal to the mark of Cain.

Aside from reasons other than practical, the person who knows most accurately that there is a lie in the grade book when a C is substituted for an F or a B for a C is Junior. One of the major causes of classroom chaos (at least I gather this to be true from my interviews with university freshmen just out of the nation's high schools) is the dishonesty involved in the attempt to adjust the student socially and psychologically to mathematics or English grammar or physics. If I can get away with this, says Junior or Jack with his adjusted C, how much further can I go? Having got a C where a D was called for, can I get a C for an F? Where Junior may have tried to make the first string on the football team, he now tries to see how much he can get away with in the classroom. Honesty in judgment of intellectual achievement would make a remarkable difference in the wear and tear on teachers. It would do more than a raise in salary, *provided* honest judgment were supported by the teacher's superiors so that eventually it would come to be valued by Mama and Papa.

Compassion? Yes. But the good teacher's compassion involves his maintaining Old Testament principles as well as New Testament ones. For the reality of human existence in our limited world of now, to which we are supposedly adjusting in our schools, cannot be denied indefinitely. We are somewhere now in our intellectual journey, just as we are somewhere physically. And the teacher's responsibility is to tell us where. The teacher's justice in giving the student his intellectual place is ultimately the greater mercy.

IV

The word has got abroad that, if the teacher is to be successful in his missionary role of helping Junior adjust to society, he must become a contortionist "personality-wise." That is, he must put himself on a level with Junior and Jack and Johnny. But the teacher, in deserting his proper role as sympathetic but disinterested judge of intellectual accomplishment, in order that he might work such adjustments, has destroyed his authority and forfeited the dignity proper to his role. The teacher must regain authority and its concomitant dignity as necessary to his position of judge, and he must do so, among various ways, by re-establishing a line of distinction between teacher and student. The teacher as regular fellow is not per se the good teacher any more than a friendly coach who lets Junior play first string end is a good coach. One slight, symbolic, and perhaps even "undemocratic," step toward the restoration of authority and dignity would be to place the teacher's desk on a raised platform in the classroom, as is done in some places now, though usually because of the large class-room and the impossibility of seeing the last rows of students other-wise. The platform is a control post, and emphasizes control. But it also emphasizes the necessary segregation of teacher and student. Desegregation between teacher and student is a thing to be earned by the student, not one to be conferred at birth. As for the "undemo-cratic" aspect, one does not put off his humanity when he puts on the judicial robe of the teacher—when he ascends the platform. And neither is one being human when he substitutes for the robe of teacher dignity the clown's uniform of motley. The teacher's plat-form, though often so used, is not primarily for the purpose of enter-taining a paying audience through professional antics.

Of course, the good teacher is haunted, as I said earlier, by this nightmare vision of himself on the platform misjudging. One has to choose his nightmare and accept it. Many teachers are reluctant to set themselves up as judges of intellect, even as trainers of intellect, who are not reluctant to draw salaries as teachers (low though that salary be). And many are not reluctant to concern themselves with pseudo-moral judgments. More teachers can be found who are will-ing to condemn cigarettes, in a mathematics class, than are willing to flunk Junior because he made thirty of a possible one hundred points on his final examination.

It usually turns out that those teachers who are more concerned with social-moral problems than with intellectual problems are actu-ally preaching moral values and social responsibilities according to the gospel of environmental determinism, whose cardinal virtue is social adjustment. It is an easy gospel to evangelize about, requiring little depth of thought. Since man is conceived by this gospel to be the product of his environment, it follows as the night triumphant that (1) man is not responsible for his *unfortunate situation* and (2) the unfortunate situation changed to *fortunate* will automatically change the man into a *desirable social entity*. The logical correlative to this line of reasoning is that the man already in a fortunate situa-tion—which generally means he who has already acquired his four-bedroom house and a college education—is likewise not responsible for his situation, but this aspect of determinism is not tolerated.

Such an assumption would be labeled quickly and indignantly as so-
cialistic polemics, if not raw communism by the haves who might be
required to give up a bedroom and a car to make their less fortunate
neighbors good. Besides, we want credit for our success. The result
of our illogical, pragmatic use of determinism is made manifest in
the schools as the necessity of adjusting Junior to social mathematics.

For the good teacher it seems a dark forest to contemplate. He
feels he has only a hatchet where an ax or buzz saw is needed. But
some light filters through if he chops at the underbrush. When Junior and Jack, and even Johnny (since he eventually feels he must be
one of the boys to overcome his social handicap of proficiency in
mathematics) see what they can get away with in mathematics class,
they are aware of one of those self-evident truths that most of their
teachers and parents manage to outgrow, a truth which the popularized environmental determinism overlooks: there are two terms in
the proposition *man* in *environment*. The boys know, however inar-
ticulate they may be as a result of native handicap or the farce of
business English, that the individual sprouts and flourishes in an environment and that, while the quantity of the fruit of his accomplishment may be affected by environment, the quality of the
accomplishment is untouched. Environment has nothing to do with
kind. If the corn seed sprouts at all, its stalk can bring forth only
corn, good soil or bad. Dog fennel grows tall in rich bottom land,
but it is still dog fennel. Consequently, in the insane environment of
that classroom which denies this sane principle of reality, where dog
fennel seems to be cultivated in the hope of harvesting corn and
where corn is expected, because it is corn, to flourish in indifferent
soil, the students mark time by playing with the environment for
amusement. They play Alice's role in Wonderland, but not as po-
litely as Alice. Thus, the teacher who sits democratically in the center of a circle of chairs to be "close" to his eleventh-grade
government students, to be democratically "one" of them, finds instead that he is less than they, that he is indeed in a cage of chairs and
is being played with. His position as judge is permanently damaged.
For, while we insist that the world's judgment of our moral and civil

misdoings be made by a committee of our peers, we resent intellectual judgment from one of our peers. The teacher who is primarily
one of the boys is not the good teacher any more than the father who
is a boy among his sons is a good father. The child is father of
tomorrow's child, not (sweet thought though it be) father of today's
man.

                                  v

Now, in closing, to connect the problem of that desired judge of intellect, the good teacher, as he faces his class in general mathematics
in the tenth grade, with his relationship to Junior's parents. Environmental determinism, the dominant American philosophy (dominant because it is the philosophy according to which we define our
lives and establish and maintain our institutions) has filtered down
through the ranks of our registered voters and become an emotional
religion which is hard to combat with reason. One who dares confront it may find himself accused of being un-Christian. Yet this
most narrowly subjective of philosophies is ultimately responsible
for undermining the area of true objectivity in the schools,
specifically those courses of study having to do with the measurable
development of mind. The philosophy has come waving a deceptive
flag emblazoned *humanitas* in the name of that mythical and illusive
god Education, anthropomorphically produced by schools and departments of education. Education's supposed grace is that it makes
one able to absorb environment rather than overcome it, to exist in
the world in an "adjusted" state. It is understandable how it was that
a majority of the registered voters came to align themselves with the
initial flag wavers following the shattering effect on religious
thought of the coming of scientific determinism in the 1800s. The
emotional adjustment of the Bible to Darwinian thought leads natu-
rally enough to the emotional adjustment of intellectual values to
social values.

   The good teacher will not be so undiplomatic as to attempt to
wrest the flag from the evangelists of Education. Such a move would
leave him unsupported on all fronts. For in the three generations

during which the present philosophy of education has come to power, most teachers willingly or of necessity deserted teaching the intellect, a most demanding occupation, for the easier comfort of helping their students feel toward adjustment. Indeed, most students of high school age have come to have a vague feeling, akin to that of their parents and most teachers, that they may acquire intellectual prowess by existing in what is supposedly an intellectual environment for from four to eight years, at the same time enjoying the pleasures of social adjustment in business English and mathematics and making crude bird houses in Shop 11 and worse than crude upside-down cakes in home economics. The college community rounds off Junior's social self, the "Whole Junior," and he is ready for the great adult world, especially welcoming the comfortable arm of the socially agreeable state with its unemployment insurance, social security, import taxes, crop supports. We Mamas and Papas have provided it all, having the necessary vote. And it is all very fine. Except in 1957, of course.

The good teacher's progress against this hydra-headed problem as he faces his mathematics class will be slow and seem slower. But perhaps in three generations, if he holds his principles, he may restore a fundamental principle to the canon of public education: the training and proper evaluation of the individual's intellect. It must be attempted. And of the possible allies, aside from a Russian scientist in orbit around the moon, the best are among the students themselves, those students who resent being subdued to the useful and the good by the Telemachuses who would feed their people bread from dog fennel seed. Some there are who honor the honesty to call a failure an F. The responsibility of adjusting to an F or an A is primarily Jack's and Junior's and Johnny's, and the teacher must stop reducing himself in an attempt to adjust for them. And the good teacher might well reassure Mama and Papa that Junior has just as good a chance of getting to heaven as Johnny—no doubt an even better chance.

2

The Fallacy of Practicality

COLLEGES OF LIBERAL ARTS attempt to occupy the vacuum created by the abdication of sound theology which, at its highest level (in the monasteries and in the medieval universities) preached to the intellect from the texts of science (in the old sense) and art. When such preaching was at its strongest, it was governed by an end to which most men, intellectuals or not, gave assent: the glorification of God. And the principles developed by intellectual training showed clearly to questioning intellects trained that there was a range of human possibility which made it difficult to suppose that all could glorify God through intellectual pursuits. This realization did not make any easier the problem which, in a different form, still confronts us: How should one attempt to share with those less fortunate insofar as intellectual ability and training are concerned, the fruits of the intellect? Should one water down the concentrated essence for the sake of the majority? The problem reached a political climax over such symptomatic issues as whether or not the Church's services should be conducted in the vernacular.

Today a similar problem is reaching an economic climax: Can the state afford to maintain school training for the masses from kindergarten through college? It is the same problem, seemingly, as that which moved John Wycliff on his crusades. But the problem is less simple now than in the fourteenth century because it is not defined within a context of generally accepted ends. And confronted by a mass of students expecting a magic initiation into the secrets of liberal training, the liberal arts teacher considers his private problem and despairs. Am I, as a teacher of humanities courses, to devote myself to translating the lyric or narrative into the vernacular? Am I to explicate only? And if I do, who is to perform the act of the scholastic? By whom will the preaching to the intellect be done? By the student in his own mind through the aid of my translation? What, the teacher asks himself again, are the uses of this poem or of this story to those before me?

I myself take it that one must see literature, even as he must see philosophy or science—the other necessaries to a liberal training—as a means. Literature provides texts to which theology applies philosophy. The insistent question is: What theology? And so, ideally, the teacher of humanities courses preaches to himself and others concerning the first and last things as defined by his theology—his view of man's relationship to the known and unknown—by presenting a range of human possibility as human actuality. Literature makes believably real that which is possible. In my own view, it does so by establishing over that common denominator of humanity— man as fallible rational animal—fictional individuals (including the poets of poems) proving (that is, testing) the possible through all the possible combinations of fallibility attendant upon man's rational, animal being.

Now the artist is the first to insist that art does its own preaching, that—accepting as true what I have said above—no justification for the humanities teacher is apparent. My answer to that is that the liberal arts teacher finds himself in a real situation; one must always work out toward the ideal from where he is at this moment. It is no doubt true that art does its preaching well, if it is good art and enjoys a proper audience. The Attic and Elizabethan stages were undoubtedly better humanizers than sophomore survey courses of world literature. But, as the liberal arts teacher discovers, he has inherited, or has had thrust upon him, the responsibilities of showing that Sophocles and Shakespeare do indeed say significant things about the human condition, toward the end of humanizing the individual student. He does not feel free to turn from what, in the innocence of his youth or the desperation of his maturity, he has accepted as a duty. In a world where, to many, Christianity is suspect and where sectarianism has so destroyed the first responsibilities and ultimate ends of human existence through the decaying effects of sociological and political and environmental theologies, the teacher of my persuasion finds himself called by conscience and recent tradition to the task of demonstrating, through an intellectual approach and to a diversity of individuals, what each individual before him is, potentially; the end is that each student may feel justified in his own aspirations. This is the basic task by which the liberal arts teacher finds himself burdened.

And unless he is a Christian teacher, unless there is a clear understanding on his part as to the ultimate end of aspiration, he is merely attempting to create in the vacuum of his own impossibility.

I

The unfortunate truth is that I have been discussing an ideal liberal arts teacher and not the liberal arts teacher as he is generally found to be. And this, too, is a reality which we must accept. One has only to read at random Caplow and McGee's *The Academic Marketplace,* a study of the hiring and firing and applying of teachers in liberal arts departments, to have this point painfully established. The "indeterminate structure of the university as an institution," Jacques Barzun says in his foreword, "derives . . . from the radical ambiguity of a profession in which one is hired for one purpose, expected to carry out another, and prized for achieving a third." That is, one is hired, ostensibly, to teach, expected to spend his time doing research, and valued and promoted to the extent that he establishes prestige through publication.

This study by Caplow and McGee is based on professorial vacancies and replacements which occurred in the liberal arts departments of nine major universities. Among the book's many unsettling conclusions, a major one is that there is really little concern for a person's teaching ability, the intrinsic merit of any research, or publication. The primary concern is for the length of bibliography and the word-of-mouth or newspaper or alumni-magazine reputation of the man to be hired. One department head who hired a man on the strength of his publications admitted to the interviewers that he had not, in fact, read even one of the applicant's publications. The primary requirement of the college teacher is, of course, as Barzun says, to achieve a status through publication which will make the individual an apt subject for publicity. This is the result of a false philosophical dogma our world is currently ridden by, a point to which I shall return, namely, that it is the act that is important and not the essence or person from which the act proceeds. Legislatures and foundations are impressed by bibliographies no less than are department heads and deans of faculties. One teacher was fired, according to one of those interviewed and quoted in *Academic Marketplace*, because he was guilty of spending too much time working with his students and not enough time producing through research.

As is inevitable, the effect of this dishonesty of the universities reflects clearly in the attitudes of society in general toward education. Dr. Keith McKean, Social Studies Department of the State College School of General Studies in North Carolina, in a newspaper article addressed to parents, asks "Why Send a Child to College to Fail?" Students flunk, he says,

> because they drift into a college where the minimum standard is above their level, when they might do all right in some other school. What parents ought to know is that there is some sort of college degree for just about everyone who cares to go. Of course, the colleges all seem to give the same degrees, but the letters stand for the widest range of academic standards. There are grade schools which are a lot tougher than some colleges; and there are PH.D. degrees which are not the academic equivalent of some undergraduate degrees. The trick is simply to find out what colleges suit your son's talents. Here again high school counselors can help and there are books on the subject, too.

This is practical advice, for it recognizes that the university degree is a symbol which has long since lost its role as symbol and has come to be, not a sign of the thing, but the thing itself, like the learned research articles one's colleagues do not read. I recall hearing a member of the board of regents of a state university in a private conversation at an alumni lunch praise my university's president for the buildings he had built and for the increase in the number of PH.D.s on the faculty. To insist upon the terminal degree was important, he argued, since the degree represented "prestige" to the school. And, he continued, to get the degree would work no real hardship on anyone, since a faculty member could go to some "jack-leg college" and get one easily enough. At least one high school I know of solves the degree problem more simply than that. A student who makes so poor a show that his teachers will not certify him goes through the graduation ceremonies and receives a blank diploma.

Now if any person doubts that this is the general academic situation faced by teachers in the liberal arts college, let him ask whether the following indictment is valid and test it by his own experience. There is a superstition underlying the magic of the thing—the published article in this instance—which is deliberately fostered by those people who as a rule argue most loudly the practical value of the liberal arts training. This impulse to encourage the superstition has its source, no doubt to a considerable extent, in the vulnerable economic and social position of the liberal arts teacher in a secular, materialistic age. With the increasing fragmentation of human existence by specialization, science and industry combine to establish as the ultimate achievement of man the immediately comfortable thing. Science is valuable primarily because it discovers, defines, and provides a serum for polio. Or it is valuable because it discovers an application of natural laws to the materials of nature which leads to an object of creature comfort and entertainment—the inner-spring mattress or the television set with remote-control channel selector. The practical value of such scientific interests is too easily demonstrated. Before it was so thoroughly developed as to become a major tenet of the American's religion, Thoreau commented on it: "We seek too soon to ally the perceptions of the mind to the experience of the hand, to prove our gossamer truths practical." Thoreau's was no new observation concerning human nature in general, but how accurate a pointer to American character in particular as it develops from Benjamin Franklin. This human inclination, which too often demonstrates itself as human failure, has been raised to the status of a national trait demanding the loyalty of all Americans. The man who dares question such "progress" risks the label of un-American or undemocratic, the latter being the more heinous heresy. What is meant by *progress* is the acquiring of a new comfortable thing in the name of the masses; it is acquired by the generous research support of the masses.

Threatened by the demand to establish a practical end to justify the practical problem of supplying it with money, the liberal arts college reacts. How? Let us look at the attitudes of the typical English department of such a college. Scholarship is honored, but the scholarship which is most honored is that which best lends itself to the best publicity—that which can be presented as utilitarian. Notice for instance the attitude toward those studies which compare one work of literature with another to demonstrate influences. It is almost as if such a study is written against the old charge of impracticality, brought against the liberal-arts man by those who can see good only in the inner-spring mattress or the television set or polio serum. Among those whom the liberal arts mind usually considers Philistine, to enjoy the poem or novel and respect it for what it is, as he (the Philistine) enjoys and respects the inner-spring mattress and television set, seems not an accomplishment worthy of financial support.

It must certainly be admitted that it is the Philistine mind and muscle whose money supports such liberal arts study as exists in the world. Therefore, with a great deal of sophistry and elaborate rationalization, the liberal arts college uses the *thing*, the published article or book, to justify its existence. It is, first of all, in existence as an object to be held in the hand as the syringe of polio serum is, and it is easy, relatively speaking, to proceed from that automatic respect among the Philistines for the existence of *things* to suggest an analogy between tracing the source of a poem and tracing the source of a disease. To have done so in an article is somehow to have explained the poem so that our Philistine patron does not feel obligated to worry about it as he might otherwise believe he should. He has provided the money to support the isolation of some mysterious virus. The poem is under control through the article or book, as the disease is under control through the serum. Therefore Doctors of Literature become not only tolerable but necessary to society, so long as they prove that they are guarding the mind through new and modern serums stored in the learned journals against possible epidemics. The one additional requirement is that it be the very latest available for the money. This requirement for the latest model article, as for the latest model automobile, works well pragmatically, if for the immediate interests of the liberal arts college. For, though in medicine the serum has the disadvantage of giving only a temporary immunity, this same limitation of the published research streaming from liberal arts colleges is actually an advantage. I do not mean to say of course, that an article published a hundred years ago has said all on its subject that can be said; I mean to criticize the liberal arts college's approach which assumes that the world "needs" a new article on the subject on a calendar schedule and should therefore finance it. All men are subject to the ravages of polio; few to the ravages of inadequate commentary on Dante's *Divine Comedy*.

Are these not true observations on the role of the humanist scholar as he exists, typically, and particularly in state universities? Is it not true, for instance, that the alumni of a university, who are by no means the liberalized body of citizens the non-alumni are encouraged by our propaganda to think them, feel that a book tracing the influence of Milton on Tennyson is a legitimate occupation for an endowed scholar, without their ever being concerned with the possibility that such a book may merely demonstrate the obvious or the necessarily true? The same group will be less likely to contribute funds to support a teacher who wishes to study and understand Milton or Tennyson. Without that printed study, without the serum, the disease is still with us. It seems futile to suggest to a dean of faculty or to the alumni during fundraising drives, as I am here suggesting, that the man himself, the studier, by the very nature of his being, his *changed* being, demonstrates his study to be worthwhile and does so in a myriad of immeasurable ways simply by being. The dean of faculty, alas, has become the universities' master computer who sees the teacher through a haze of distorting statistics prepared to be published by the president's annual report in pursuit of an enlarged budget. And the alumni are assured of the teacher's value through these statistics which appear as news stories datelined "State University" or as stories in the alumni bulletin—*speeches given this year*: three (On what, to whom, and whether worth the price of transportation?—questions not to be asked) *recent publications*: two articles on the influence of *Howl* on the presidential elections and a book tracing Donne's indebtedness to the New Testament. The legislature is persuaded, the money flows, the college prospers, offering degrees to more and more by a faculty less and less interested in the art of teaching.

I am not, of course, arguing that none should write critical papers. What must be re-emphasized is that a purely utilitarian approach to the satisfying of intellectual needs is doomed, ultimately; that what the liberal arts approach has to offer to the training of the mind is quite different from what it is popularly said to offer or seems to offer. The liberal arts teacher must, for conscience and sanity, examine the title his college generally bears and argue that the *College of Arts and Sciences* has come to represent a division and a manifold specialization where unity was once implied by its name. If the liberal arts teacher who is serious about his relation to society does not see as a starting point, for instance, that the sciences involve a human orientation toward the universe whose prime necessity to perfection is the removal of the human element that science may be perfectly objective, then how may he himself see the necessity of the complementary arts which offer one way of putting humanity back into the universe. He must restate and give an equal emphasis to the *arts*, that he may abandon the dishonest attempt to encourage the superstition that liberal arts training is of general utilitarian, pragmatic value to the man in the street.

But a warning to him: The proper way to relate arts and sciences is not through a scientific measuring and evaluating of the arts. Such weighing of value lends itself too easily as a means of surviving in the economic world. That approach insists finally upon a utilitarian virtue in liberal arts training at the expense of the arts it serves. There must be no deliberately created or innocently maintained blindness to the proper end of the human being. The humanities teacher of my persuasion is apt to hold against Plato of the *Republic* just such a pragmatic use of art, suspecting that good physician Plato of purging his patient's bowels by too much letting of his blood. That is certainly what one holds against the article-factory scholar who subordinates through self-pride or the pressing needs of academic survival the aesthetic, moral, and intellectual qualities of art, and who uses as a justification the argument that such concerns are themselves immeasurable. Of what virtue, or practical use either, is it to compare Samuel Pordage's *Mundorurti Explicatio*, precursor to *Paradise Lost*, and Milton's greater poem if the concern is not at least with the point that history is generally a sound enough winnower to preserve that human work which best reflects the best mind—aesthetically, morally, and intellectually considered. But finally, what must be said and insisted upon as the end of all our endeavor to promote liberal education—the ultimate earthly end of liberal arts training—must always be to prepare a particular man to hear, really hear, Oedipus's agonized cry so well that he knows agony as never before.

II

What is the reaction of the student, innocent enough and Philistine enough to measure what he is told by what he sees? There is an honesty forced by innocence which is difficult for a teacher to "adjust." To argue the pragmatic value of liberal training is to present such honest students an absurdity which their experiences and observations easily show to be absurd, though they maybe unable to articulate the absurdity and though they may be discretely polite enough not to attempt its articulation. What any semi-literate student can see and hear is that at this particular juncture of history, the rewards of the comfortable home or of public veneration do not in fact go to the literate, humanized intellectual. A student has only to name those people he knows who are making money. He has only to look to the offices of government from the local to the national level to see that the argument is fallacious. He has only to listen to those in authority at universities and colleges themselves.

I have said that the liberal arts colleges have occupied the vacuum created by the abdication of sound theology addressing the intellect on the subject of first and last causes of human being. I have also said what seems to be undeniable—that most members of liberal arts colleges do not have a clear sense of the end of liberalized education. How many professors of liberal arts faculties would accept and govern themselves by Whitehead's statement: "Your learning is useless to you till you have lost your text-books, burnt your lecture notes, and forgotten the minutiae which you learnt by heart for examination. . . . The function of a university is to enable you to shed details in favor of principles." But one cannot be a member of a faculty for long without realizing that a surprisingly large number of those who do not seem concerned with principles nevertheless conduct themselves and speak as if they are members of an elect priesthood guarding sacred principles. Faculties should feel themselves to be such, of course. But there is something deathly wrong in one's pretending for purposes of economic survival or in his assuming shallowly that he is possessed of the only true means of becoming the ideal human, if in fact he has no sense of the ends of ideal being which the liberal arts are argued to give one. The professor of geology, the professor of English literature, the professor of bacteriology, to listen to the run of them, speak as if each alone were guardian of the true and lively word leading to the salvation of the human race. Although a student may not understand such falseness sufficiently well to reject it intellectually, he senses it and becomes emotionally suspicious, wondering how one god, the liberal arts college, seems to have so many seemingly unrelated manifestations.

I believe I know the causes of the cancer that makes civil war inevitable among the cells of the liberal arts college, though I see no cure that is not facile. The immediate historical cause lies in the divorce of humanism from Christianity. Humanism became a freed cell. Released from Christianity, it ran wild from Christianity, began to exist as an independent theology during the Renaissance. For a period of time, the more thorough its freedom, the more powerful it became. It made possible a secularization of man's ends which was not possible earlier; it made possible the abandonment of the glorification of God as the final end of human existence. Such freedom made justifiable the intellectual and political imperialism of that day. But it also made inevitable the fragmentation of human being toward diverse secular ends, a fragmentation which followed the heady and impressive and tempting glorification and edification of man. To this day we suffer the consequences of that all-too-successful revolution which began six or seven or eight hundred years ago, a revolution which preached an appreciation of immediate human values and earthly truth, a revolution which at once used the intellectual mechanism which was preserved and refined by the scholastics out of our Greek inheritance and ridiculed that preservation and refinement by labelling stigmatically the age of the scholastics as the "Dark Ages."

But the immediate and inevitable consequences to us? Robert Frost says, in a wise poem,

> *once comparisons were yielded downward.*
> *Once we began to see our images*
> *Reflected in the mud and even dust,*
> *'Twas disillusion upon disillusion.*
> *We were lost piecemeal to the animals,*
> *Like people thrown out to delay the wolves.*
> *Nothing but fallibility was left us.*

and, Frost's point is, even fallibility will not set us aside from the rest of creation; the white-tailed hornet he writes of is fallible. Matter itself seems to err. For *disillusion* in the line above, read *fragmentation*. That has been the history of the individual's value in that unified span of human history from the repudiation of the scholastics to the 1960s. Fragmentation of human *being* into specialized human *action*—art, science, multiple sectarianism going separate ways.

Industrialism rose and declared its independence from the ultimate ends that once held society together in a way that our substitutes—social science, advertising, or the Community Chest—cannot. The argument that such fragmentation was made inevitable by the sudden blossoming of discovery, geographic and intellectual, is not conclusive. Milton is supposed by this argument to have been the last completely educated man in that he compassed within his mind all known knowledge. Aside from the fact that it seems questionable that Milton actually did encompass the world's knowledge, the point is that fragmentation of being follows upon the loss of a sense of the ideal and not upon the impossibility of encompassing all knowledge toward an ideal end.

And the evidence of this fragmentation so far as our liberal arts colleges are concerned? What is more specialized than the departments of liberal arts colleges? One has only to listen to departmental jealousies exhibited in the deprecation of American Literature specialists at the hands of English Literature specialists or the smug self-assurance of the American Literature specialists. One has only to see heads of departments patrol departmental borders in faculty meetings. One has only to watch the growth of departments which are successful in the competition for students through the offering of more "practical" courses or more specialized courses. From departments grow schools whose internal factions then become departments; from schools come colleges whose departments become schools. Departments of Economics become Schools of Business Administration. Chesterton says, looking at Chaucer's world as opposed to ours, that in Chaucer's day, life was considered a dance, but soon afterward it came to be considered a race: ideally we should dance with each other, but instead we race against each other.

Let us consider further the recent history of this basic error of the liberal arts attitude which has led to the decay of the liberal arts college. The liberal arts college has become more secularized, which means more a servant to the business world, than it is convenient to admit in our statements of principles. But our university catalogues give the lie to these high-sounding (and often sound) principles. The ends of studying literature must be justified in terms of the job with the publisher, or of a position as teacher in high school or college. It is true that at one point in human history the liberal arts training was desired not only as an end in itself nor only as a means of helping one to that Dark Ages ideal of the proper glorification of God, but also as a purely practical bread and butter concern. It became obvious to the man who had eyes to see that he must train his mind in the trivium and quadrivium if he expected to transcend the role of his father, a mason or cobbler.* Hawking and jousting and crusading with the sword made room for grammar and logic and rhetoric as the practical requirements of the world changed. A new slogan was born and nurtured and came to power: The pen, in fact, did become mightier than the sword. And finally the gentlemanly pursuits ceased to be hawking and jousting. The gentleman was one who, among other accomplishments, could write an effective lyric. Today, having "progressed,"—and we must accept this as a starting point—the well-turned steak at the cook-out replaces the sonnet.

The point for the liberal arts teacher to keep in mind is that the trivium and quadrivium were established *before* the pragmatic advantages of those disciplines appeared, developed out of the natural desire of man to know, not because they were immediately practical. At the point in human history when liberal training could be of practical concern, the system was ready and waiting for whatever abuses were attendant upon its worldly uses. The value of the ideal was in no means negated by the fact that its uses were suddenly found to be practical because of the change in what man could see of his world. During the Renaissance such training as the liberal arts are said to give one became more and more practical, not practical only in the worldly service of the Church, but also as a means to position in the State. It is this latter tradition of the practical end of liberal training

---

* One of the popular superstitions of many of us is that in the Dark Ages only those that had, got; that education was limited to those with means. My colleague, Professor Lindemann, tells me that he had occasion to check the matriculation list of the University of Leipzig for the sixteenth century and that where there were very few of the nobility enrolled, slightly more of the substantial middle class "cives," the overwhelming number of students were enrolled under the column labeled "pauperes," that is, lower middle class.

which survives today and which is so helpful in creating those arguments on behalf of liberal training which even the semi-literate student rejects. For one does not need to know Homer to be governor of his state. The Scholastics who fathered the system were at least aware of the end of man as one which transcended service to Bishop or State. And it is their old faith in a transcendent end that the liberal arts teacher must repossess if he is to preserve and advance the true nature of liberal arts training in a pragmatic world.

For though once indispensable to the statesman, who in the instance of Milton must know Latin and Greek at least, this training was never one required of the many; wherever it remains a valid course of intellectual pursuit, it continues to be available only to the few, the few who have not only patronage but intellectual potential. The public argument that a liberal arts training is desirable for the generality is a specious one, since the general concept of man and his end has changed through our decay into a materialistic anarchy, which we are pleased to call "democracy." One does not need to write or speak well, much less intelligently, to be a newspaper reporter or columnist or to be the politician or statesman about whom these reporters write. Since every man has been told that all men are equal in the eyes of the State, as they were once said to be equal only in the eyes of God, and since all men have been instructed that they *are* the State, as they were never allowed to suppose themselves equal to God, the ambiguous democratic doctrine *all men are equal* comes to mean *all men are potentially president*. And since the shadow of the old practicality of liberal arts training lingers and grows, one is urged by those with vested economic interests in the myth to conclude: *Each man must be liberalized through formal education in case he becomes president.*

But the truth is that all men are not equal in their potential availability as president, even in a democracy. Nor are all men equal in their potential to absorb liberal arts training, in spite of all the votes that may be mustered in support of this "democratic right." Furthermore, the men of power, who articulate the argument and persuade the voters in its support, consider the common man not as an equal —not as a literate, intelligent citizen, even potentially—but as an integer representing a vote, an accumulation of which is necessary to maintain power. There is a romantic glow cast over Lincoln's career which is so powerful that it subordinates all considerations of his achievements and failures to the fact that he was born in a cabin and walked miles to borrow books. The myth demanded a folksiness of Franklin Delano Roosevelt to overcome the political handicap he suffered by not being born in a cabin, the distinctive disadvantage he had of being able to buy books he wanted without having even to walk to the bookstore. Indeed, his having been crippled by polio was one of the most fortunate events in his life, so far as his political career is concerned. Our romanticism about the individual's relation to the State—to the town and country and state and nation— scarcely provides for realizing that the significant thing is not the *walking* or the *sending-for*, but the *kind* of book fetched and how it changes a man. We ought to spend less time teaching that Lincoln walked miles for the books he read and more time reading the books he walked after.

The vote becomes the common denominator of man: the common man becomes president, as he has become his own God. Or rather a man becomes president who seems to be a common man, who may actually be so in those few disastrous flukes of history that put an Eisenhower in office. Thus the irrefutable evidence against the argument of the pragmatic advantages of the liberal arts training. (Consider the fate of an actual product of such liberal training, at the hands of some of his critics.) What the supporters of the tradition do is keep alive the traditional sentiment for political or economic reasons, making it impossible for such training ever to be effective. I heard Robert Frost tell of chiding Roosevelt for always bringing God into his speeches; Roosevelt's reply was that he tried to leave Him out, but got so many protests from little old ladies across the country he was forced to include Him. The argument in favor of a liberal arts education for the populace in general is little more meaningful, if we take the blinders off, than Roosevelt's use of God in his speeches.

III

It has been possible, then, to keep alive the popular superstition that a liberal arts education is desirable because that argument has been presented in the name of a democratic right of the citizen and as the means to a happy social adjustment to the State. But the ideal human condition I hold is the perfection of the individual. By the very fact of individuality, which our contemporary democratic arguments at once postulate and deny by actions, there is a range of unequal human beings. It is politically expedient to make *equality* a vague and all-embracing term. And it follows undeniably from such confusion that wherever the public institution is involved, every taxpaying citizen has equal and inalienable rights. With such deliberately muddled thinking, there can be no common reference to an end of man's perfection which transcends his relation to the State. The "Dark Ages" view that man's proper end was the glorification of God through the perfection of the self made acceptable the undeniable fact that there are many ways to the realization of the potential self, even as there are many individuals seeking perfection—that the liberal training of the capable mind is not a special privilege in any way other than that those so schooled have been graced by special abilities. This view of the individual—secularized, then sentimentalized and sold to the American parent—is John Dewey's principal contribution to the disintegration of society. As Darwin refined the Chain of Being and removed the angels and God from it, helping make possible the new primacy of the State, Deweyism adapted the Aristotelian and Thomistic theory of potential being but removed any reference to ultimate ends other than the happiness of the individual in society, to be brought about by frictionless adjustment to society. The following note printed on a first-grader's report card is an obvious extension of Dewey, not a distortion of him, as is popularly argued in his defense: "It is the purpose of this report to describe your child's progress and needs, rather than to compare him with other children. This is because we know that children differ in interests, abilities, past experiences and rate of growth." Impressive? Of course it is. And the teacher, in this case one whom I know of directly as incompetently trained to judge, nevertheless grades the first grader on such categories as "growing in appreciation of beauty" and, in arithmetic, "understands meaning of numbers; uses numbers with accuracy; knows necessary number facts; solves problems."

The supposedly democratic argument evidenced by the report card is as specious as would be the argument that all citizens have the right to be skillful bricklayers. It would seem to be a self-evident truth that the bricklayer who has found himself as bricklayer—who makes himself, perfects himself, through building a good wall—may be as "humanized" as the good user of rhetoric who teaches or studies liberal arts. It should be obvious also that the perfection I am speaking of has nothing to do with the acquiring of split-level houses and second family cars. The point is that the act of raising the wall may be a gesture of human worship which is equal in the eyes of God to the act of guiding logical argument to a forceful conclusion. Thus, individual salvation is possible by means other than the high school diploma or the AB degree, though salvation to certain individuals may be best achieved through the pursuit of the diploma or degree. Chaucer makes my point extremely well in his portrait of the two brothers in the prologue to the *Canterbury Tales*, portraits which all parents should know as they concern themselves with the training of their children. The good Parson has a highly trained mind, presumably an Oxford-trained mind, while his brother is a lowly plowman whose devotions are confined to carrying many a load of dung to his fields. And yet Chaucer shows in each a spiritual dignity and goodness that makes us understand that they are not only blood brothers, but spiritual brothers as well, suitably accompanying each other on the pilgrimage to Canterbury. Chaucer does not establish them as "equal" to each other in their potential, as we attempt to do through our confused distortion of the term *equality*.

Our denial of this principle of inequality of abilities has important business advantages. For one thing, it ultimately helps provide both a market for inferior products and the inferior products to supply that market. For equality finally boils down, in our view of it, to *access to things*. Equality is Progress, and Progress is the new car each year, and every third or fourth year the new house in a new place.

What happens is a kind of anarchic economic communism, advanced by industrial power through advertising. Everyone must be equal, not living in the truth.

Such a pursuit of freedom and equality has had a decided effect upon our moral fiber. The symptoms are reported regularly by the news media and social agencies, with only an occasional cry concerning the disease itself. An instance: One of the automobile industry's problems is to convince its workers of the validity of its product, an attempt made necessary by the obvious recognition by the worker that what he is doing is less well done than his conscience and desire demand. A friend of mine, a very excellent mechanic who would give John Ruskin and Eric Gill cause for pride by his integrity as mechanic, told me of a visit he paid to an assembly plant of one of our largest automobile manufacturers. The man who conducted him on tour was quite emphatic in saying that the last person in the world they wanted to try to train for work on the line was a mechanic, since a mechanic would be dissatisfied when he saw something being done shoddily. The line would be slowed down for the presumably minor concern of correcting bad work. The novelist Harvey Swades reported some years ago on his experiences in working in such an assembly plant. There was deliberate sabotage of the automobiles by the workers—by such devices as putting loose bolts in inaccessible places to cause rattles. Sabotage, not because the workers were being paid substandard wages or driven to hard work, but as a sort of sadistic expression of dissatisfaction with the quality of the work demanded of them. This I take to be our Hungarian revolution and I find it encouraging. It once more demonstrates that virtue lacking which a man cannot be at peace with himself: the virtue of doing well what one is capable of.

It becomes necessary for the person who is devoted to liberalized training to realize that he does not hold a monopoly upon the one true way to human perfection, and that by its very nature liberal training has been, is, and will continue to be a rather limited approach if one considers it in terms of the number of persons of a given generation who may be properly affected by it. What he must realize is that the impulse that prompts him to preach his doctrine, insofar as the impulse is good, is the quality of his being that he shares with mankind in general: that his impulse is prompted by the common desire for human perfection. He distorts this impulse by attempting to make a particular talent or gift a general and universal requirement. And especially must he realize that the recent revival of interest in liberalized training on the part of the business world is not basically a concern for liberalized training, but a means toward human perfection. There is at bottom the immediately practical concern. What the business world wants, with rare exceptions, is effective basic training. The AB degree must indicate a minimum of proficiency in basic skills, not a humanized employee. The executive has learned that in the arts and sciences colleges, one finds teachers generally better able to teach basic writing and basic mathematics than in those schools of business administration that have grown out of arts and sciences into departments of economics. He is interested in the graduate who has, through the AB degree, acquired the training that grammar schools and high schools were originally intended to provide. What the liberal arts colleges have to offer to the business world are those preliminary skills that are, in the light of the old ideal, merely prerequisites to the liberal arts training.

The English mathematician and philosopher Alfred North Whitehead defines culture against our tendency as the "activity of thought, and receptiveness to beauty and humane feeling." Some segments of the business world recognize such a definition as valid, but feed upon the innate desire for the beautiful and sympathetic inclination to the humane that is in some degree a part of each individual's nature. They *are* interested in an AB graduate with a thin veneer of culture, but any thorough concern for "activity of thought" as Whitehead means the phrase is an unhealthy complication, as is the mechanic a complication on the assembly line. For the veneer is conceived of as a skill, like typing or bookkeeping, whose end is the fooling of the intellect. The proof of the charge lies in examining the general procedure in the advertising world. The pious concern for general welfare, publicly expressed, is about as convincing as the piety of a Tartuffe. Aldous Huxley presents a forecast of this business world's concern for culture in *Antic Hay*, published in 1922.

Here is a more devastating revelation of the advertiser as enemy than any found in Dos Passos's *U.S.A.* or in such non-fiction accounts as *The Hidden Persuaders.* Huxley's shady promoter of products, an advertiser with a diabolic adeptness at manipulating our receptiveness to beauty and humane feeling, says, "There is no better training for modern commerce than a literary education. As a practical businessman, I always uphold the ancient universities, especially in their teaching of the Humanities."

The graduate with an AB in the liberal arts, unless his training is so thorough as to make him incapable of the intrigue necessary to success, makes the most effective public relations man or advertising agent, though even with a superficial layer of culture there may be enough inclination in him to the good and beautiful to give him ulcers. For a person who undertakes to serve as public relations man in an automobile assembly plant has first to convince himself and then the workers that what they are doing is somehow connected with the creation of beauty, an attempt made necessary by the workers' recognition of unbeautiful, unsatisfying products. And the humane feelings? It is best not to consider that problem too deeply. That is, it is best to consider only the shibboleth uses of the term. Humane feeling is what the employee should have for the employer, who is doing his best to provide for the "good" of all—his worker and the public. If one goes too deeply into the concept, examining it in terms of the reality, he may discover that the argument does not fit the reality, that the system dehumanizes even as our present liberal education is likely to do.

If the holder of the AB degree were really liberalized (as the company's hiring representative is increasingly arguing that he must be), he would be capable of examining, undoubtedly forced to examine, the foundations of a system which is not basically humane, though it pretends to be. In fact, he would realize that he himself is largely responsible for the pretence that strives to hide the reality (and thus he is blood brother to the unhappy assembly line workers and the liberal arts teacher who make similar discoveries). For the basic duty of the public relations man is to disguise and distort reality—whether as a writer of stories about his company which he must persuade newspapers to print as "news," or an editor of a house organ smoothing relations within the company, or the man who demonstrates through the seductive cigarette ad that one who smokes the latest weed is the man who has a way with women. The public relations man, upon whom the survival of our economic system is said absolutely to depend, must be dedicated to a principle that Barnum enunciated: All men are suckers; all men are capable of being manipulated without their realizing they are being manipulated. The basic concern of public relations—the priesthood of our government, our business world, our educational institutions—is to devise the necessary deceit to sell the product, whether toothpaste or political party or degree, and to oil the waters of public reaction when or before the public discovers it is being had.

Such deceit is manifestly distasteful to the humanized person, whether humanized by liberal education or his sense of the proper way to make a thing well. That is why some liberal arts minds are driven out of the business world to the liberal arts colleges, the first monastery that suggests itself. And there?

There such a person at first finds himself in an extension of that world he thought to escape. Then he discovers what is even more depressing: that the world he has entered is a primary creator of that world he thought to escape.

IV

There are more ivory-tower teachers than our glib promoters of the academic world as pragmatic, materialistic servant to society would have us believe. Finally, then, let us look to the problems of such an individual, one who has perhaps renounced our national religion, pragmatism, in the interest of becoming a "priest" in the service of liberalized training. He may soon give up the popular idea that such training is generally desirable, if he ever entertained it. Then he finds himself supporting a system that is temporarily prospering by arguing that very point—prospering as a business prospers. He is inclined either to give up his ideal or blind himself to the reality. For he finds himself confronted by a growing number of students—each year more and more—who are quick-minded enough to sense the falseness of his position. He knows that, when he attempts to present *Macbeth* or "Go, Lovely Rose," he is dealing with students, young adults, who are or seem to be already old men and women. They respond mechanically if at all, except for one or two, as if life were already over and they some contingent of the citizenry retired from business but interested in Continuing Education—students to whom the beauty of language and the significance of abstract idea is so foreign that a teacher feels alone in the crowd of faces, even when they are turned respectfully to him.

And so despair. Disillusionment. Bitterness. Cynicism. He knows that the faces are indeed masks prepared for his especial benefit, behind which boredom and bewilderment and hostility lie smoldering. He knows that the responses are largely conditioned responses built in by twelve years of inadequate primary and secondary education, that the interest which is displayed is displayed because the faces suppose it to be expected of them as the price they must pay for the degree that presumably is the prerequisite to their doing the world's business. It is only rarely, when the mask is down, when the teacher has gained, by some lapse or trick, the confidence of this or that student, that a real relationship comes into being. The sign that such a personal relationship exists is likely to be a question that shocks the teacher, usually an aggressive question: What good does it do to read Shakespeare? This is the question—from those whose homes subscribe to facile magazines, who watch generally wretched drama on television, listen to impossible music which has not even the virtue of being honestly barbaric. Or the teacher may know the fact of the mask by the constant question asked by the ingenuous: *Will we be responsible for this on the final examination?* The system, through its persuasive advertising of education creates the mask. The conditioned reflex to liberal training is falsely maintained.

And then one day this teacher, this believer in the ideals of liberalized training, who has perhaps fled the world, wakes to the realization that he wears the mask also. His own response has become the conditioned reflex of one who once believed. And the terrible agony of futility drags him down. If there is no *visible* harvest of his devotion to self-evident values, if the monastery is really only a worldly factory and the *abbé* a vice-president in charge of production skills, are the values self-evident as he once thought? Are they even values? By deeds do we know virtuous men? By the effects of acts do we know the virtue of the principles?

And it is now that the central Christian principle, that one's first responsibility is to himself, must return to save one. Not that it means that such a person wasting in despair goes into business again, carries the mail or lays brick walls or gets him to some of the variety of possible monasteries—though he may do so and properly so. One must save himself. He must begin by realizing that his value in an absolute sense is not dependent upon the value of his actions nor the value of his actions upon their effect. In spite of the rampant superstitions fostered by Sartre, a man does not exist because he acts: he acts because he exists. Acts are not the source of being: they are only a sign of being. One's acts are not valid because they are effective: they are valid because they proceed from a valid being. Nor is this concern with self an indication of selfishness. One might more wisely argue that a concern for the *effect* of acts is a destructive selfishness whose roots are fed by hubris or pride. To the extent that one is what he might be, he is good; and to the extent that he is good, he will act. The act of a good person is good, though its effects may be invisible, as the effects of valid liberal arts teaching generally are. The good effect may even be accidentally evil: one may give a drunkard needed food, which he exchanges for whiskey. The point again is that the world is as it as because men are what they are: fallible rational animals, each distinctly, and thus individually, so. A person—doctor, lawyer, bricklayer, liberal arts teacher—has as his primary responsibility to attempt his own perfection, his own salvation, as preparation for, and the act of, glorifying God. He should not, he dare not, define himself by the worldly consequences of his acts, which not even the latest science is capable of measuring. Therefore he should not question his validity only by the world's response to his acts. It is because a good bricklayer sees his good wall in a way that a teacher cannot see the result of his act that bricklaying is so illusively tempting to the teacher. It is because the farmer measures his harvest and thus knows the potency of his seed, because he watches them mature, as the teacher cannot his seed, that the teacher is tempted to think the farm an oasis and long for a little place in the country. Whether bricklayer, farmer, or teacher, it is first and last the actor and not the act nor the end of the act—the wall, the growing seed, the disciple—that is important.

To conclude, what the liberal arts colleges must do is accept as fact the fragmentation and specialization of all our human institutions, but of the liberal arts colleges in particular, and go from there to define more clearly the specific responsibilities of particular institutions. The function of a grammar school is to teach the grammar of language and mathematics and science; the function of high schools is to teach the logic and rhetoric of these to some, not all: to those with the potential to learn, reserving to others specialized training—trades and crafts and so on. The function of the liberal arts school is to take the few with potential and give them what liberalizing values the individual liberal arts teacher can give them, through the virtue of his own perfection. While working toward this as an ultimate ideal for the liberal arts college, the college must admit the disparity between the goal and the actuality rather than pretend the disparity does not exist or is not a grave one. Then it must accept the undeniable tasks attendant upon the recognition. That is, such a college's English Department for instance should admit that its immediate opportunity lies, not in attempting to teach the unscreened freshmen the appreciation of literature, but in attempting to teach them to read simple prose exposition while hoping and working for the day when the grammar school may be forced to accept these responsibilities once more. This is the course of action. Or the school must institute such sound entrance requirements that it can assure its freshman instructor a class sufficiently prepared as readers to make possible the attempt at presenting the virtues of "Go, Lovely Rose."

And what the unhappy idealistic liberal arts teacher must himself realize first and last is that he is a part of a civilization not unlike that crumbling around Augustine, who said finally with Paul the fact of all history: "We have here no abiding city." He must believe in himself as valuable because he is oriented toward a transcendent city. He must preserve the virtues of liberal training, as the monks did in those ages which we in our blind glory have named the Dark Ages, knowing that when the world has a genuine practical worldly use of them they will be ready to supply the need. If the temple is to be destroyed, our contemporary Augustine, T. S. Eliot, has reminded us, then it must forever be rebuilt that it may be destroyed. Provided only that the builder does not suppose, through pride or simplicity, that the rebuilding is the end. It is simply his own private means toward the Eternal City, as it is a public means toward an orderly society within which individual virtue may flourish.

PART II

Now

3

Wanted: A Better Reason as Guide

ALLAN BLOOM'S POSITION in *The Closing of the American Mind* is provincial to such a degree that it is inadequate to a sufficient re-opening of that mind. The danger lies in part in Bloom's persuasive description of a mind unquestionably inhabiting the academy, but presented as if it were indeed *the* mind. A rarefied specimen from the world of intellect is presented as the species. There seems to me also a presence in his argument of an irritated nostalgia, exacerbated by a constricted view of liberal arts in relation to community. I am tempted to conclude that Bloom is an intellectual antiquarian whose sympathies lie so decidedly with Enlightenment constrictions of reason that his portrait of the American mind can be partial at best. The position he takes is that mind can remove itself from the complexity of existence by an exercise of reason. The suggestion is that, in our current intellectual confusions, the intellectual's best recourse is such a removal. It is a position which (for the sake of concision) Eric Voegelin has explored at length in *Science, Politics and Gnosticism* (1968) and in *From Enlightenment to Revolution* (1975). That is, it is the position of the secular gnostic.

After an initial celebration of the book on its publication, including a generous attention to it in op-ed pieces, there seemed to follow a momentary euphoria, typical within the conservative spectrum, I fear, whenever firm words are spoken and assumed to mean that action is thereby already accomplished. That has been the flaw in current conservative quarters. Disillusion within conservatism is the consequence, the lesson not adequately learned that a considerable distance lies between the action in the Word as announced by St. John ("In the beginning was the Word") and the word in the mouth of fallible man.

There was a moment of relief when Bloom's book was published and talked about: the academy must necessarily right itself, having been so roundly exposed as anti-academic. Euphoria threatened to transform into intellectual ennui, but then dissident voices began to rise against Bloom within the conservative camp, voices quite distinct from those of the fanatical Left such as the feminists, the Marxists, or the Darwinian naturalists of the NEA. Russell Hittinger very properly raised a warning to us dissidents (in the Fall 1987 issue of the *Intercollegiate Review*). His warning is that we must be careful not to throw out reason in our argument because we have reservations about Bloom's version of reason. What I intend to speak for here is a better reason as guide to the intellect than the one advanced by Bloom.

Hittinger agrees with Bloom's assertion that America lacks a traditional literary culture and is, therefore, at a considerable disadvantage in the throes of the rampant egalitarianism that threatens democratic institutions. I suggest that, to the contrary, we do have a literary culture championed by the intellectual community but one at such variance from social and political realities as to become antagonistic to the "American mind," whose good instinct in the matter is unsupported by that intellectual community. The traditional literary culture is one spawned by and disseminated from the twenty or thirty academies that are the special concern of Bloom. Just how radically removed from the "American mind" this culture is becomes increasingly a concern, as indicated in Russell Jacoby's recent *The Last Intellectuals: American Culture in the Age of Academe* (1987).

Hittinger makes in passing a very telling remark, wondering why "the role played by medieval men in constructing universities which are recognizably similar to our own is never mentioned by Bloom."

As to why the roots of academe should be so ignored, I suggest that it is because Bloom's position is more indigenously that of an American intellectual than of a European one, in spite of his considerable attention to Rousseau and Plato. His position is compatible with the very intellectual tradition he seems to call in question. Bloom's schematic reading of natural minds, seemingly derived from Plato and especially from the *Republic*, is rather a reading of Plato limited by an Enlightenment reason further restricted and filtered by Transcendental vagaries that have been a longtime infection in the American academic mind.

I find it not only notable that the medieval roots of the Western academy are not a part of Bloom's concern, but also even more surprising that he makes no mention of Ralph Waldo Emerson or of Emerson's own version of his argument, "The American Scholar," a mind and a work underlying Bloom's view of the academy. One needs only to examine Bloom's categories of students to see my point. There are those, he says, who are much concerned with the "relevant," which is to say (as I understand his category) those students concerned with topical events as immediately pressing upon personal circumstances. The anti-war turmoil in the 1960s illustrates the destruction of the academy by the "relevantists," with the academy becoming a staging area for contrarevolution in the social and political countryside surrounding the academy. Then there is a second category: those who "will have a spirit of enthusiasm that subsides as family and ambition provide them with other objects of interest." One ventures to say, incidentally, that this category actually supports the American academy at its economic level. This category may well prove restive when called upon to maintain the academy for Bloom's third category of student—those for whom the academy finally exists in Bloom's schemata. This is "a small number" who "will spend their lives in an effort to be autonomous. It is for these last, especially, that liberal education exists."

There is, by the assertion of these categories, the seeming assumption of separate species of mankind determined by an inherited mindset; thus one's inclination to be concerned with the "relevant" or with "family" is prohibitive of the mind's flourishing through the vir-

tues of liberal arts. The coloring given is that of abstractionism exercised through naturalistic presumptions about existence, a more recent intellectual grounding than Plato's *Republic*. Thus Bloom's
elevation of the "small number" of elect minds would not likely find
a point of analogy in the medieval scholastic. But these objections
are not my immediate concern. Rather, we should note the signal
word describing the end to which these elect are to devote themselves: They are to become *autonomous*. The description makes quite
clear the presence of reason truncated from the larger understandings of reason in the history of philosophy. Now if Enlightenment
thought in its liberal manifestations has largely collapsed into our
current intellectual chaos, as I contend, Bloom nevertheless maintains its validity as a means of restoring the academy. In my view,
such a restoration would make the academy a reservation for the isolated mind, rather than an institution vital to a community of souls.
What is to be rescued through Bloom's argument are conditions
suited to an autonomy of mind maintained by its own reason. It is
mind sufficient unto itself, as argued by Emerson.

One can sympathize with this longing, given the intellectual
chaos that erodes mind. But that sympathy is more out of an instinct
for mind's survival than a thoroughly reasoned understanding of
mind's role in the community of mankind. We must recognize in
Bloom's position a species of the deconstructions of reason that have
brought on the chaos of mind in the first place. The problem is not
with reason itself but rather with the presumption that the proper
end of reason is the elevation of mind to an autonomous survival in
the jungle of lesser minds. What is advocated is the self-sufficiency
of Emersonian thought. Alas, on the principle that autonomy is the
desired end, one can establish any number of temporal justifications
of any number of categories of self-sufficiency. Our second category
of minds must, in the light of such a principle, be excused a reluc-
tance to support the academy, having other and more pressing "objects of interest." The nineteenth-century German philosophy
underlying Romanticism, which Bloom examines severely, rises
against this same Enlightenment version of reason, but it does so on
the grounds of autonomy of the self as well. When autonomy as the

principal end of mind is pursued through a faith in the self-sufficiency of mind, the extensions of this principle allow no grounds to distinguish between the mind in its "solitary quest" for autonomy through reason and the mind on that same quest through "feeling."

In the name of the "autonomy of the self," then, all manner of actions by mind against the complex reality of the self and of the world emerge, including those very minds against which Bloom directs some of his most effective criticism. I am suggesting that the root source of the perversions of the self he laments is the very position he would recover. Feminist, Marxist, Deconstructionist, Libertarian, Neo-Conservative—the list might be easily extended—any and each justified by Enlightenment reason on this principle of self-autonomy, whether the position is advanced in the name of reason or of feeling. Hence the spirited attack against relativism mounted by Bloom does not in the end have any sufficient ground to distinguish it from the species of more spectacular relativism bringing chaos to the American academy.

One need only cite the eloquent introduction to *The Closing of the American Mind* supplied by Saul Bellow. Bellow recalls having been drawn when young to "the world of the streets" rather than to "a life of pious observances," a calling considered legitimate on the ground that he had the "tastes and habits of a writer." Those tastes and habits, as explored in the introduction, led him to eschew intellectual and spiritual disciplines in the interest of the randomness of enthusiasm. There is much truth in Bellow's assertion that "the book of the world . . . is being closed by the 'learned' who are raising walls of opinions to shut the world out." But the difficulty is that Bellow's "learned" are not truly learned. Nor is there any sure safety in the assumption that the isolated mind called to "the world of the streets" will itself be sufficiently open to the complexity of those streets. The literary movement associated with Bellow's Chicago, Naturalism, is ample warning against abandoning "pious observance." To abandon piety toward existence may lead to a "relevancy" that quickly distorts the rich complexity of the world of the streets.

To reject reason because of Enlightenment reductions of it to autonomous ends, in the name of unreasoned autonomous ends—

the "romantic" reaction to "rationalism"—is but to pose one partial dimension of mind against another in a struggle for power over the world of the streets. What needs saying is that reason, as Bloom seems to understand it, is not the final issue. What is needed is a recovery of a pursuit, through reason, of wisdom—a pursuit requiring the collective faculties of mind, of which reason is certainly the principal one. But reason is a gift of means in the created nature of man. Its full operation is not man's end, however much man prides himself on being distinguished within the orders of being by his gift of reason. Means reduced to an ideal end no doubt explains the strange conjunction of heroes for Bloom, as for instance of Rousseau and Plato, whose minds are not so easily made compatible as his joining of them urges. One is well advised to explore as a corrective to such yoking Voegelin's analysis of both Rousseau and Plato; Voegelin's counterargument is most revealing of the inadequacies of Bloom's Platonism and Romanticism.

Plato's *Republic*, Bloom says, is "for me *the* book on education, because it really explains to me what I experience as a man and a teacher." If I can depend on some of my own teachers, including Voegelin among the moderns and St. Thomas among the ancients, and also on my own reflections, I believe the *Republic* to be a portrait of the philosopher as a young mind and therefore to be taken with caution. Where Bloom finds in it "a teaching of moderation and resignation," I myself find in it a reduction of the quest for order and for the structure of the *polis* to an abstract definition of a savior, the philosopher-king whose ragged manifestations in the political affairs of this century of all centuries ought to require our looking more skeptically at the dialogue. One might better recommend Plato's *Seventh Letter*, at the end of his growing life, as far more resonant of moderation and resignation, especially after his many experiences with would-be philosopher-kings in Athens and Syracuse. Plato, in the wisdom of age and experience, advises that it is the second category of Bloom's mind that provides health and order through a wisdom gradually acquired by those men who are "in the first place advanced in years, who possess wives and children at home and can reckon the most and best and the most famous ancestors, and who own all of them sufficient property."

The root sense of order through which Bloom would have us restore and justify the academy is insufficient except for the preservation of the isolated, autonomous mind. That such a mind is capable of distorting idea and history in its quest for autonomy is witnessed in the book itself. One must feel a considerable sympathy for the assertion that "the most successful tyranny is not the one that uses force to assure uniformity but the one that removes the awareness of other possibilities, that makes it seem inconceivable that other ways are viable. . . . [T]here is what might be called an official interpretation of the past that makes it appear defective or just a step on the way to the present regime." This statement is pertinent to the arguments Voegelin makes in his analysis of tripartite reductions of history from Joachim of Flora through Hegel and Marx into our own day. It also fits the tyranny of Darwinian evolution in the face of cogent arguments from Gilson, Barfield, and Jaki.

One is surprised, then, by Bloom's own illustration of his generalization: "An example of this [tyranny] is the interpretation of Rome and the Roman empire in Augustine's *City of God.* Rome is not forgotten, but it is remembered only through the lens of a victorious Christianity and therefore poses no challenge to it." This statement contains Bloom's only mention of St. Augustine, whose influence on liberal arts in the Western academy is very considerable. Nor was Christianity triumphant when Augustine was writing his great book, for both Rome's civilization and Christianity itself were being threatened with extinction by barbarians whose analogues one finds in our own institutions ever since the end of World War II. Neither can it be said, in the light of Enlightenment rationality followed by the rise of nineteenth-century mechanistic science, that Christianity has been a triumphant tyranny of mind during these past two or three centuries—and most certainly not in the Western academy. There was perhaps a brief moment in the history of Western mind when it was dominant, in the thirteenth century. But one notes that the great academic mind of that moment, St. Thomas

Aquinas, is remembered by Bloom only once, and only for having read and taken Aristotle seriously.

There have been minds hardly respectful of viable ways separate from their own, but minds Bloom understands as greater than Thomas's or Augustine's: "[I]t seems absurd to me to say that Bacon, Descartes, Hobbes, Leibniz, Montesquieu and even Voltaire . . . were less deep than Jacques Maritain or T. S. Eliot—to mention two famous contemporaries from whose mouths I learned as a young man that the Enlightenment was shallow." We are to conclude from this remark, presumably, that Maritain and Eliot advanced themselves as deeper thinkers than these Renaissance to Enlightenment thinkers. But once more the history of intellectual argument in this century hardly supports such a suggestion. When Bloom was a young man learning from these "mouths," both Maritain and Eliot were struggling to recover other viable ways from the tyranny of two opponents: modernist rationalism and romanticism, divisions of mind directly out of Bloom's heroes.

The proper parallel here is, first of all, Maritain's and Eliot's minds to Bloom's. Surely neither of these teachers was so superficial as to have charged Bloom's figures with being simply shallow; the destructions of intellect everywhere about them were too conspicuously evident in their continuing influence. On the other hand, and rather certainly, Maritain and Eliot would have pointed out how partial and narrow a vision of reality those minds advance. But Maritain and Eliot would very likely detect some shallowness in Bloom's caricature of their position. Maritain especially might wonder at Bloom's conception of the discrete individual, as when Bloom says that "there are various kinds of soul" with "various capacities for truth and error." One might expect a student of Maritain to be more cautious with such a complex term as *soul*. One suspects here a residual and vague Platonism, arising more nearly out of Emersonian imprecisions about the soul than out of Plato.

The concept of the *polis*, to which one must at some point relate the academy as institution, is equally vague and residual of the more precise thought of Plato, Aristotle, Augustine, Thomas. Consider this passage: "Country, religion, family, ideas of civilization, all the sentimental and historical forces that stood between cosmic infinity and the individual, providing some notion of a place within the whole, have been rationalized and have lost their compelling force. America is experienced not as a common project but as a framework within which people are only individuals, where they are left alone .... The advanced Left talks about self-fulfillment; the Right, in its most popular form, is Libertarian, i.e., the right-wing form of the Left, in favor of everybody's living as he pleases." Such a description, seen in its narrowness, is accurate enough, though the antagonistic tone (given the ideal of autonomy) is surprising. But the description of the Left and the Right is most inadequate in light of the realities of those factions within the American polis at this juncture of history. Indeed, the Right is perhaps more peripherally "Libertarian" than allowed. Is it accurate, proportionately, when one considers the Fundamentalists, the Traditionalists, and even a considerable portion of the Neo-Conservatives on the Right? Here again is a tunnel vision, which is not necessarily conclusive evidence of shallowness, though Bloom's rhetorical stance is at times decidedly inclined to a shallowness. Consider the blanket dismissal of anything "Southern," the "Southern" mind as seen by Bloom set more in the mode of a nineteenth-century abolitionist reading of it than by an advocate of reason.

What begins to appear is that Bloom's vision of the academy is from a limited personal experience. He has lived in a rarefied intellectual environment, that of his academies. He finds a betrayal of mind in those institutions, a true finding to which I would add the extension of that betrayal to the American academy generally through the mechanisms of intellectual imitation. But my reading of the betrayal finds it beginning much earlier than the current collapse and closing of mind. I hold the betrayal to be that of the Western intelligentsia since the Renaissance, insofar as that diverse community of mind has turned more and more to autonomy of the individual as the principal end. So I am less than impressed by Bloom's limited critique of the American mind; the instrumental mind at work here seems to me flawed by its narrow reading of mind's betrayal. Bloom can see "country, religion, family, ideas of civilization" as merely "sentimental and historical forces" protecting an ambiguous individual from the threat of "cosmic infinity." To see in this manner must qualify at once what that mind can make of such institutions as country and family and religion, let alone what is to be made of the relation of the academy to them—that is, the relation of intellect to community.

Here is a final, but crucial, instance to the point from the concluding pages of *The Closing of the American Mind*: "The real community of man, in the midst of all the self-contradictory simulacra of community, is the community of those who seek the truth, of the potential knowers, that is, in principle, of all men to the extent they desire to know. But in fact this includes only a few, the true friends, as Plato was to Aristotle at the very moment they were disagreeing about the nature of the good." Bloom's conception of the Platonic *spoudaioi* would surely prove unacceptable either to Plato or Aristotle, because finally it is content with the autonomy of the individual, an autonomy self-generated by reason and refined by elevated friendships that are at a considerable remove from the ragged concerns of community. Self-satisfaction can be the only end.

Little wonder that Bloom as teacher is interested in "the kind of young persons who populate the twenty or thirty best universities." They constitute the "greatest talents," in evidence of which they have somehow chosen to pursue liberal arts, though not liberal arts as conceived by the medieval institution. Here the conception of liberal arts education is much closer to the version established in America by Harvard out of Emersonian thought and programmed by Charles W. Eliot—a deconstruction of liberal arts resisted by Irving Babbitt, George Santayana, and T. S. Eliot. For Bloom, other students (and faculty?) "have their own needs and may very well have very different characters from those I describe," that is, from those "greatest talents" bent on establishing and living the autonomous mind. Once more the use of *character* here reduces the high questions of mind in community toward the level of spectacle, as does speaking of *soul* as various in kind with "various capacities for truth and error."

Little wonder, too, if in consequence of such abstract conceptions of person to be imposed upon community in the name of the highest thought, we find E. D. Hirsch's *Cultural Literacy: What Every American Needs to Know* (1987) so often coupled with Bloom's book. A "Great Books" attempt at community was spawned in Bloom's twenty or thirty institutions in an attempt to conciliate Babbitt's Humanism and Charles W. Eliot's pragmatic Emersonianism. Now, through Hirsch, the tendency in the continuing crisis of intellect in community is to reduce the "Great Books" program to a "Catechism of Cultural Phrases," aimed primarily at the provinces in which "the American mind" feels itself isolated as if on outpost duty.

Conservatives and liberals alike are well advised to observe that Bloom's view of the academy is a very narrow one, a very partial view of the complexity of community. A considerable sorting out of argument is in order, requiring precisions of reason in pursuit of a larger wisdom about the nature of man in community and nature than Bloom perceives. Otherwise the argument must degenerate into the shallow surface conflict between a gnostic elitism and a gnostic egalitarianism, both of which operate from the principle that mind is of value because it defines, establishes, maintains, and defends the autonomous self. That is the problem we begin with at the first alarm over the failure of the American academy. But as of this moment we are not much advanced beyond that beginning recognition.

4

Scalawags and Carpetbaggers:
Higher Education as a Royal Nonsuch

DAUPHIN: What's your line—mainly?

DUKE: Jour printer, by trade; do a little patent medicines; theatre-actor—tragedy, you know; take a turn at
mesmerism and phrenology when there's a chance;
teach singing-geography school for a change; sling a
lecture. . . . it ain't work. What's your lay?

DAUPHIN: I've done considerable in the doctoring way
in my time. Layin' on of hands is my best holt—for
cancer, and paralysis, and sich things; and I k'n tell a
fortune pretty good, when I've got somebody along to
find out the facts for me. Preachin's my line, too; and
workin' camp-meetin's; and missionaryin' around.

Mark Twain
The Adventures of Huckleberry Finn

O
N ONE OCCASION a kindly critic, surveying my literary criticism and poetry and fiction, described me as being, like
Flannery O'Connor, a "hillbilly Thomist," a phrase she applied to herself. I do not disclaim that characterization of my pre-

sumptuous intrusion into philosophy in the interest of literature, a foray beyond my more comfortable environment of poetry and fiction. But my conscience demands of me some distinctions here in the name of that neglected intellectual virtue prudence, for the reader's sake but most of all for my own. I will admit that my prudence is somewhat shadowed by pride. For pridefulness is not easily escaped in any circumstances of our complex life. When I find myself likened to such presences as Flannery O'Connor and Thomas Aquinas—the one a consummate poet, the other the consummate philosopher—warning bells go off deep in my conscience. Prudence, then, demands at least an attempt to lighten that shadow of pride that is peculiarly pervasive of intellect. Peculiarly pervasive—that is, amalgamously inherent in intellect, but with a behavior unlike a shadow in sunlight, in that it is interiorly pervasive. Peter Pan's difficulty is not even a circumstance compared to this false light of intellectual pride, that *ignis fatuus* glowing deep within the process of intellectual action, and most disturbingly, preceding out of the action itself.

To my own present point, then: My pride is a false glow born of the assumption that I have been so persuasive through my words that my kindly critic is justified in praising me as "hillbilly Thomist." In justifying that pride, I remember Dante at the outset of his journey into the darkening Inferno, reporting himself made a sixth amid such intelligences as Homer and Virgil. The shadow of pride becomes almost set in the substance of intellect from such reflections, through the facileness of an analogy whereby I imagine myself companionable to Dante. And now Dante, no less than O'Connor and Aquinas, becomes of the company I keep. Who could ask for anything grander by way of self-evaluation? Any committee appointed to consider such a proposition, a committee carefully drawn so as to be balanced, would hardly concur with me or my kindly critic. It helps but little to know, as long experience has revealed, that by a "balanced committee" in respect to matters academic, one means rather a body self-neutralized in their conflicting, separable judgments, thereby giving to the uninitiated the illusion of objectivity, without which illusion academies across our nation would collapse.

They would collapse, since then it would be necessary for responsible and particular minds to declare judgment in intellectual matters. Most of those holding academic positions intended for such judgment have been so long removed from viable principles of judgment that they are lost without what they call the "input" of committees. Nor is it full rescue from my intellectual dilemma, occasioned by my pride, to review once more the motto I keep over my desk: "For God so loved the world that he did not send a committee." Certainly, the popular fate of my recent *Liberal Arts and Community* and its companion forays, attempting some rescue of the academy, as of my work in general, seems hardly encouraging to myself as "hillbilly Thomist."

Perhaps, says my conscience's antagonist, not content with self-indictment—perhaps there is a correlation here. Pride sputters to life, considering the possibility: perhaps to be ignored is to be right. To be ignored is evidence, if but indirect, that *this* intellect bears witness to the truth in false times. Certainly such an engaged intellectual activist as Kierkegaard used just this argument, making a virtue of Copenhagen's neglect. The evidence that I myself am a prophet without either honor or honoraria in my own country, the Deep South, is undeniable. Bringing Kierkegaard to my company, then, I consider the present fate of such labors of mind and spirit as my neglected books a hint of validation of that work. *Liberal Arts and Community* in particular seems to have fallen off the edge of the flat world of intellectual geography—a world defined in my estimation by those untenable modernist presumptions about intellect itself, of which I have spoken, presumptions which allow no round world constellated with diverse others within the larger mystery of creation. The more widely neglected, the greater the work. And so the struggling "hillbilly Thomist" finds refuge in the proof by neglect.

I

By now, what I am doing may be more clearly apparent: I am acting out the ambiguous movements of intellect in its journey, an intellect whose peculiar calling (or so it supposes) is to a service in the academy. It pursues the truth of how things stand, within conflicting circumstances such as the intrusion of committees or administrators whose self-justifications have obscured that first principle of intellectual action. But that principle is also subverted from within intellect itself by the corrosive acid of self-love which is anciently termed pride. St. Thomas reminds us of the first principle: "The purpose of the study of philosophy is not to learn what others have thought." Which is to say to us, such "others" as committees neutralized in their response to reality by a balancing of internecine ideologies, or administrators who are concerned with alumni or legislative or media support. No, says St. Thomas, not even what Plato or Aristotle or Thomas himself have thought, however necessary that we should know their thought. The end of intellectual action, he says, is to know "how the truth of things stands." Understanding the limits of my powers of rescue may lead to the suppression of pridefulness, under a current necessity of dealing with those untoward circumstances of intellect. For those circumstances are, like St. Paul's poor, always with us, to be handled with whatever charity proper to the reality of the circumstances themselves. Again, this does not mean the necessity that I *accept* the untoward. This is a lesson difficult to learn, and even more difficult to live by, as a teacher. For instance, it is difficult to hold firmly to the realization that true charity requires my giving a C or and F to a student who is a C or F student, rather than violate reality by giving him a B or a Pass. "Tell it like it is!" cry our young, in response to which we lie about reality, which is what grade inflation amounts to—a formalized lying justified by socialized rationalizations.

Now let me be as open as I may, telling it like it is in respect to my own position as teacher, an action seldom tolerated by an academy. Mine is a position, come to after long intellectual journeying, which denies my own intellectual autonomy. It is a position grounded, insofar as I am able to ground it, in Christian orthodoxy. That is my intentional position, whether actual in all parts of it or not. What that means is that mine is not a program to be advanced, but a deportment of intellect governed by a continuing concern for the truth of things. It is a position emerging from my faith that existence is real, that it has meaning beyond any prideful suppositions of my finite intellect. Thus, intellectual suppositions are suitable only as warily pursued, lest intellectual pride reduce creation to a flat world, as has progressively developed in the West since the Renaissance.

Flat is a term metaphorical here, representing that limited metaphorical position—that of Modernism—which nevertheless thinks itself *round* and thereby ends up with the curved lines of its own thought intersecting as a closed universe, leaving that intellect rotating upon the axis of its prideful, self-declared autonomous self. That entrapment is almost absolute in the academy at this point of history, so intensified by centripetal reductions of reality as to have made of the academy something very like those black holes that fascinate astronomers, though those holes lie at the outer reaches of our closed or closing universe. The implosive force of intellectual autonomy, which is assumed the governing principle of reality, removes the academy more and more from the rest of creation, human and other.

Most ominously, it supposes itself removed from that community of humanity in which the academy willy-nilly is embedded. The academy, once characterized in its removal from social dependence as the "Ivory Tower," now seems—at least from my perspective—rather a black hole at the outer boarder of the social body upon which it feeds parasitically. And *because* it necessarily feeds upon that body in increasingly conspicuous debilitations of that body, that sustaining social community more and more recognizes the academy as parasite. Or perhaps, rather, it appears a cancerous presence—to shift our metaphor from those black holes remote to us among the stars to a closer concern for the community's local *embodiment*. For we are more generally acquainted as a community with cancer as ravenous of discrete beings than with black holes in the heavens sucking the universe into non-being.

How may such forces turned randomly malignant, destructive of the proper ends to our intellectual journeying, be dealt with by the affected community? The question, cried louder and louder by community, unfortunatly is answered by some program, some five-year

plan of abstract construction, promised to be established and moni-
tored by authority, usually as associated with Congress. We want an
"Education President" and an "Education House and Senate," by
which we mean we want a centralized, detailed plan for directed action, funded by public monies—the sort of solution we turn to in any
emergency in this country. But that is in the end only to exacerbate
the problem. One rushing off to Washington for solutions is like
rushing down to Mexico in pursuit of a magical scientific cure for
cancer of the liver. Whatever help such cures might afford—and
there is sometimes some help—is help only when ordinately taken.
Which is to say, when taken in relation to the disease—the *dis-*
ease—in the communal body. It is that *dis*-ease which must be first
understood, and my understanding of it is that it lacks fundamentally that spiritual deportment proper to reality as required of intellect in consequence of intellect's real, finite nature. Intellect is
neither the cause of its own existence nor the first cause of any actual
existence of any thing. That is why my approach to the difficulty
attempts to act out, as it were, a recovery of a proper intellectual deportment. One reviewer of *Liberal Arts and Community* is quite right
in charging that it provides no program, but whether that is a failure,
as he supposed, may be yet an open question. Nor does the book
gather up critical evidence by researchers into the general surplus of
academic idiocy—the by-product of our larger community's careless,
unreflecting support of higher education in this century. That careless, well-intentioned community support leads to excesses whose
analogy might be to those tons of butter or corn or soybeans that
accumulate through federal crop supports, external intrusions into
economic realities.

But my metaphor is not apt in its correspondences. Butter and
soybeans and corn clearly have intrinsic virtues, even when stored
and rotting in warehouses. They are not properly related analogically to the surplus of academic idiocy that abounds, stored in computers or libraries. For, in another dimension for accumulating
idiocy, what university, pretending to national and international
prominence, lacks a multitude of "Institutions for the Study of X"

the blank filled in yearly with new *ad hoc* specialties? This species of subsidy to intellectual "crops" promises to submerge the academy, to hide it, as kudzu hides an abandoned house. I might better seek metaphor in relation to surplus city waste, that residue of daily life which threatens to submerge our once habitable earth. For Institutes and specially designed Programs certainly threaten to overwhelm a once intellectually habitable academy. Recall, in relation to this analogy, those stories about the odyssey of those barges loaded down with Eastern city garbage, set afloat in quest of a dumping ground, with no place allowing an unloading. For all I know, those barges are still drifting up and down the Eastern seaboard and into the Caribbean, like ghost ships, the crew growing older and older—sort of our version of "The Ship of Fools." That is a metaphorical picture, increasingly seen as turning literal, from the disquieted community's perspective, of the academy. As for the academy's accumulation of intellectual detritus, I might be in favor of setting it adrift on the prevailing winds tending toward harbor on the Potomac. But then I am at this moment being rather caustic, less possessed of that charity which at once calls garbage *garbage*, without that inclination to a revenge that would innundate the White House and Congress with it. After all, they have as much and more locally grown than they can accommodate.

One could by researches into such academic residue make a telling indictment of the academy as polluting the body social and political, through intellectual malfeasance. Indeed, it is an indictment repeatedly registered in the past decade, in such books as Dinesh D'Souza's *Illiberal Education: The Politics of Race and Sex on Campus*, which even made it to the *New York Times* Best Seller list. This says something of the growing restiveness of the larger community. Still, such indictments have so far led to no decisive trials of guilty polluters. At best an indictment seems only an arrest of the question at issue, yielding therefore no corrective effect. Corrective action is delayed, lest the trial itself be prejudiced and all potential jurors discredited by premature judgment. One must have time to assemble a jury and make sure that collectively they cancel each other out in the name, not of truth, but of objectivity.

And so my approach to this impasse is somewhat different, presenting no ordered indictment as such, nor program of recovery which—if steps one through thirty-three are followed—will restore intellectual health to community. A sure-fire patent medicine derived from technological reductions of humanity itself is the usual procedure of such programs; for such is the naïvete of the community in our day that it easily consents to magic potions, of which there are always providers. Snake oil specialists operate often, though with more subtle finesse, like Huck Finn's unsettling partner, the Dauphin, who has "done considerable in the doctoring way," his "best hold" being a "laying on of hands . . . for cancer and paralysis." What I require of the potential juror, with myself considered surrogate of him, is a concern for reordering his own intellectual deportment. And so my approach attempts to dramatize, through its rhetorical structure, the manner and bearing of the teacher who would be the good teacher as he finds himself physically and emotionally drained by modernist circumstances in his attempt to feed himself and thereby the community at large. My professor must remember that the food properly required for the common health, for the health of persons in community, may be husbanded and somewhat multiplied by a proper cultivation of reality, in the Thomistic sense of reality.

Mine is intended to be an address to the cultivation of *personhood* within the complexity of reality, and from a Christian perspective upon that complexity. And witness is by imitation of that deportment of intellect which recognizes that we have here no abiding city or academy within the city of man. This approach is not likely to provide spectacles of alarm, a crying of "fire!" in the crowded halls of academe whose dry-rot makes it most inflammable. I recognize that always a slow fire smolders, dry rot being a continuous condition to the context of intellectual community. The fire is already long underway, initiated long ago—or so I contend—in an old garden, as the poet would say, before which time the indifferent virtues of fire were unnecessary to distinguish. That was long before Prometheus and his ambiguous gift by man himself to mankind in defiance of the gods. Dry rot in intellect is ages and ages old, initiated then and continued since by the friction of free will in man and God's largesse to man. The issue of that friction we term, from my perspective, Original Sin, whose most potent reminder of its continuing presence is the subversion of self-love.

Of course, I have pointed to, and shall on occasion point to, spectacular decay. I assure you that I do recognize intellectual barbarians not simply at the gates of our city but occupying the seats of power in the academy itself, that center assumed responsible for the good health of a civil citizenry by that citizenry's residual, unexamined consent. The recognition is sufficient cause of alarm, justifying the ringing of many bells backward. For once more we remember from of olden days that the orderly bells, punctuating the rituals of orderly community life, when rung in backward sequence, sound alarm. Such are those books like Bloom's *Closing of the American Mind* and D'Souza's *Illiberal Education*. From the perspective of my surrogate professor, my *agent donné*, the barbarian is in charge of the city's pretenses to order and most likely himself has too heavy a hand even on the bell rope. What that professor—myself—might say metaphorically, especially should his interests lie somewhat largely in literature, is that the academy has fallen into the hands of a new species of scalawag, though only seemingly *new*, and increasingly is being administered by a new species of carpetbagger.

II

My mischievous metaphor of carpetbagger and scalawag, aimed at characterizing certain occupants of the academy in the 1990s, is prompted by my own experience of the academy as very much an occupied territory. And my surrogate self, my struggling professor, exists in that environment as in an internal exile, if he has not been actually expelled from his academic place. One could cite specifics to show that I am not being fanciful here. One has only to read carefully the flood of reports out of the academy for example, perhaps, in the *Chronicle of Higher Education*. My professor, then, who may be deprecated by his antagonists with the epithet "traditionalist," a most ambiguous term, suffers an exile. And though it is in my own view an exile more ancient than our "modernist" moment, the victim experiencing the immediacy of his exile may at first think it otherwise.

That this exile is ancient, however immediate in consequence, is suggested by the haunting lyric lament of the Psalmist in Old Testament days. And Euripides was such an exile from Athens, making an embittered retreat. Socrates, refusing that internal exile of silence, paid a considerable price through that first teacher evaluation at Athens in 399 B C. Of course Dante, to whom I turn often, was another such, roaming Italy but held to Florence by the tenuous threads of his love for that city of his origin through all his wanderings. So the question occurring to my professor in exile, whether literally expelled or internally isolated, is first of all how he may come to terms with the immediate conditions of his exile. That is a first consideration when anyone comes to himself lost in whatever dark wood. But my professor must come to terms with his immediate place in the world if there is to be any hope of his serving somewhat in the recovery of the academy from the exploitations of carpetbaggers and scalawags.

To set his own house in order is the first necessity for our professor, then, if he hopes to recover intellect from the exploitations of carpetbagger and scalawag. First he must reach a sufficient confidence in his position as anchored in reality—in the true nature of intellect itself—as distinguished from what appears as the presumptuous confidence of his adversaries. Those adversaries know the convenience for their exercise of power in assuming the intellect autonomous and so are indifferent to complex reality, except insofar as that reality may be manipulated to the satisfaction of their ever-growing hunger for power. But reality may be manipulated as they intend only through intellectual reductionisms practiced on it. That is why my professor's recovery of confidence in his own ability, at once to oppose reductionism practiced on reality and to move toward an understanding of the complexities of reality, lies not in establishing systems or processes. It lies rather in his deportment of openness to the truth of things in themselves, to those realities of existence which must be denied by his antagonists if they are to exercise autonomous power over things, whether those "things" be persons or institutions such as the academy. This does not mean, of course, that through such an openness my professor does not come to recognize or value structure or system. It rather means that in doing so, he does not confuse his own recognition as the necessary and primal cause of the orders discerned in complex reality. This distinction is crucial, if he is to avoid the illusion that his own intellect is the first cause of any order within a thing or among things. Put in another way, my professor's recovery of intellect through a proper orientation to reality lies in his recovery of the validity of his intuitive recognitions, strengthened by rational understanding of them.

Such a recovery as I advocate is an occupation of a lifetime, not that of a moment. We are speaking, then, of the continuous conduct of responsible intellect which is traditionally spoken of as that of the philosopher, the lover of wisdom. In accepting that calling, whatever his subordinate devotions to particular systems or programs within the operation of intellect, which we may describe as *specializations*, my professor pursues knowledge. But because of that larger perspective on knowledge he is intent beyond knowledge to arrive at understanding, so that he may become in some degree wise. He may, indeed, become not only a lover of wisdom but in some degree possessed of it or, under the aspect of grace, possessed *by* it.

An intellectual vision holding in due relation to each other the true, the beautiful, the good: that is the labor of a lifetime required of my professor. And he finds confirmation of his deportment as proper only through his arduous journey within complex reality, and at many levels in complex reality. He sees confirmation, for instance, in the great artist who shares his intent. William Faulkner is famous for his portrayal, through dogged characters, of the virtue of endurance as prelude to a character's prevailing over his always untoward circumstances. As dramatized in Faulkner's fiction, endurance is a sort of unreflective hanging on to slippery existence, with an inexplicable stubbornness which the actualities of the circumstances enveloping such a character make comical because seemingly hopeless. Such a character in such circumstances, it would appear, has little prospect of surviving the circumstances, let alone prevailing over them. Again and again, however, Faulkner shows his dogged character coming through with some rescue of dignity to his humanity, moving thereby beyond the exegencies of circumstance. The character who keeps on keeping on gains our respect, however grudgingly we may award it. Even a Flem Snopes is never quite freed of his humanity by his gnostic intent toward creation. For if he were, as Faulkner well knows, he would be merely a flat character bearing no dramatic contingency to reality as fictional character.

My professor, unlike a character in Faulkner's fiction, must not only keep on keeping on. He must as well *profess* the virtue of the tenacity of intellect in its pursuit of the truth of things. In doing so, he may increasingly gain some degree of certitude as to the nature of intellect itself and of its limits, and most to be desired, a recognition of the limits of intellect in its ordinate relation to existence. In discovering, by his devoted action, the principles that underlie his own finite intellect, he arrives at the devotion required of him as an intellectual creature in service to that community of creatureliness which we sum up in the term *creation*. And he discovers himself not only steward of things in themselves actual, but of those permanent things, the truths essential *in* things, as St. Thomas would say. Such discoveries of essential truths in things sustain him in more confident action as husbandman to intellect itself, whereby he recovers through grace an acceptable self-love. Now to put these concerns in such a way will appear, at least at this juncture of our concern for the academy, as most vague. But if we recover from these reflections an intellectual context of what men have thought of the human condition through the centuries, they will appear to us less vague when summoned by intellect to a present recognition. That is why my remnant professors are so much alarmed by the current intellectual barbarian's strategy of conquest, which would root out and burn what some men have thought, in the interest of their own dominance in the moment as pretenders to thought. As intellectual barbarians, they rather cultivate a spirit of feeling to supplant thought, in order to establish the randomness of their moment's desire as the supreme intellectual principle, which they assert requires our unquestioning submission.

Since I have alluded to Faulkner as ally of my professor, let me recall his own stirring testimony to the endurance of intellect against its destructions, words from his Nobel Prize speech. Faulkner is speaking to the fiction writer, but what he says speaks as well to the actions of any intellectual creature attempting to deal with those "problems of the human heart" which concern the fiction writer. There is no room in the intellect's workshop, says Faulkner, "for anything but the old verities and truths of the heart, the old universal truths lacking which any story is ephemeral and doomed—love and honor and pity and pride and compassion and sacrifice." In our terms, what is required is a concern for truth in relation to the nature of, the truth about, man himself as a limited intellectual creature moved intuitively—by the heart—toward ends proper to his desire. Such are fundamental intellectual concerns, and until they are recovered we will, in Faulkner's words, labor "under a curse." Man will stand witness "not of love, but of lust, of defeats in which nobody loses anything of value, of victories without hope and, worst of all, without pity or compassion."

Without a recovery of a community of mind within which to hear such words as speaking a healthful truth, mankind accomplishes only its own abolition. My professor's dominant responsibility, therefore, is the recovery of this community of mind, without which the words themselves remain but clichés. For valid terms at once become cliché when we neglect the truths out of which they rise. As we recover somewhat the context of such terms, lying in the human condition, we may find the exile we experience, each in his own way, at last tolerable, and may even be able to accept our present position as a member of a remnant. But then a strange, if not mysterious, shifting occurs in our understanding. For instance, in relation to our academic carpetbaggers and scalawags and their ascendancy in the academy, we realize that it is *they* who are more fundamentally exiles. They occupy a place, this immediate academy, but it is a strange and even threatening place to them, which they hasten to imprint with accidents of their own making to hide the apparent strangeness. Elaborate building programs and landscaping are sometimes symptoms of their sense of exile.

What follows is their gradual assumption of totalitarian authority over place, as Genghis Khan was required to exercise in his
doomed conquest of places in his westward conquering. It is this
aspect of Modernist, deracianated intellect, its sense of but not understanding of the causes of its exile, that led Allen Tate to characterize our moment as that of the triumph of the provincial spirit.
And in making his indictment of that spirit, Tate was looking most
particularly at the American academy. The provincial spirit "sees in
material welfare and legal justice the whole solution to the human
problem," Tate suggests. It is an attitude of mind "limited in time
but not in space," occasioned when men "lose their origin in the past
and its continuity into the present, and begin every day as if there
had been no yesterday." Long after Tate's words in 1945, prophetic of
the provincialism which would come to dominate the political and
social arena and settle upon the academy in such devastating ways at
the end of our century, Solzhenitsyn said much the same thing:
"Spiritually all intellectuals nowadays belong to a diaspora. Nowhere are we complete strangers. And nowhere do we feel quite at
home." The difference between my professor and his antagonist in
respect to this provincialism is this: the antagonist sees provincialism
as a virtue instead of a spiritual deracination whose end must be the
despair of his alienation from all places, all existence.

Our carpetbagger in the academy, in this view, is a species of that
most hapless exile of all, the provincial intellect self-exiled from the
realities of existence, even the realities of his own existence. It is a
condition, incidentally, requiring little intellectual sophistication to
accomplish. One need not be degreed from Harvard or Yale or Ox-
ford or the Sorbonne to arrive in that provincial estate of mind. For
any junior college in any state is a likely enough place for such self-
displacement. Our carpetbagger nevertheless seems always in transit, from junior college to college to university, then to universities of
national or international reputation as decreed by the provincial
spirit dominant at the national level. He moves from no place to no
place, with the false dream of autonomous intellect that it may make
its own place, may make a Harvard of any regional university. But
that dream, which he mistakes for a sufficient form, will allow no

substantial reality established through the totalitarian will of the dreamer. On the other hand, the fervor of his totalitarian dreaming allows a desubstantiation of whatever place upon which the carpetbagger (or scalawag as well) practices his dreaming.

All this is to prepare for a reflection upon the abiding problem of exile, whether that of my professor or his carpetbagger-scalawag antagonist. Exile is a reality consequent to either, by virtue of man's existence as a created intellectual creature. For to exist at all as a finite creature is to be in some degree in exile in the finite world, if intellect itself is a part of the nature of such an existent thing. And this condition of exile is spoken of by my professor as consequent upon the intellectual violation of existence committed in that old, pre-Promethean garden. Adam, as patron of my professor, is thus to be accepted in the light of his failure, and by that acceptance there comes a certain understanding of the haunting sense of deracination in intellect, its desire for a proper end—a home, a place of certitude of its own nature. Prometheus, as patron to the provincial antagonist, understood not in his tragic dimension but as the heroic deliverer of divine fire to man—the fire of autonomous intellect in the transformation of the Promethean myth—justifies a remaking of the world to the gnostic antagonist of reality. But my professor's memory is deeper and more ancient, bringing father Adam to the present moment of our exile.

What my professor sees in his circumstances in the academy is his own role in *seeing* the nature of exile, a contingency to his *willing* a belief in the limits of his existence as exile, his being circumscribed by reality itself. Or, its alternate, *willing* a belief that exile mean no limits to the intellect's manipulations of reality—the gnostic temptation. My professor's is a recognition of his own willed separation from existence itself through having willed a separation from the Cause of existence. In this recognition, his recovery of a known but forgotten knowledge, lies the potential of an annealment of separation. He will respond quite differently, then, to that succinct formulation of exile which Milton's Satan expresses:

> *The mind is its own place and of itself*
> *Can make a heaven of hell, a hell of heaven.*

For my professor there is the terror of oblivion in such a perverse formulation. But for his antagonist, there is rather an illusional promise of endless programs in the restructuring of creation by the willfulness of intellect as autonomous. An annealment of the separation that his terror speaks, my professor comes to realize, lies in an intellectual accommodation to reality, a return to the truth of things, including the truth of himself as finite creature. That is a recognition through which he may remove obstacles to the grace of that Love that holds and sustains all being and all beings. Prophetic sense is recovered: a seeing of existences, things in the truth of themselves, a recovery whereby one hears the voice of that Calling ordinate action in creation. That Love and that Calling are spoken to most movingly, incidentally, in Eliot's *Little Gidding*, and in a direct relation to the importance of our recovering a proper intellectual deportment toward existence through words, through signs, whose reverent keep is the academy's charge.

The second provincial sort of exile, allowing no returning to the place from which we set out, I characterize as the exile of Gnostic Modernism. It is the willed separation of intellect, not only from that Cause of existence toward which Eliot moved after his own willful, provincial separation from it. It is also a separation from existence itself in its actualities, a turning from the truth of things in themselves, in which lies the truth that things are caused, but not by finite intellect. It is the intellectual action characterized as modern Gnosticism, which, as Eric Voegelin observed, is intent upon a power over being. But by such intent it voids itself, lacking that openness to being which is anciently termed *love*. Thus consumed in its closed nature by its disoriented desire which confuses love with power, it stands revealed, in Dante's explication of it in lower hell, as *perverted love*. And by that perversion, it presumes that any place or anything is a no-place or no-thing except as dependent upon its own power. Thus a no-place—say a provincial academy—becomes an arena progressively cleared of recognitions of being. The illusion, however, is that such a no-place is not absolved of being as supposed, for only the intentional gnostic intellect itself is emptied of reality by its action. Still, the place as perverted by gnostic intellect becomes the arena within which that gnostic intellect would dream a new creation by its autonomous will, supposing that the dream itself makes the intended creation substantial.

Such is an analysis of gnostic intellect, which might be supplied at one level with an argument of its psychological nature and at another level by the data of its deconstructions of the place or places it seizes for its purposes, in our immediate concern the place of a particular academy. Data of actual deconstructions of actual academic places is now constantly reported in the media: strange events occuring on campuses across the country. But what is more fundamental to our concern for the attempted emptying of place is the spiritual level of such action. It is a spiritual destruction through intellect that results from the presumptuous denial of any existent thing except as that existence is dependent upon finite intellect itself. Intellect so possessed by a perverse will denies existence but intends by the denial its own godhead. It intends a creative power whereby it makes its own *something* of the *nothing* that is residual only to its own intellect. For that "nothing" is never actual in its "nothingness" except *in* the perverted gnostic person. We might remember here that moment of despair in Mark Twain in recognizing the dilemma. Thus he has his own Satan in "The Mysterious Stranger" declare as the only bitter truth that "all is a dream" because the dreamer himself is but "a thought—a vagrant thought, a useless thought, a homeless thought, wandering forlorn among empty eternities!"

III

The Gnostic condition, I suggest, is that of spirit consumed by *acedia*, rechristened—or perhaps better put—resatanized as *ennui* in our century. We remember Baudelaire's sardonic remark that Satan's cleverest wile in the modernist mind has been to convince that mind that Satan does not exist. And we remember once more that the spectacle attendant upon *acedia* is not necessarily an arrest from activity, for the soul in such a state may be most busily employed in doing things in the world, in order to distract itself from considering its condition. If we turn this general observation toward the carpetbagger in the academy, we may recognize his spectacles as disguise, certainly in some instances. The species of administrator I have in mind as carpetbagger is a floating contingent in the body academic. He moves here and there, we said, going up and down in the earth, never quite at home anywhere. In his estimate, his principal virtue is precisely an intellectual deracination, whose supposed complement is a pragmatic skill in manipulating available resources, whether bricks or scholarships or academic chairs. To hear him perform before trustees or legislative committee or Rotary Club is hardly to suspect, except after close examination, that his business may indeed be symptom of an accidic spirit.

A symptom to the diagnosis of spiritual gout, of *acedia* struck in, might well be his profession of neutrality in all matters intellectual, except inasmuch as he holds responsibility for the "facilitating" of ideas, which work requires of him much busy-ness. He is expeditor of products intellectual. His neutrality on intellectual questions is why such an administrator is so constantly beholden to the committee, partly as a necessity, having little facility in intellectual discourse, and partly as strategy, whereby he is in some degree protected from unexpected consequences since he has a committee to blame. Little wonder, then, that the carpetbagger is increasingly embroiled with committees. For at least on some occasions, at least some members of such committees may object to his indifference to things in themselves and his devotion to merely marketing and distributing things. Even so, committees themselves are strange creatures adrift in the academy, from whom little rescue of the academy is to be expected. Like the carpetbagger, the committee may well reject that wisdom caught in a verse from a recent country song: "If you don't stand for something, you'll fall for anything."

Now it has been the scalawag who recognizes the carpetbagger's vulnerability in refusing any position, and he exploits this weakness, recognizing in doing so his own advantage within the safety of the committee. From such a vantage point he may advance his own dream of what this no-place, the particular academy, may become, himself anonymous within committee. Certainly committees have an increasingly destructive effect upon the academy, managed through that sort of intellect I characterize as scalawag. Committees come up with never-ending sequences of programs and curricula adjustments, to be expedited by the carpetbagger, whose neutrality in respect to the content of such programs or curricula is the handicap which allows the advance of ideology over idea. Such an administrator, because he sees no solution to his difficulty, falls for anything, in an act of wily self-preservation or in an ignorant obliviousness to the realities at issue.

There was a time, of course, when the carpetbagger was rather exceptional in the academic community, though surely always represented. What held him in check was the common sense of place relative to the academy, its relation as academic community to the larger community upon which it depends ultimately. Even I can remember a day when the president of my institution, or deans of our colleges, were integral members, not only of the intellectual community as such but of the actual community in an actual place. The old relation of "town and gown," including its traditional contentions, seems now most faded. In that older time the ceremonies of intellect might require such formalities as the academic gown, and those ceremonies served to maintain a relation to the larger community, giving a healthy perspective even when there was that immediacy of local frictions. Now, the graduation exercise is reduced to empty gesture. The community recognition of a student's passage, once signified by the "sheepskin," is handled by mail. It is evident that the academy itself has lost its relation to the community as a real existence. The academy's purported service to the "public" understands the public as an abstraction. Abandoning the "gown" is followed by abandoning the "town" as well. And in that abandonment, the carpetbaggers flourish.

Now if the carpetbagger was in a minority in those good old days, so too were the scalawags. But soon enough they recognized, if not a common interest then a common end desired. A complementary alliance emerged. The question of who should ultimately occupy the seats of power was deferred, in the face of their common obstacle—the traditional academy or the remnants of that traditional understanding of the nature of higher education. Under that new subversive alliance, an internal decay set in—within the academy—until a point where the carpetbagger and scalawag became sufficiently powerful to determine matters academic in consort. And that is the point where they began to fall afoul of each other in an internecine struggle over power, a struggle which reaches the level of spectacle in the 1990s. It was inevitable that they should become antagonists, the one holding no intellectual position on principle, the other having committed itself to a very limited, self-centered, agenda of power.

Nor could there be much doubt as to which would be ascendant, since a false position resolutely held will eventually carry the day against no position at all. The limited, the self-centered, however clothed by a rhetoric of high intention such as the current devotion to the mystical "politically correct," will collapse at last, but it will also initially prove dominant by the very arrogance of its presumption. A symptom of the gradual inception of collapse, which occasions my statement of hope, I hear from old friends and colleagues here and there in the academic humanities. Very recently, new candidates for position would be insistent in presenting their credentials to show themselves as well versed in "deconstruction." Now they have to be prompted if one wishes to know what they might think of de Man or Derrida. Of course, such hesitation makes the fresh candidate vulnerable to the old hard-liner deconstructionist, now elevated to tenure though increasingly recognizing his own internal isolation. The realities of language that make his position untenable in respect to the validity of idea begin to reassert themselves. Still, protected for a time by that traditionalist's contribution to the academy, the system of tenure (which the scalawag has been most careful to preserve for his own benefit in his forced intellectual retreat), he is for the moment safe, if lonely. He may even enjoy the carpetbagger's new dilemma. The carpetbagger was once himself protected by tenure and so able to retreat to some university department under pressure. But the academic trend at the moment is to deny tenure to administrators first. Presently it will be denied to faculty.

The state of the academy is at the moment in such doubt as to raise the specter of external auditing of some ideas entrenched and

defended in that sanctuary which has enjoyed till now an intellectual
"King's X" to protect its ideas from reality itself. My professor may
watch with wry amusement to see whether the carpetbagger submits
to today's agenda as daily advanced by an isolated faction of scalawags, represented by a committee in a show of power. For the supporting community grows impatient with the spectacle. Committee
justifies a loudness of voice, as if loudness were itself sufficient authority in the daily skirmishing, but when the community's ears begin to ring it will demand a noise ordinance or the carpetbagger may
stumble about trying to discover both principles of and means to a
resistance to any new program. Those experienced in the academy,
as is my professor, know all too well how often they themselves are
wooed to support one or the other—the carpetbagger or the scalawag—usually with private assurances that the one or the other recognizes in full the absurdities of the position held by the other or the
one.

Just why such a remnant as my professor should be so solicited
may be variously explained no doubt, but there is most likely to be at
least an intuitive recognition by the wooing carpetbagger or scalawag that this member remnant has yet some authority in respect to
the reality rejected, an authority based in principles to which the
common sense of various intellectual constituencies may yet be
roused. Put bluntly, my professor is articulate, through the degree of
his confidence in principles anchored in reality, so that he will the
more likely say the persuasive thing to common sense, sometimes
even when member of a committee. That the persuasive thing is
likely to be destructive of the position of carpetbagger or scalawag is
not of immediate consequence to that rascal, since what is at issue
for him at the moment is a survival at this instant of danger. His is
the sort of desperation one finds in the midst of fire, flood, or earth-
quake. When a Sputnik goes up suddenly, or the legislature under
public pressure questions regents or trustees and they in turn question carpetbagger and scalawag: that is a moment to seek new, more
solid allies for survival if one is scalawag or carpetbagger. My professor, grounded in principle, becomes in those circumstances an
honored exile, though exile still. His wry humor at his own situation

is like that humor he experiences when a colleague, say in physics or chemistry, and even in history or sociology, on occasion calls him (if he is in "English") to ask whether a comma or a semi-colon is required at this point in the latest article underway for scholarly publication.

If it is the carpetbagger who solicits support of my professor as mediator, as a sort of persuasive public relations agent in his moment of stress, it is because he would rather not cave in and grant the scalawag today's agenda, put forward by that isolated faction which has successfully commandeered the authority of a committee. As committee, there seems a larger contingent of power than the professor alone might wield were he himself to put forward any agenda. Not such an agenda as the scalawag's, of course, for my professor is rather likely to be more radical. He might even urge the responsibility of biologist or sociologist, chemist or historian, to require a suitable use of language in oral or written discourse by the specializing students in their charge. But that expectation would require not only that the professor of these disparate specialities be responsible for his own and his student's use of signs: such a radical program would also obviate the English professor as authority in the uses of the comma. For that reason, there is not likely to be much support for an agenda demanding elementary responsibility in language, at least not from my professor's own colleagues in his own English "department." To remove "remedial" responsibilities would more than decimate most departments of English, robbing them of both faculty and graduate students.

The carpetbagger needs support in his resistance to grandly conceived and so expensive agendas which may be advanced by the scalawag, since if he fail to resist such programs he is obligated to expedite them and his resources are shrinking dangerously. He knows as well that, if he consent to the present proposal in lean times, tomorrow there will be yet another persuasively advanced to his consideration. There will be another necessity of program from the same or a newly constituted faction with its own rarified agenda for a semi-private program, justified as "specialized," as opposed to any community validity in the program. The proposal will, of course, buttress its demands with arguments pointing out that such is the way things are done at Harvard or Stanford or Michigan and even add that the benefits down the road will be of value to the community, even the local community.

The failure at least two decades ago to depend upon my professor and his associates in withstanding the struggle over curricula in the academy accounts in large part for the present radical destruction of curricula. The carpetbagger, who first emerged as academic power over both my professor and the restive scalawag, began to welcome the "new," the "innovative," without considering what such terms designate. For they justified a spectacle sufficient to his own need of public money poured into the academy. The marveling media, aided by his own extensive "PR" staff, made great stories of what is happening at State U under his aegis. That such innovation as spectacle might likely prove destructive to the academy emerges rather slowly, after the destruction is pervasive. The child at table, decorating the cake with a bottle of catsup, arrests the assembled adults with amused delight for the moment. But then the gathering realizes the cake is ruined, and may well look to the roast beef and potatoes to see whether they have been reconstituted with sugar and frosting, or perhaps an excess of salt. Such is the moment of disturbed wonder in the general community, concerned with the intellectual fare prepared by the academy in the name of community.

That community is baffled in its response, in large part because it has long since been conditioned, by the intellectual establishment itself as empowered by gnostic principles, to believe a liberal arts education in the old sense to be at best a luxury for minds removed from "reality," when reality is seen pragmatically. (Such, I think, is the weakness in Bloom's concern for the "closing of the American mind," a failure to see beyond the popular response to the virtues of liberal arts to the healthful service of liberal arts to the community itself.) Under the increasingly awkward failures of the academy, the demands for pragmatic virtues restored through education become louder. My professor knows that loud demand from of old, when it was not a demand but an assumption about his own responsibility to the community: he was expected to be responsible first of all to teach grammar—to show where commas belonged. After which, in part as reward for that devotion, he might look into Shakespeare or Milton with some few students.

Never mind that my professor said long since, "Look out. He's going to ruin our food with his random catsup." By *he*, I mean most particularly the scalawag, whose appealing demeanor to the patrons of chaos, particularly the media patrons, has been that of the lively, "exceptional" child. Destructiveness practiced in the academy by such children was quickly sentimentalized in the 1960s by the media, who were ill-prepared to recognize in much of that destructive activity accompanying the crying out against the "Establishment" a reaction to the denials of reality. And instead of recovering intellect to order, to the measure of intellectual acts by reality after that chaotic encounter of "Youth Culture" and the "Establishment" in the 1960s, what remained instead was the elevation of destruction as ideologically justified. That impulse from vernal youth became the principle which above all justified the academy to itself, requiring little exploration of the causes of sudden disorder. Youth must be served, and not the maturing of intellect.

There is in our carpetbagger as administrator, though only residually, elements of an egalitarianism long since used for the deconstruction of community, focused since the 1960s upon restless rebellious youth to placate that youth. There is, as well, a direct and intentional use by the scalawag of egalitarianism as an ideological weapon. In his hands that weapon becomes a sort of "agent orange" used in the reductive defoliation of the rich variety of existential intellect. The reductionism in its effect is represented at this moment by the descriptions of the ideologically required landscape of the academy as "politically correct." This is to say, then, that there are differences in the uses made by carpetbagger and scalawag of this antiquated, failed ideology of egalitarianism, which was born in the nineteenth century after a long political gestation and came to flourish in sociological and political manifestations after World War I. Egalitarianism is in collapse before our common sense recognitions of ideological absurdities in the final quarter of the twentieth century, but it intends to end with the bang of "PC." As still manifest in the academy, which is always behind the actual circumstances of the "real" world, observe the carpetbagger, interviewed for an academic position. He uses the abstraction, though in respect to himself as its agent he denies its applicability to himself in the issue. For some are more equal than others. Egalitarianism is universal, but he must stand outside the universe so decreed. Consider:

At the request of the duly constituted "search committee," our drifting carpetbagger is likely to present his version of the dream of reconstituting the host institution so that it becomes "equal" to those institutions in which the worship of intellect as autonomous is long since established. Podunk University or Junior College must be re-made in the image of a fabulous Harvard or Yale or University of California or Michigan State. If only Podunk U had the pragmatic advantage of a Yale or Harvard as represented by endowments! A legislature persuaded of the necessity of such largesse will be re-warded by a flow into its social body of trained intellects, the egali-tarian premise being that any intellect sufficiently treated with state-supported material advantages will prove an exceptional prod-uct out of that support. There is in the carpetbagger's presumption of the nature of intellect itself, upon which he builds his dream of Podunk U as at least a little Harvard or Michigan, an assumption of the "egalitarian" intellect as a sort of undifferentiated raw material upon which education is to be imposed. But the assumption is nei-ther intellectual nor egalitarian with respect to the reality which is the inevitable issue of such assumption—the reality of intellectual chaos which now clouds the academic air—the polluting effect upon the academy of an intellectual ozone, distorting the sunlight which would reveal actual circumstances in actual—not abstract—intel-lects.

Meanwhile, our carpetbagger, presenting his dream of the acad-emy, a dream untouched by intellectual principles, practices his dream but a moment at a place. Then comes the invitation to ad-dress another "search committee" or even perhaps occupy a position in the Department of Education, state or national. A part of his dream is that he himself might draw nearer and nearer his imagined Mecca. He will move to any institution which has an appearance of possessing more "resources" than his present academic address affords. The mobile administrator, whose name I fear is legion, has in his own heart of hearts an ambition to be president of Harvard or Yale or California or Michigan. On occasion, such unanchored ambition results in a comic spectacle, to the outrage of the patrons of education who themselves are the principal contributors to the outrageous, spectacular event they decry.

A president of one of the institutions of higher education in my home state was suddenly very much under attack in our media, though by that point he was actually an ex-president. In renovating the "President's Mansion," he had allowed cost overruns so startling that they appeared to faculty and staff, themselves "frozen" in their raises by economic recession, to be very like those overruns by defense industries who develop bombers or submarines. There was the expected storm of protest, but the object of protest had already moved on to head a similar institution in a neighboring state, then replacing its own ex-president who had come under criminal indictment for malfeasance in office. Within weeks of the public outcry at home, the story broke that the same sort of excessiveness had occurred already at the new "President's Mansion," or that was the perception advanced by the agitated and agitating media.

To live in a mansion as president of a large academic institution is perhaps some consolation for not being president of Harvard. But with that ambition thus consoled, lacking intellectual principles sufficient to order the ambition, the carpetbagger will still not be able to recognize the magnitude of his betrayal. The pretense to an institutional egalitarianism of intellect, whereby a faculty of "international reputation" is promised in a province, is (says our common sense recovered from exile) to suppose silk purses made of sows' ears. Nor will the more immediate, palpable evidence that a Harvard or University of California have fallen on perilous academic days themselves, in respect to promised educational alchemy, be evident at Podunk U, either to carpetbagger or—lacking spectacular event—to his supporting alumni and local general public. Even a Jonathan Swift would be hard pressed to survive except as a simple reporter of that academic world all about us. His Grand Academy of Lagado, outrageous in its exaggeration in the eighteenth century, is hardly sufficient as mere description of the American academy in the twentieth. Lagado's scholars as dramatized in *Gulliver's Travels* have sufficient representatives among our scalawags, but Swift, a spirit sometimes sustained by dismay, might despair before the reports of the antics of our carpetbaggers.

President Donald Kennedy of Stanford University, for instance: Kennedy, tolerant of those scalawags who are desperate to destroy curricula in order to destroy Western civilization, stands suddenly exposed as enjoying as reward for his participation in that destruction such "perks" as a yacht at public expense. Then there was the public monies spent on his wedding reception, and the two thousand dollar monthly allotment for flowers for his presidential mansion, or seven thousand dollars to enlarge the president's bed and provide designer silk sheets for it. One can only imagine, given this, President Kennedy's protests of innocence, his confused wonder, now that a state legislature and federal auditors press him sorely.

IV

Given such spectacles of carpetbagger violations, the carpetbagger being a species one encounters as well among the faculty itself, what of his collusion with the scalawag? If each makes the other for to win, as do Chaucer's apothecary and doctor of physic, the auditors of financial books can at least bring the carpetbagger to bay, individually, before the public pack. We know the "bottom line" in matters financial. But to confront the scalawag with a sufficient public support: that is another matter. For who is to persuasively audit intellectual bankruptcy? Still, it is the scalawag who, in an initial collusion with the carpetbagger, but now increasingly in open conflict with him in the academy (witness events at Stanford), most thoroughly plunders the citadel of intellect, often in the name of overthrowing the corrupt carpetbagger. The scalawag is increasingly manifest in the 1990s, not clothed excessively to our first sight as is his principle facilitator, the carpetbagger, that manipulator of means financial.

The carpetbagger expounds upon a yellow brick road he would build toward a fabled future institution, paved by high salaries and academic chairs and impressive technological facilities that will appeal to "the very best minds." That is the promise, and it is made in arguing that by so doing all minds may be eventually elevated as the very best. Meanwhile, the scalawag, more wily, adapts as disguise (in order to court the residual idealism in us all) a rhetoric and terminology out of the older and still valid paradigm of intellectual community. For it is thereby that he would enlist my remnant professor as ally. In doing so, he may the better subvert the valid for the sake of his own limited, elitist concern, such programs as represented by the radical versions of Feminism or Deconstruction. Of course, that elitist manipulation is made in the name of his opposition to *elitism*, the term thus made ambiguous at best, since distorted toward rejections of reality. That some minds are better than others is a reality intolerable, though the scalawag assumes his own better if not best. His wily manipulation of reality replaces and serves, through rhetorical confusions, a purported moral deportment of intellect in respect to reality. But a truly moral deportment begins in openly recognizing that gifts differ, though without an implication in such difference of moral superiority or inferiority. Again, my professor will be acutely aware of his own danger if he is manipulated by a gnostic power disguised as if it were acting with moral authority. Such is the deceptiveness at the heart of the current program of the new academic principle of the "politically correct." In my professor is an old understanding: truth is the end to which his educational journey moves, an end indifferent to special dispensations of any sort by the accidents of power. He is, so long as he holds that understanding, somewhat immune to the carpetbagger's violations and will not be overwhelmed by despair when the evening news reports yet another instance of those violations. He is also in some degree immune to the distortions of reality by the scalawag, who speaks loudly such rubrics as "race, color, creed, sex" in a pursuit of that power which denies the existence of those named accidents that accrue to a person's intellectual existence. To supplant those accidents, inescapable to the essence of things, is to make possible a substitution of accident imposed upon essence as if accident itself were significantly determinate of essence.

And that is the necessary strategy of any gnostic manipulation of being. For a person as person is also male or female, white or black or brown or yellow, believes or does not believe, and so on. It is with those particularizing effects of accident that intellect must come to terms, not by denial of their existence, but through understanding. To pretend that a particular intellect exists unrelated to the accidents of being is to become vulnerable to the insistent demands of accidents made into the ghosts of being by gnostic separations, ghosts of being which we must worship. A thing is not a thing by intellect's dissociating its accidents, as if by that action intellect thus rescues the thing, becoming its savior by Gnostic action. Such is a species of unmaking, and nowhere more disturbing to the prospects of communal love than when practiced upon person in the name of moral necessity. To suppose that a person exists as a person by virtue of a denial of the particularizing accidents of his being is to deny his personhood itself at last. For where in the annals of intellectual experience does there exist a person who is neither male nor female, neither black nor white nor brown nor yellow nor red—or some combination of these and other accidents of particularity? To deny *race, sex, creed,* and the like by denying their existence as actually accruing in persons as the realities which such terms designate is to deny in the end the existence of the person in whom those accidents adhere, however moralistic the argument of denial. We have only to observe tensional antagonisms, festering in the political body in response to these nominalistic manipulations practiced upon our personhood, to realize the inevitable consequences of intellectual confusions in our necessary response to the realities of existence beyond such intellectual manipulations of reality. And so we may consider that such denials constitute a species of sacrilege to being itself. The disorder resulting is inevitable in its effects upon the body of humanity, since what is at risk is the loss of personhood itself, for "humanity" is constituted at its primary level only by persons. That is the danger intuitively perceived by a person. When not understood as such, he will be set at odds both with his own existence and against other persons within the community. For a person to take such a position in opposition to the gnostic carpetbagger or scalawag who is feeding parasitically upon the body of being is at once to be disfranchised in the academy. That is why my professor will be isolated by both carpetbagger and scalawag, or employed at best as mercenary to the moment's necessity of survival by the scalawag or carpetbagger. Increasingly, he is actually driven into exile from the academy. For he is a clear and present danger to them if he sees as the central purpose of the academy its service to the larger body of the community we call, vaguely, humanity. That service is through a direct engagement of those persons—students—electing intellectual training. The larger community, always in the making and never made, is a body in whom membership is to be harmonized to the limits of discretely existing creatures, and thus further harmonized to creation as a body. In response to that harmony, one begins to understand members of creation in their differential modes of being. One not only accepts, but values the truth that things differ, one from another. Through such recognitions, difference dissolves in a vision of creation as complementary in its parts, in its members. And nowhere is the recognition more necessarily valued than in that part of the body of community, the intellectual community. Such is the labor of structuring "humanity" to a concert of being which is realized, not by intellect's denials of complexity or assertions of identity of beings beyond differentiating accidents, but through love, and in response to that governing Love which is the Cause of all being.

There can be no pride of place or of person in response to such a Calling heard through the gift to man of his intellectual nature. But neither can there be a denial of a place as *this* place nor of person as *this* person whose particularities are under the supporting grace of Love and requiring an answering love from man. There can be no pride in "inequality." But neither can there be a denial of difference between things discretely existing and discretely seen. For by existing at all, any *thing* is necessarily unlike any *thing* else. Any person, by the actuality of his personhood, is specifically unlike any other.

Indeed, any person is by his very given nature a distinct species of existing things, in which respect persons differ from other creatures in the inclusive complex of creation.

In this perspective upon creation, one sees that intellectual virtues as manifest in particular beings are not morally decisive. Rather, it is the essential natures for discrete things, made discrete by the realities of existential limit, which is decisive of our intellectual virtues in knowing as opposed to judging with moralistic intent. With this understanding of the limits of knowing, my professor will also know that the scalawag's use of such terms as "race, color, creed, sex" constitutes but a stalking horse in his pursuit of power. Those terms are but means unrelated to the end of understanding the truth of things, which understanding leads to an ordinate love of things. They are, rather, appropriated to an appetite for power over things. The truth that each creature is anchored by its accidents of being in complex reality is circumvented. But intellect may not obliterate any thing or elevate it as if conferring essence by its act of knowing. It must come to terms with each thing through the accidents of that thing's being, despite the confused or devious distractions from that necessity to which intellect is susceptible because of its freedom. To deny accident to being is an act of abuse. It is a transgression upon particular beings.

We do not therefore conclude, of course, that such creatures as "chauvinists" or "bigots" or "elitists" do not exist in the pejorative sense of those terms, or that such unacceptable habits of being as designated by those terms when truly applied are not themselves derived from an abuse of existing things. There are some persons to whom the terms are apt. It is rather that the virtue of a coincidence of thing and term is so easily manipulated by the intellectual scalawags in the ascendant at this present juncture. He is able to do so with some impunity through nominalistic subversions that have become habitual. It is the responsibility of intellect to make these distinctions in honoring truth, and nowhere more pressingly necessary than in that refuge of intellect, the academy. For in the violation of the truth of things at this moment, the actual chauvinist is rather the scalawag or carpetbagger than the caricature so commonly associated with the pejorative terms. The intellectual bigot must be appropriately designated as such, even at the risk of brawling in words. What is required in the attempt, of course, is a demonstration of the appropriateness of a term to the thing so termed.

Intellect must make and profess and stand by distinctions through a knowledge maturing to wisdom, confident that in wisdom resides his love for the truth of things. Thus it is that complex reality becomes intellectually tolerable beyond violations of reality practiced by carpetbagger or scalawag, by chauvinist or bigot. And thus only may my professor escape despair. He knows that the radical nominalism which now makes the academy intellectually chaotic and barren will not in the end serve the truth, which is abiding. He knows that gnostic manipulations by intellect will in the end restore neither a moral community nor an intellectual community in which a common responsibility to the true, the beautiful, and the good binds intellect to reality and intellects thereby in a viable body. The nominalist manipulations we suffer must be seen, then, as perversions of intellect. Their effect is a degenerate elitism established through the disparity between gnostic intent and those high intellectual principles proper to intellect which that degenerate elitism mouths to hide its program of conquest.

We must recognize that perverse intellect is adept at mouthing formulae derived from old legitimate recognitions of the truth of things, including the truths about our intellectual nature. What it would deconstruct toward devious ends is the nature of humanity itself, and so the final product of such a deconstruction can only be the less-than-human, the less-than-person, however colorfully described in terms commandeered to falsify reality. It is as if we have forgotten the cogent exposé which George Orwell's *Animal Farm* gave us: Some animals are more equal than others. That such is the presumption of the gnostic manipulator is made evident by the variety of methods used to prevent the free and open debate of intellectual issues which are assumed settled by the advocates of "political correctness." Students incited to riot supply physical intimidation of any attempt to recover language to viability in restoring intellectual order. And students rioting are soon followed by official sanctions of their actions by duly constituted committees, by some promulgated administrative fiat pretending to rational justification of intellectual anarchy as the principle of higher education. We might, as an instance, cite the verbatim copy of Smith College's guide to entering freshman, reprinted in *Academic Questions*, Spring 1991.

That document anticipates the freshman's puzzlement over terms that are at the center of her coming academic encounters. Thus she is given brief definitions of those terms. *Ethnic identity* is a governing term, from which follows "Factors of Oppression in General," under which appear definitions of *prejudice, discrimination, institutional power, oppression*. There follows next a brief listing of "Specific Manifestations of Oppression" to which a vocabulary is supplied to lead the freshman aright. There is the acceptable term *ableism*, defined as "oppression of the differently abled, by the temporarily abled." There is *ageism*, which is "oppression of the young and old, by young adults and the middle-aged in the belief that others are 'incapable' or unable to take care of themselves." (The infant, therefore, must supply its own milk and the infirm aged their own comfort of body when bed ridden, lest any gesture to them be an act of oppression.) There is, inevitably, *classism*, the "oppression of the working class and nonpropertied by the upper and middle class." *Heterosexism* is "oppression of those of sexual orientations other than heterosexual, such as gays, lesbians, and bisexuals." Thus to be *heterosexual* is to be an oppressor, that term a "devil" term (as Richard Weaver calls such), while the document supplies "preferred terms" (Weaver's "god" terms) *bisexual, gay, lesbian*. Our baffled freshman must also know the god term *differently abled*, "created to underline the concept that differently abled individuals are just that, not less or inferior *in any way* [my italics] (as the terms 'disabled', 'handicapped', etc. imply). *Physically challenged* is also accepted." There is also to be found by that entering freshman class the "Non-Traditional Age Student: A person whose traditional undergraduate education was interrupted and who made the decision to return and complete it."

The subterfuge in such an "official document," by which the differentiating accidents of a *person's* being are declared null and void, leads to the confusing contradiction of strange campus festivals in which, once differentia have been set aside, the differentiating aspects as abstractions are then elevated so that all participate in worshiping particular abstractions. A day for the handicapped might, in such a perverse comedy of the human condition, require that heterosexuals wear blue-jeans as do the erstwhile sexual deviates, or themselves suffer a discrimination or ridicule or worse. Or perhaps on days celebrating the Differently Abled, one might tie up one foot behind one, or put one arm in a sling, and smile in the wonder of the celebrations. For there will follow upon the confused distortions of the reality of handicap, whether physical or intellectual, a necessity to make those inescapable distinctions an occasion for special celebrations.

The confusions practiced upon reality are such that we are now at a stage in our conduct of higher education analogous to that in the French Revolution, when Robespierre and others found it necessary to incarnate abstractions upon which to center the necessity in the soul to worship *something*. Having destroyed the ground on which true worship is possible, such a necessity results. For without a release to the frustrated spirit, anarchy prevents all management in the reconstitution of existence itself by gnostic intellect. And so in the academy there occurs those necessities of holding a Black History month, or a festival celebrating Asian Cuisine, or a justification of Woman or Homosexual, and so on and on. Those from whom the aspects of their being have been removed will otherwise feel robbed, but know not of what. What is operative here is the psychological management of our disorientation, which disorientation occurs when we deny differentiation.

v

The issue of the scalawag's perversions is the totalitarian reduction of intellectual virtue, a constriction of the intellectual community in order that he may advance intellectual mediocrity to his own advantage. For what he knows is that, like the one-eyed man in the country of the blind, the wily, clever intellect at large among mediocrity will have its way. In addition, it is only intellectual mediocrity in the end which will submit to such manipulation, this nominalistically managed severing of the naïve intellect from reality. It is, for instance, only by establishing a climate of intellectual mediocrity that the embattled carpetbagger or scalawag can be reconciled in compromise with each other, whereby each accepts the inferior but calls it superior lest they lose general support of both the academic body and then of public funds. Even the unlettered recognize that some minds are better than others, whether lettered or not. It is often the unlettered—or perhaps we might say the less sophisticated mind, the mind not distorted by the letter as deconstructive instrument—who recognize the grace of individual, particular existences whereby they differ one from another.

We have come to a point, in relation to the intellectual capacity of the community, in which it is neither sophisticated (though it quickly pretends to be) nor natively attuned to reality by common sense. It is an intellectual climate possible when community has been disfranchised by the lettered Gnostic, who presumes to an ultimate intellectual sophistication more often than not. The disfranchisement has been accomplished over a period of time, beginning in the early Renaissance, as a consequence of knowledge specialized. That specialized knowledge which is possessed by the particular "expert" becomes generally acceptable—and properly so—in consequence of the desirable effects for the community that the expert produces. For we do not mean at all that a productive system of "accountancy" of nature is to be deprecated, an accountancy through which for instance the medical profession has made such remarkable advances in delineating the causes and cures of particular diseases.

The difficulty comes, however, in what follows from the community's changing attitude toward the bearers of specialized knowledge. What is lost in the change is an understanding of a sufficient prescience in relation to complex reality to keep that welcome ordinate. Either by this failure, or by the wile of intellect's catering to the carelessness typical of community in its general intellectual deportment, the credentials of specialized knowledge provided by the "expert" lead to a transformation of the "expert" to "philosopher" in the public's estimate. That is, the expert's specialized knowledge justifies an enlargement of his authority beyond his limited "field." Thus an unwary community will submit to the expert as wise beyond the common ken by virtue of his particularized knowledge. It is as if to know completely a little thing, to know that thing beyond our common knowledge, were to know all of all. For, says our unsophisticated response, look what this expert has provided us by what he knows of this thing. It must be, then, that he.... Such is our deference to expert knowledge. If we consider, in relation to the fate in this century of lower and higher education, the facility with which the "educationist" as expert has had his way with our education, we find him empowered by the community precisely because of his limited view. For decades, he was protected by a pseudo-scientific language beyond any easy common grasp. Lest a local citizen, and especially a citizen active in the P T A, be considered intellectually gauche, he may quickly grant to the resident expert a larger wisdom, even when common sense is restive, saying secretly beneath the level of his effective articulation that foolishness is afoot and treading down the green intellect of youth.

Eventually the disfranchised generality will come to see the error in such an easily granted consent to the expert, whereby he is taken as philosopher, though that eventuality is slow to come. Even Congress solicits expert testimony on rural farm problems from a cinema star who has played the role of a depressed farm wife. At some point of the near collapse of community, in part the consequence of its own consent to its intellectual disfranchisement in deference to the expert, it will realize that it is in collapse. By careless consent it has become rarified as community to a mere abstraction, the product of a multitude of experts. It may then once more long for a philosopher, though it may not have available to it the term to name the person for whom it longs. And this is the point of community collapse when it discovers itself a chaos of memberships, in which the difference is not simply that of demonstrable differentiations of its membership but a spiritual estrangement one from another through its habitual denial of differentiations. That is pretty much the present state of community in its intellectual circumstances, the large and disturbing manifestations of which are played out daily on the campuses of our institutions we thought consecrated to higher learning. Of course, if by *higher* we mean only a more rarified and limited specialization of knowledge, unrelated to understanding or wisdom, those institutions will continue their farcical displays of that chaos whose toxic intellectual waste will continue to erode community.

Our chaos is held tenuously from collapse through a growing refusal to completely surrender by the ordinating, discrete power of the particular reluctant person—lettered or not—who longs for a restoration of significant order to the human community. The refusal of complete surrender is from a nagging common sense. The person that we each are knows an order not only possible but desirable, and he knows it through common sense out of his daily experience of reality. It is a thing known even if only by its absence. A person knows what is necessary intuitively, though he be unable to name it. And he will also recognize it when he sees it, though misled by gnositc illusions telling him that he desires or ought to desire a contrary thing. He is like the wanderer in the desert who is tormented by mirages of water, of quiet coolness beyond desert sands. That there is no water in the desert does not prove that water does not exist. To begin a recovery of the actual reality from the distortions of reality by Gnostic intellect: that is the task to higher education. And it must begin with our recognizing and accepting the distinctions in things as consequent to their creatureliness.

In respect to those "things" called *students*, by its acceptance of reality higher education must accept and declare as well that distinctions in no wise effect the loss of dignity in a person, by his being either more or less gifted intellectually than his neighbor, in being distinguished from his neighbor on the grounds of peculiar gifts. That is the wise point Chaucer makes to us, at the threshold of our descent into our present disorder. We see in his portraits of the Parson and the Plowman, in the "Prologue" to the *Canterbury Tales*, a dramatic rendering of the point by the complementary portraits. These are natural, family brothers, sharing a community of equality within the Church, a spiritual equality which does not, however, deny the reality of their differing gifts as intellectual creatures. The

Parson, himself of humble station in the Church hierarchy, had proved suited by intellectual gift to attend Oxenford. The Plowman proved suited to the hoe and plow, in the fields adjoining that institution of "higher education" as it were. What both know, accept, and are joyful in is that their differing gifts do not affect their moral and spiritual value as persons. Chaucer shows that point in reflecting the companionable charity of each to the other.

I am quite aware of an immediate objection which we have been conditioned to raise, namely that a *system* imposes the distinction upon the brothers. Perhaps the Plowman possessed an IQ that, if supported by SAT scores, might open Harvard or Yale to him. Certainly systems can be and often are arbitrary. That is one of our continuing, often legitimate, complaints, not against systems per se but against false systems or systems falsely managed. But an automatic objection such as I anticipate is most probably based in denial of any distinctions, when the denial is pushed back to its principle. And such a position, operating under the color of a compassion for all, would elevate every intellect by that principle to an equality—virtually to an identity—in the face of inescapable differences in intellectual capacities. This is the habitual sentimentality practiced by an intellect either through its own submission to the unreality of its position (justified by vague feeling) or practiced by a manipulative intellect intent upon drawing others into that sentimentality in order to use them to gnostic ends. On either hand, the distortion occasions not only the considerable social unrest we are heirs to at the moment but immeasurable spiritual miseries in specific persons. Such persons confuse intellectual gifts with spiritual gifts.

By supposing themselves victims of a perverse "discrimination" which denies to them their intellectual "rights," they further may suppose those rights circumscribed unjustly but only by externally imposed denials of their rights. It becomes some system, or even some particular teacher or teachers, who thus reduce them. That such external violations of intellectual gifts is both possible and often actual may not be denied. Indeed, such is the burden of our own argument against modernist thought as pervasive of the intellectual community itself. But that is a complication, not an explanation, of the problem. The problem is not resolved by denying other possible or probable circumstances to the limit of one's intellectual potential, primarily that of an intrinsic limit. Given actual external violations, however, it becomes easy enough to any beleaguered intellect to conclude that all limit upon its desire is external. Intrinsic limit thus becomes a reality not to be admitted.

We are all in some degree tempted by our restless desire. One would be as Beethoven or Shakespeare or Einstein. One would be as Elvis Presley or Rod McKuen or Lee Iococca, if desire alone were determinate of the fullness of our discrete gifts of being. But denied our dream fulfillment by circumstantial realities and the limit of our specifying gifts of being, whether admitted or not, we may come to resent our limitations, and by a failure of accommodation to both gifts and circumstance conclude that a moral transgression upon our "rights" has occurred. This may lead to confusion of our spiritual worth as person with the determining gifts of our actual worldly being. The confusion is most ancient, but there is a modern complication too general among us to be ignored. Most of us no longer believe in existence as created, and so we no longer believe in the Creator God. And so we no longer have God to "blame." An immediate substitute must be found, perhaps among our fellows, against whom we may then protest. That substitution, a consequence of modernist reductions of personhood, is the root cause of the growing factionalism in community whose end is an anarchic pluralism. (The tendency toward pluralism as native to humanity was seen clearly by the Founding Fathers, who attempted to engage and control it to our political health under the rubric of "factionalism.") By now we know all too well how various and numerous are those self-sovereign, detached persons who wait to manipulate us through our confusions. Those agents would exercise a totalitarian power, and at whatever level possible to them within circumstantial complexities: at the level of family or committee; of party or sect; locally or statewide or nationally or internationally.

It is not easy to be persuasive in reassuring any person confused over the relation of his spiritual gifts and his physical or intellectual gifts that his spiritual gifts are themselves inalienable, however much intellectual or physical gifts may be abused by the world, the flesh, and the devil. Certainly it is difficult in an age in which the spiritual dimension of human existence has been excised from our intellectual address to the nature of community itself. Our world would rather insist that the Plowman is "lowly" because of some transgression by a system or group or force of history that determines him to be plowman in spite of his virtues. He is at every hand encouraged to set his will against that determinism as unjust. But if it should prove rather that the limits are intrinsic to his peculiar nature, he is left then with only the recourse of bitterness, since there is no satisfactory accounting for his peculiar discreteness by natural or social determinisms that will satisfy his head and lighten his heart.

The justness of any grounds of discrimination is, of course, a complex problem, though imminently proper to intellectual pursuit. But that pursuit must be made in the light of what is evident to common sense: some distinctions signify differences native to discrete intellectual creatures, without those distinctions signifying a determination of moral worth to the existing soul. To deny this distinction is to prepare for such disorder in the person as to breed chaos in the body of persons. To insist, as our educators have been foremost in insisting, that "everyone can be whatever they want to be" (this is the too familiar formulation), is to lead to a frustrated citizenry as the young become adult in years but not in their understanding of their disappointment in not having become what they wanted to become through emotional whim as encouraged by *expert* authority. In such frustration, the idea of discrimination becomes burdened with pejorative connotations (the manufacture of which connotation keeps many "experts" in positions of power) till the term submits at last to only one formulation: *discriminate against.*

VI

One knows at an elementary level of encounter with reality that differences exist inescapably. And it is the young person, turning adolescent and moving toward adulthood, who is acutely attuned to difference. It was ever thus, leading to the perennial conflict of gen-

erations. But it became a collective recognition in the 1960s, leading
to a civil war in the family itself, from which we have little recovered.
If one is ill-prepared to discriminate among differentiating realities,
one is likely to object to all differentiation. The second grade teacher
cannot sit on a low chair in a circle, denying the grotesque figure she
makes thereby, without consequences along the way. For the second
grader knows with immediacy this fantasy pretending to be a reality,
a game in which an adult pretends to be a child. Taking that incident
(once a popular "educationist" ploy) as figurative for a whole complex
of such sympathetic distortions of reality, against whom will the
child in middle or high school revolt if not against the immediate
grotesque adult confronting him with lies about reality?

Difference is accepted as actual by the young, but they require a
knowledge of difference toward an understanding. Their education
hardly prepares them to gain that understanding. Even the magic of
genetic theory cannot solve the disturbance in their personal engagement of reality. For even God, now denied them, was a more
acceptable target of objection than the illusive gene. The gene requires, not faith, but specialized learning if one would approach it.
Given faith, at least blasphemy becomes possible. But God the creator supplanted by the gene as creator, the gene delivers no commandments speaking to moral hungers in us. It signifies in a
radically different way to the hunger for personhood to be commanded "Thou *shalt* not lie in God's name" as opposed to "Thou
canst not lie in the gene's name." Denied the risks of blasphemy,
what is one to do? *Blaspheme* and *blame* have the same root, we remember. One may blame a god, but what profits it to the agony of
the soul to blame a gene for one's agony? In addition, the gene is
most coldly unforgiving. Still, to some intellects, the gene is more
promising of solution to social problems than God. Through control
of the gene comes the engineering of a perfected polity—with the
gene manipulator enthroned, of course.

Meanwhile, the unfortunate persons become subject to their
genes, like an Eastern caste, and must be controlled as the ready
force to be manipulated in building the biotechnological Eden. In
that uncertain present, such abstractions as "establishment" or "sys-

tem" are handy devils out of which the eventual good is to be drawn in the fullness of time engineered by autonomous, self-elect intellect. With sufficient pressure in the political sector, unlimited resources to experimental ends may be commanded. But in those ends as seen by Gnostic abstractionism there will not appear my beginning, to echo Eliot once more. There will be only my reduction to an indiscriminate identity. I shall have become a duplication out of gnostic idea in the final abolition of man. There shall then be only a social machine, differing in parts but differing only in relation to the machine as machine. Huck Finn's complaint against the Widow's "Heaven" will then prove a more appropriate complaint against socio-biotechnology's Eden. For there would be yet a Parson and a Plowman; only they would be differentiated by mechanical principles. That they could share in a companionable charity, each for the other and both for creation at large: that is the gift of gifts to created humanity which will have been removed from nature. That will mean, in C. S. Lewis's term, that man has fully abolished himself.

The difference in particularizing gifts among persons does not affect the Parson's or Plowman's moral and spiritual value as persons, since personhood is not determined by particular gift but by specific gift, actual and transcendent of the particular. It is in this mystery of our existence as persons with which we must come to terms within ourselves in resisting that temptation of final refusal, *non serviam*. That *non serviam* is the hidden motto operative in the progressive abolition of man. Chaucer's characters, reflecting the possibility and probability of persons in his world, recognize and accommodate the mystery in complex ways, the Parson and Plowman being an instance of the possibility of difference bonded in a companionable charity. They blame neither circumstance nor establishment nor each other nor God for the distinctions within their enveloping personhood. Thus the point: Charitable love is possible, one of another, beyond the pride of intellect which dwells inordinately upon the exceptional as known in the orders of nature. From an inordinate concern for the exceptional rises a bogus egalitarianism to be imposed upon created things. The gnostic in his operation is bent upon an egalitarianism as tempting as in that ancient garden, in which a transgression of the orders of nature promised to make mankind equal to the gods. It is from this perspective that the refusal of distinctions in the orders of being, the modernist approach to existence, will be seen by my surrogate professor as a species of the diabolical, however much clouded by its pretenses to a concern for the dignity of persons. For the pretense to that concern is the means to the dismantling of charitable community, a pretense widely used in the perversion of personhood in our day. The pretense of that high concern is admirably represented by Milton's Satan in his argument to Eve in *Paradise Lost*, whereby the ground in which the dignity of person, independent of the range of the accidents to personhood, is destroyed through the intellectual nominalism practiced in conjuring Eve's incipient pride.

The confused and increasingly violent response of our young Adams and Eves to the so-called "Establishment" since the 1960s, aided and abetted in their confusions of the issues by manipulative intellects, is nevertheless initiated by their own intuitive response to violations of personhood. But the director of that violence turns out to be, again and again, the self-elevated leader of revolt against the order of reality, an order implicit in creation itself. What must be remembered is that the revolt against the nature of and limits of order in creation is practiced by both "Establishment" and "Anti-Establishment" intellectuals. It is out of that war between agents contending for dominance out of the same perverse principle that our carpetbagger and scalawag emerge. With respect to the academy, then, we might discover the revolt early in our century, leading to the enfranchisement of our carpetbagger. And subsequent to World War ii, the revolt leads to the enfranchisement of our scalawag, now conspicuously locked in decisive battle with the "Establishment" carpetbagger. On this view, one might recognize the negative correspondence in the perversions of reality whereby carpetbagger and scalawag, in respect to the gifts of each, are dark reflection of Chaucer's Parson and Plowman. (In such a bold analogy, the Carpetbagger corresponds to the Plowman, the Scalawag to the Parson.) By such a juxtaposition, one sees a grotesque figuring of the potentials of decay, whose positive potential are fictionally represented in Chaucer's portraits.

Of course, it will become increasingly difficult to make such a point to the lost and rebellious young, once they have had their intuitive recognitions of perversion distorted through radical dislocations of academic curricula. For they will have no familiarity with Chaucer—and certainly not with Milton. Out of that dislocation, they will be left to discover such persons as the Parson and Plowman as best they may, unaided by the academy. And they may no longer share with my professor this literary heritage of testimony to the abiding conditions of the reality of person, the potentiality in each for either decay from or growth toward moral, spiritual, and intellectual virtues. For, once they have been denied the great witnessing to that potential as dramatized by Homer, Sophocles, Virgil, Dante, Shakespeare, Milton; by Plato, Aristotle, St. Augustine, St. Thomas Aquinas, and so on—once they have been denied that witness to the realities of *humanness*, there will be a chasm between them and my professor, at least at the outset. Actually, however, that possibility is encouraging, almost to the point of making one call for a final collapse of the academy. For in that intellectual resilience we credit to youth (but which is no less available to age), they will discover, in their immediate world, Parsons and Plowmen along with their dark opposites and all combinations of intellectual deportment to existence in between the extremes.*

---

* In an age which is doggedly disinclined to believe in the saints or to accept aspirations to sainthood, our young at least impose expectations of sainthood on mortals whom they have chosen as heroes. But in doing so, they prepare their own disillusionment, since heroes and saints differ through differences in their envisioned ends. Heroes are always discovered to have feet of clay. It is the possibility of sainthood deferred, the possibility of moving beyond the entanglements of clay (which we used to speak of as the entanglements of the world, the flesh, and the devil) that make the hero a tragic figure. They are tragic, in that they reflect our aspirations to a perfection of actions transcending the entanglements of the circumstantial necessities to action in the world which are not fully oriented *beyond* those necessities. Not to recognize the

The immediate differentiations in our proximate environments do not obliterate basic, elementary points of departure to intellect in its pursuit of reality, for those constitute the accidents of existences through which the whatness of existent things become at once available to intellect, insofar as it opens itself to the complexity of reality. That is a very ancient secret, though it is not gnostic. And it is a secret that lies at the center of great art, from Homer to Dante to Chaucer to Shakespeare to Eliot and Faulkner and to lesser servants of that secret who mediate it through art in the membership of the body of humanity. To reduce that devotion to the level of *culture* in the pejorative sense in which that term is presently employed is to betray particular intellects, particular persons, and leave them disconsolate in relation to their own reality. It leaves them disoriented in anger and frustration, and so makes them easily available pawns in displays of power unleashed against any academy's recovery of its obligation to the truth of things. Look, to illustrate the point, at the resurgence of "demonstrations" in the academy in the 1990s, in which noise and violent action once more supplant discourse. Hapless souls, persuaded by their manipulators, believe the recovery of reality depends upon their rejection of any inheritance they may have received from "Western" civilization. They are in grave peril.

VII

It is much bruited abroad at the moment that the obfuscation of intellectual realities, the proper concern of the academy, is daily accel-

---

hero as existing on the border of sainthood, rather than to suppose him to have crossed that border, will lead in the end to our disappointment in heroes. In that disappointment too often rises a cynical rejection of both hero and saint. In cynicism, charity is excluded from the soul, the error lying in the tipping over into self-love by the cynic himself, a pretense as it were of his own heroic sainthood had he but been brought to the same trial as the fallen hero. Cynicism refuses that purgation of the soul which Aristotle sees as the tragic effect, the purging from the "self" of both pity and fear. In the cynical response to hero or saint, then, one is left with self-pity and self-fear, the desperate hell within the alienated soul.

erated toward good resolution by those who peddle pseudo-virtues as precedent to, and so preparative of, all virtues. Those pseudo-virtues are for the moment collectively termed the moral deportment of any intellect when it is "politically correct." The term will be quickly abandoned in the interest of some more recent and catchy name for the same perversion of intellect. But for the moment this Gnostic shibboleth is so pervasive as to be recognized at once by its reduced symbol, PC, an acronym suggestive of a rallying banner for the pragmatic execution of the programatic, and so extensively recognized as to appear in comic strips in the evening paper. This latest magic concept, demanding one's fealty, has for the moment thwarted the displaced exile, members in that diminished remnant of intellectual community who still hold and use and believe in the good, the true, and the beautiful as terms significant of realities. It is those lost realities, justifying the terms by their reality, that orient our intellectual journey, when those terms are properly taken. This is a journey toward an end not illusional. And it is through holding firmly to such an orientation that one may escape disorientation in the present intellectual swamp called the academy, aided and abetted in its swampness by the idolators of chaos.

The idolatry which is the doctrine of the "Politically Correct," naturalistically attractive to the young, attempts to manipulate public consent in general through a rhetoric more wily than witty. It would touch in the general public a vague, residual sentiment which has lost its proper object, that inclination to being through love that is part of the soul's nature. Or it would stir a vague guilt which lacks any possible recognition of cause in the troubled conscience, since sin is long ago reduced to a naturalistic disposition which requires only an adjustment in response to natural and social forces. The ends intended by such manipulation are those which common sense would reject, and if need be violently reject, if understood in their true intent—the intent of exercising collective power. In this intellectually decayed community that is ours, conditioned to defer common sense in the name of "experts" removed both from any governance by common sense and from community itself, the exciting question seems always plausible. Who would not desire to be

"Politically Correct"? Having long ago surrendered its responsibility for educational institutions, the general public has embraced instead the "expert" and through him given consent to gnosis as determinate of the truth. For after all, as we have said, such a surrender has yielded back such material conveniences as never existed before. If gene therapy yields control of cancer, politically correct therapy will surely restore community.

Little wonder the public hesitancy, however, as these virtues of the "Politically Correct" are espoused by radical "experts," established by tenure or administrative office as expert. For common sense is intrinsic in our natures. Still, those experts know a thing or two about our residual sense of guilt, which yet remains although we have been conditioned through determinisms of various sorts to deny the reality of sin. Thus they declare that one may blame one's fathers for "psychological" disorder, so long as the line of succession of the fathers is not pursued too far back in history. The cave man may be honorable enough antecedent, but it is to be disallowed that one suppose any Adam lying somewhere behind that anthropologically demonstrated generator of our descent. To go before the cave man in speculative concern for origins requires a limited pursuit, a pursuit limited to our animalistic origins. The mystery of intellect itself as somehow possibly intrusive into nature, along with willed intentionality—such speculative question is not comfortably entertained. Such questions are suited only to the expert for his "scientific" speculations, the limits defined by his particular intellectual specialty: as anthropologist or neurologist, as geologist or sociologist, as astronomer or nuclear physicist. It is thus that ontological questions are frozen at an immanentist level. Lacking the guidance of the philosopher, that lover of wisdom for whom those specialties are valuable departments of knowledge but require an integrative understanding, what are we to do at this distant remove from the academy as viable to potential intellect?

Such is the circumstance of the general public, reading in the evening news an account of disturbances at State U. Certainly PC seems spoken for authoritatively by academic experts, presumed by us to be expert by virtue of office held at State U. Supporting PC, then, appears similar to supporting the flag or apple pie or mother-hood as those old opaque symbols may be vaguely remembered as operative in certain quadrants of the body social at an ancient day. (Those old symbols have been made largely opaque by manipulative uses of them, so that the realities they once designated to a common consent are seen only as symbols, if at all; seen only as a glass darkened by intellectual violations of reality itself.) A term like *politically correct* was itself once a term naming a manner of and deportment toward, an ideal, to which Plato and Aristotle and Cicero speak wisely. But these wise men are to be discarded from remembrance, disallowed to speak for the ideals of civil order, so that civil order may be decreed by the expert now turned intellectual totalitiarian.

The supposition by a naive but well-intentioned public is that such a program as that of the "Politically Correct," if established as academically required, may move us beyond fear or greed or passion. It supposes the position founded on intellectual principles demonstrated as valid in that place of intellectual demonstration, the academy, since that is the academy's responsibility. But the responsibility has been unmonitored by common sense. The cadres of experts have effectively disjoined intellectual responsibility from the public, and reserved it to the purview of institutions. That has proved one step in the reduction of man in general from his reality as intellectual creature, wherever we find him in the body of humanity. The public as *well-intentioned* is a reality perceived by the gnostic manipulator. He sees the reality of will as intentionally operative in the deportment of individual persons. However, the truly radical nature signaled by that intentionality—an intuitive desire for the good—must be avoided, which is one reason that to go beyond the cave man in human lineage becomes dangerous because of questions put by the non-expert. But still there are "good intentions" to be used, in relation to a residual sense of guilt. Thus community may be conditioned to the ends intended by gnostic will, if one can prevent those questions proper to the philosopher, though only puzzling to the "expert," from being raised.

The general public, that reservoir of intentionality required for the gnostic restructuring of the community, has not yet recognized its own betrayals, as it eventually will. For in the end it is protected against infinite manipulation by its common sense. Common sense is intrinsic to the created nature of the soul, resting in intellect itself. If the public is solicited largely by intellectual scalawags, it will come at last to recognize them as such. At the moment the public is solicited by these scalawags to be ally against the intellectual carpetbaggers, or by the carpetbagger against scalawag. But it is being called to support one false alternative against another, in order to establish a new species of totalitarianism over the person as person. Common sense recognizes a false dilemma, even should intellect lack the formal term.

If *Adventures of Huckleberry Finn* has not been excised completely from our common curriculum, it is worth rereading to our point chapters nineteen and twenty, in which the Duke and the Dauphin maneuver against each other in order to gain Huck's and Jim's service as slaves. Through the distorted language of address, they would accomplish that end: your *Grace* and your *Majesty* and so on. Huck and Jim here are parable figures for the general public now caught in the clutches of those Dukes and Dauphins consented to as experts. For the naive consent Huck and Jim give is a trust in those scoundrels' honest use of terms in relation to reality, out of naive good intentions. Only experience shows Huck and Jim the error in their trust. And so will experience lead to our own disillusionment in respect to the Dukes and Dauphins of the academy.

In our parable, the "Royal Nonsuch" is used to bilk the country folk in that one-horse Arkansas town, but we must remember Jim's and Huck's own roles in their own deception, for they are not guiltless. They are participants in the scam, despite degrees of naivete in them comparable to those in the general public in its relation to higher education in our analogical comparison. We might well remember the public response of the citizenry to the "Royal Nonsuch": the first audience is baffled and outraged, but they turn conspiratorial. For, having been themselves duped, they decide to talk the "show" up and "sell the rest of the town," lest they be the town's laughing-stock for having been duped. (For interesting extensions of correspondences in this episode as parable, see Bryan F. Griffin's

Panic Among the Philistines.) The whole town deceived after the second performance, there is a mob reaction in the offing for the third. But the Duke, a clever scalawag, anticipates the action, knowing the public to be "greenhorns and fatheads." And so the theatre riot (in the local courthouse, such are the appealing correspondences) misses the Duke, Dauphin, and Huck, who by then are floating on down the river out of reach.

But parable correspondences are not exact, and our Dukes and Dauphins in the academic analogue are not likely in the end to escape so easily from the rotten eggs and cabbages and dead cats available to the public for its evaluation of their performance. A curtailment of economic support is more certain to reach at least some of the perpetrators of fraud along the way. One might prove prophetic beyond merely wishful hope in assuring an inexhorable, if slow, recognition by the general public, with budgetary consequences at least, though it itself shares responsibility for the "Royal Nonsuch" currently advanced under the billing of "Higher Education." The very recognition of its own culpable participation, indeed, may exascerbate the reaction. That such a growing recognition is well underway is evident. We have already suggested something of the dead cats and rotten eggs aimed at our intellectual con-men, as for instance what has been happening at Stanford in response to President Kennedy's manipulation of public money. Auditors at Stanford are as thick as grasshoppers. And there are other portents, encouraging to my exiled professor. For even Harvard and MIT are not beyond formal scrutiny.

There was a considerable stir when Allan Bloom published his *Closing of the American Mind*, a book whose analysis of the academic milieu is persuasive, although his understanding of the relation of the academy to the community is in my view less acceptable. And there has been Charles Sykes's *Prof Scam* and his *The Hollow Men*. We alluded already to Griffin's *Panic Among the Philistines*. Dinesh D'Souza's devastating critique of the new ideology of the "Politically Correct" stirred public response as none of the others. His *Illiberal Education: The Politics of Race and Sex on Campus* received such a response at the "grassroots" level that the book became a best-seller, as we mentioned, as did Bloom's. These and other engagements are welcomed public alarms, stirring as they do some recovery of common sense to our common intellectual responsibilities as the academy's supporting citizenry.

But my own address intends, as I said at the outset, to be within a larger perspective. My concern is with what may follow, once the beseiged and occupied academy is either recovered or totally collapses. The academy will then lie largely in ruin and the rebuilding will be slow and costly, but not in terms of money alone. Nor will it be freed ever of the continuing guerilla forays of what will then have become intellectual barbarians in exile, who are with us always in one way or another, those who seem at this moment to command power in the academy. And so what I have rather attempted in my own *Liberal Arts and Community*, even as in this essay and the next ones, is a sort of acting out of the gradual recovery of a deportment I believe proper to the teacher, his deportment to student and to public in the interest of the recovery of community in our trying moment of history. I intend a testimony of my own understanding of the proper conduct of intellect through sign—sign as grown out of concept. Concept in turn arises from intellect's encounter with *reality*, a term which we have used again and again, and to which I shall turn in our concluding explorations of the proper intellectual deportment that I think necessary to the academy.

I recall something Josef Pieper says to my concern: "All speech by its very nature refers to something that is not speech. What is it? It is reality." He adds, "I attend Church, not because of all the talking and preaching but because something happens there." What happens for Pieper is his encounter with ultimate reality through the Mass. It is an encounter whose analogy, at a lesser level of reality than the one he means, occurs when professor or student moves beyond all their talking, whether in defense of liberal arts or against liberal arts, whether in an attempted rejection of Western civilization or its rescue to intellectual health. Academic talking, out of the various and disintegrated specialties now burdening the academy, distracts us—teacher and student alike—from the obligation of intellectual action to recover reality, to know insofar as intellect may know, the truth of things. And to know that reality in a quietness of heart and mind beyond the limits of signs, of words.

That is the end St. Thomas declares as proper to philosophy, to the love of wisdom: the end of knowing and understanding the truth of how things stand. In the labor of recovery which is now ours as teacher and student, we shall find it both slow and painful, and the way lies necessarily through those departments of rational intellect designated as *grammar* and *logic* and *rhetoric*, as appropriate to our talking about reality. In that possible recovery, there may follow a reorientation of intellect to reality, to the truth of things, beyond ideological warfare as currently engaged in the academy by forces under many banners, though such a warfare is ancient: then and now and tomorrow.

If the poet's highest office is, as Eliot declared, to "purify the dialect of the tribe," then the philosopher's must be to orient that purified dialect in respect to the realities of human nature, within the matrix of the creation out of which such dialect rises. To do so will require at once our accepting the realities of our own finite intellect, if we are to recover within community those safeguards against the manipulations of persons as persons by other persons who are perverse by neglect or intent. That manipulation is in varying degrees always diabolical, in that it denies the truth of things for ends that are self-elevating of this perverse manipulator of being itself, who again and again turns out to be our very self. It is a perversion possible at last only by intellectual manipulations of our common dialect, and we are responsible not to practice that manipulation, nor to allow it to be practiced against us without calling it to account.

The signs we call our common dialect are made opaque by manipulative intent, but they are also made opaque by our own neglect. The cliché has lost its anchor in reality, but it may cease to be merely cliché when returned to its proper mooring in reality by intellectual action. That is the first responsibility the academy must recover. It may do so only, or so I would hold, when we accept the wisdom that says we bear false witness when we use words carelessly, no less than when we lie with deliberate intent. To refuse a responsible attention to sign is to reject that intellectual piety proper to intellect's relation to reality. That is why I have insisted, in *Liberal Arts and Community*, that a contentment with sign as cliché is ultimately a service to the diabolical. It is servitude to the diabolic, to quote from that work,

> since it is, whether by accident or intention, a destruction of reality and the solicitation of a destruction of reality by the young. We hesitate to call it diabolic, the more's the pity. . . . But acknowledged as diabolic or not, we witness the effects of such destruction of being at every hand. Though we shield our sight from it through a vaporous sentimentality, its effect is palpable in the withering of those discrete gifts in our sons and daughters. Anyone who teaches in public secondary schools or colleges or universities, if he pause for reflection, will recognize at once that it is this distortion of actual existence, the denial of the particularity of gift whereby one is a discrete and most valuable being in a community, that makes effective public education virtually impossible. He will recognize the confusion of morality with mind training; a pervasive heresy against reality which can have come to dominate community only with the academy's and the community's consent.

My concern now is to become somewhat less playful, given the magnitude of the challenge to regaining the academy from the barbarian captivity. But playfulness in dealing with such serious matters, even to the extent of such outrageous uses of terms on my part, such as *carpetbagger* and *scalawag*, for instance, may be more than a substitute for sardonic irony under the burden of despair. It may well signal a hope vital to the life of intellect in exile from its true country and resisting that exile.

5

The Journey Toward Wisdom

L EST I BE MISTAKEN in my meaning of the term *philosopher* in
addressing the reader as philosopher: I assume the term
proper to all serving the academy. For unless we are as
academicians "lovers of wisdom" first and last, we serve under false
pretenses as professors of higher education. To love wisdom is not,
of course, to be wise, as if our beginning were our end. To love wisdom is to desire and labor toward wisdom through the gifts of intellect, each according to his gifts. Without that enveloping desire,
whatever our specialty, we are at best technicians and not teachers.
We may in addition be renowned as "expert" in any of several technical specialties, within that enveloping desire. There are virtues to
such accomplishment of expertise. But we are not made sufficient
thereby to be active intellectual witnesses to that journey toward wisdom which is the proper fulfillment of the gift of intellect. And that
is the principle most centrally to be nurtured by any institution that
pretends to a devotion to "higher education."

The epigraph to this book, from St. Thomas, would, in some
places or times, appear a commonplace, a statement of the obvious
concern of the philosopher. But the history of intellect in its service
to the community of mankind since St. Thomas is such that the
words prove rather foreign to our own decayed assumptions about

intellect and its responsibilities to the truth of things. Words seem particularly so on those community-funded reservations devoted to endangered intellect, the academies of higher education, though one might suppose such a first principle of intellectual action to be valued there above all else. The current restlessness, however, speaks quite the contrary. The natives are disturbingly restless, or so it appears to the patron society which itself grows increasingly uneasy about those reservations and its automatic support of them. There, removed radically from any attachment to the larger supporting community, there has occurred a retrogression to an intellectual primitivism, threatening any concern for the truth of things, whether expressed in isolated pockets on the reservations or abroad in the larger, enveloping community. The new war cry is for intellect's submission to the "politically correct," which necessarily involves a rejection of the concern for the truth of how things stand. Those war dances, complete with initial sacrifices of local victims on the reservations, are reported from Stanford and Berkeley all along the chain of reservations to Princeton and Harvard. The formally appointed agents of order, the administrators and regents, have lost all control and either join in the dance or surrender as sacrificial victims.

I

Now, from such a preamble, it becomes immediately evident that I address the current situation in higher education from the position of the poet, through metaphor, at once both serious and playful in my address. For if a concern for the truth of things as central to the growth of intellect is to be recovered, it seems necessary that I find some way to call attention to the fact that those revolting natives wear no intellectual clothes, and the poet's way is anciently effective. One cannot make the point with the old innocence of the child pointing to the naked emperor, for that requires a community of common sense sadly neglected in our day. Though I speak through the limited innocence of the poet in the presence of things as they are, I often as well speak presumptuously as if a confident philosopher of the old school, the philosopher who was once central to higher education. As for my seemingly divided role—betimes poet, then philosopher—I do not take that personal division as unique to myself. It is an abiding problem whenever intellect attempts to bear witness to glimpses of the truth of things as to whether the poet or philosopher is the better witness. And so my cautionary assay upon the problem, treated in a mode as if peculiar to me, is rather an exemplum of the possible or probable to any intellect in its progress, whoever the particular journeyman, whether he be of those reservation natives or that native's disquieted overseer and community agent, whom we usually call administrator, or the detached but increasingly threatened patron citizen of the larger community.

Consider initially, then, that I address the present confused moment in my own journey as a discrete soul. Mine is a concern with my own understanding of reality in present intellectual circumstances, addressed from a position as a Thomistic realist concerned for the restitution of order to the intellectual and community, and in the interest of the health of the general community of mankind. Presumptuous to present it so publicly, this witness of mine. And doubly presumptuous if I suppose my experience of the circumstantial complexities not unique, but instead common. I believe mine a common experience, if in common we but turn our intellects to a pursuit of the truth of how things stand. As for the presumptuousness, I remember a downhome saying, intended to caution pretensions to greatness beyond what is warranted by a person's peculiar gifts: "Me and Dan'l Boone killed a bar." I would not intend to foretell how me and St. Thomas Aquinas expect to survive the 1990s. Yet this seeming playfulness promises a serious entry into the subject of my debt to St. Thomas. In this mode, mine is the playfulness of the poet, who is always tempted to manipulations beyond reason, especially when threatened by his sense of exile from the intellectual community. Playfulness affords a leavening by humor of that sardonic irony so typical of a Kierkegaard or Eliot in their reactions to higher education, or of that pathos of desire sliding into despair which we find in John Keats, who longed for, but could not come to, the philosopher's metaphysical understanding. Remember in your kindness what will have become apparent to you: that I speak to philosophers more comfortably when I am as a poet, though I believe the two disciplines of intellect, the two callings, both companionable and indeed intrinsic to any intellect, whatever robes of office one may wear. Nor does my greater comfort in speaking as poet justify that for which I speak. For I am forewarned by St. Thomas that each intellect is ultimately responsible for its failed or safe acquisition of the truth of things, truth being the proper good of the intellect. The need for a comfort in signs, to each according to the gifts given, is a part of our nature as persons, and through signs mutually held we witness to each other the truth we hold. Since we know together Keats and Wordsworth and Eliot and Pound, whether we know them as ourselves the philosopher or poet, I have asked these to represent me as images of myself *in medias res*, that being in the middle of things which is the continuing condition to our existence, whatever our calling or age. We are always in the middle, which we designate as this present moment. These poets I have discovered bound to this very conclusion, whether or not they arrive.

Keats, at a moment of indecision, retreats from London to Margate, as Eliot was to do when he experienced his "nervous breakdown" a hundred years later. And at Margate, Keats very like Eliot was distressed to discover that he could "connect/Nothing with nothing" on Margate sands. No trained philosopher, as was Eliot, Keats wrote a plaintive letter to a friend back in London. Please send three or four books on philosophy, he begged, for he felt very much the need of a metaphysical position. How typically Romantic, one wants to say. But how typical of any "poet" when seen from within the robes of the "philosopher." It is as if the poet would turn to the *Summa Theologiae* as if it were the Sears & Roebuck catalogue. Not that philosophers do not themselves sometimes act as if poets in this respect. That is the heavy burden Thomism has had to bear. Which brings me as poet to observe of this inclination, to which I do not deny being susceptible, that it may be put more accurately thus: how typically "modern." Keats's plaintive request finds a parallel in that later, stranded poet, Eliot, it seems to me, though their terms are not strictly parallel. Keats expects of "metaphysics," as Eliot of "myth," that it will be simply a "way of controlling, of ordering, of giving a shape and a significance to the seemingly immense panorama of futility and anarchy" (to use Eliot's own words describing his own sense of myth in 1922) which was his own contemporary history. But more immediately, his concern was not with a contemporary, modern history but with his own intellect.

If poets in their passion for passion are sometimes given to saying such simplistic things, the poet in turn may suspect a comparable simplicity in any philosopher's or scientist's rational intent upon rationality, so that perhaps the philosopher or scientist may in the event practice much the same thing, too easily committed to controlling, shaping, ordering present confusions. On occasion, I fear using St. Thomas or Einstein as a sort of wrench to tune the world. Understand, I am not suggesting that you yourself do so. I am only concerned that such a possibility would serve to obscure the ends proper to poetry or philosophy or science. And I am most directly characterizing an inclination I find in myself, a temptation to an unearned dependence upon St. Thomas and to uses of him that are not to be blamed upon that spirited intellect who is everywhere present in those words surviving to us in well-ordered signs under his name. It is a temptation to take the words as authority, disregarding the spirit present in them no less than we may disregard the reality toward which that spirit speaks. I gather that this is a distinction that describes the perilous ground named "Thomism," which Gilson explored in warning us of such dangers. I approach the danger with a playfulness of metaphor, with a seeming dependence upon attributive analogy in that playfulness, in comparing a possible use of the *Summa* to recollections of old uses of the Sears & Roebuck catalogue. Seemingly attributive, I say, for my intuitive intellect tells me that there underlies my metaphor a sufficient anchor in an analogy of proper proportionality, which anchor St. Thomas would insist necessary.

The danger in attributive metaphor makes me wary as well of the dangers in my taking terms separately, divorced from other terms in the rich texture of Western thought. For attributive metaphor easily becomes an escape to the poet, whose temptation is to forego the

rigor expected of the philosopher. In our day, as in any day, the philosopher is certainly committed to a responsibility to know what
men have said. The audacious poet might bring a charge against the
philosopher—especially the academic philosopher as we know
him—that this necessary means (the knowing of what men have said
of fundamental principles) has rather become an improper end in
itself, and philosophy thus reduced to description. But to know what
men have said—whether we speak of Plato or Wittgenstein; of
Copernicus or Einstein—is not therefore to know how the truth of
things stands.

Our inherent desire to know the truth of things, a gift to intellect lying in our very nature as intellectual creatures, will not be satisfied by mere description, even when presented by those professing
themselves philosophers. Such a pretense to the truth reduces philosophy to an archeology practiced upon ideologies, for things in
themselves are overlooked in the interest of merely ordering concepts, intellectual artifacts. Instead of philosophy's leading to an
encounter with reality, it effects in the end an isolation of intellect
from reality, with an intuitive recognition—not an instinctive recognition as the term is likely to be in a Darwinian climate—of exile. It
is this recognition that is prevalent on the intellectual reservations at
the moment, the academies, where intellect has atrophied to a primitivism. Of this peremptory judgment of mine, let me urge its consideration in the light of Gilson's *Methodical Realism*, which
considers Cartesian Idealism in its progressive usurpation of Western philosophy.

Little wonder, then, that there is a restive, growing rebellion
among young intellectuals, who are little content with "objective"
rationalizations that allow little commitment of themselves as persons, in the Thomistic sense of the term, beyond a merely witty detachment. The mischievous poet, indeed, might suggest that the
computer is now a much surer philosopher, more than compensating
for the possible loss of wit by its capacity of instant accommodation
of infinite contingencies of the merely descriptive. The most insistent cry of our young, as they come to the threshold of intellectual
responsibility, has for two decades now been that we must "tell it like

it is." But the old have long since lost the craft of telling, having surrendered that responsibility to technology, conspicuously represented by the computer. Hear the president of a Southern university, pretending to speak wisdom: "The products of our educational system [degreed students] are the raw material for industry." On another occasion, to his faculty: "An integral part of our mission must be to push back the frontiers of knowledge." Such metaphors speak ill of knowledge as enemy, of students as raw grist for the mills of industry. Or hear the dean at Binghamton State University, pretending to unquestioned authority, announcing the necessity of a "purge" of "logocentric modes of discourse," by which she means that she would isolate and excise any faculty who may yet profess a reality to which intellectual signs are significant. Instead, only those feelings agitated by intellectual claims are to be considered valid, feelings to be realigned under the rubric of the "politically correct." As one commentator on this intellectual barbarism remarks, one is hard pressed to discover how such a purging of the "logocentric modes of discourse" serves one's understanding of the table of the elements of chemistry.

Such a flourishing of argument by the poet against the pseudo-philosopher, through whom the intellectual barbarians have emerged as power in the academy, nevertheless makes me wary of the dangers of terms taken separately, out of context, as the poet is tempted to do. Terms removed from other terms and used attributively, in the interest of metaphorical spectacle, become problematic. Such a poet might as well be a "modern" philosopher, so far as his getting at the truth of how things stand through such audacity. In matters intellectual, it is as if one should take the thing itself away from all other things—out of the body of creation in its wholeness—without noticing that by such action the thing so taken is affected by the removal. Pinned and wiggling on the wall of language or on the lab slide, it is no longer the thing itself. Nevertheless, the necessity is that we must take *from* in one way or another, given the reality of our intellectual finitude. It is a necessity which I believe consequent upon Original Sin, not a very popular perspective to hold at this moment of our long wandering called "history." Original Sin: a term now held suspect, unless one present it as an attributive metaphor, thereby saying it does not speak a reality of the soul. To speak of Original Sin is only to speak of a present problem to be solved by objective analysis.

II

Now, whether or not we see our intellectual act as a taking-out-of in our pursuit of the truth of things, that is the point of departure of rational action. We start with the *thing in itself* whose actuality as itself is embedded in the whole of creation. So we must, once the obligation of a rational deportment toward our own existence as intellectual creature is accepted. And insofar as we continue mindful of our finitudes as takers of things, a steady remembrance of our intellectual nature as limited, we are somewhat protected against intellectual pride. For in that remembrance lies the possibility of a piety limiting intellectual excessiveness. To take is not to make, though that becomes an easy confusion under the influence of our will, whose temptation always, in the popular slogan for the temptation, is to be "number one."

With suitable piety, we know that the thing as we *take* it exists in its full truth beyond the inevitable reduction committed in our act of taking. In its full truth any *thing*—whether in existential reality as encountered by the senses or in concepts or signs of existential reality encountered in thought—is larger than our partial comprehension of it. This proves true, even of a favored concept in which we may invest our consequential being as if thereby the concept were the cause of our being. For concept is tangent always to an incomprehensible whole, insofar as the finite intellect is capable of comprehension. That whole includes both the thing taken and the intellect that does the taking. With such a recognition, our intellectual act holds any thing loosely, as it were, lovingly as in the open hand. A violation of the necessary piety toward things leads to a grasping of things, and by the grasping a dislocation of things to perverse ends, most usually to a self-justification as our own ultimate end. Such is the violence practiced upon things by pride, which

Dante calls perverted love—love turned back upon the self, and so no longer love but an appetite for power over all things taken. And the intellectual presumption in such a taking is the pretense to *comprehension* in the root sense of the term. It is in sharp opposition to that action of intellect through grace, properly termed not *comprehension* but *understanding*, that way-station toward wisdom in St. Thomas's account of our proper intellectual journeying in creation.

We discover quickly enough through piety that the truth of the taken thing is not fully excisable from the whole of creation. Thus understanding, and not a prospect of full comprehension of any thing, is the limit of our relation to each thing taken, a limit determined by the finitude of intellect itself. Wisdom, beyond understanding, is the loving and open acceptance of that limit, a joyful deportment to both intellect and soul. Our best poets are most often concerned with such a fundamental distinction, however various and seemingly different the things taken by them from the whole to give corporeal presence to their concern as makers of things—of poems. We know how constant a concern the poet has that his poem share, at least analogically, the conditions of created things insofar as his signs may share. His poem strives to be substantive or concrete or actual or such, weak terms that attempt to speak to the importance of his made thing's anchor in substantive existence. He would thereby bear visionary witness to the truth of things, however confused his premises or his conclusions as examined by the philosopher. And in that witness he is more likely than scientist or philosopher, one ventures, to defend the thingness perceived in an intuitive way.

Perhaps the point is clearer in instances of the poet's objections to philosopher or scientist in their deportment to existence. For instance, Wordsworth complained that our "meddling intellect" is much given to murder things in order to "dissect" them. His is a concern for that ambiguous realm of nature—the whole of creation, which seemed increasingly a victim to empirical science, though the murdering of human nature itself for the advantage of dissection was not so far advanced in Wordsworth's day as it has become in ours. J. Alfred Prufrock is more cowardly in his deportment against such deconstructions than Wordsworth might be, and is not above adapting the deconstructive instruments himself in a defense against the whole of creation on one hand and the reducers of that wholeness on the other. He retreats from other intellects, lest he be left "pinned and wriggling" as a specimen collected by indifferent intellects. He would much prefer to have been, out of the accidents of time, merely a pair of ragged claws scuttling across the floors of silent seas, a specimen below the threshold of self-awareness. But he treats all other intellects with an indifferent mode, pinning them with his clever intellect. He is skillful in manipulating metaphor, for instance, in that mode the scholastic would conclude attributive and not anchored in the actualities of being. We remember his dismissal, vaguely put, of those uncertain collective women who come and go, talking of Michelangelo, in relation to the terror raised in him by the actual presence of a particular woman, whose arms are downed with light brown hair. Such encounter with presence does not lead to an openness, but rather Prufrock does an intellectual version of the crab threatened, scuttling backward into the chambers of his own remote self-awareness.

Even so, Prufrock at least recognizes, though cowardly in his recognition, that the pin intellect uses to mount things taken from the whole of creation—the intellectual sign or word—though forced by will through the wriggling actual thing, is in the end a reduction intolerable to reality. The poem is heavy with pathos since Prufrock recognizes at last that the thing of nature reduced from the potential of its wholeness is J. Alfred Prufrock himself. The terror he experiences is consequent to his recognition that he practices self-violence, while attempting to preserve himself through self-love. The recognition does not yield tragedy, only pathos, for as he remarks of the issue to his position, "here is no great matter."

To see the thing itself, whether a J. Alfred Prufrock or the hazelnut Dame Julian of Norwich holds on her open palm: that is the intellectual difficulty, complicated because of our spiritual nature itself. The difficulty is to see the thing not just *against* its background of creation but as integral to that larger inclusiveness. Our day's growing concern for "ecosystems" is a step toward a desirable recovery, though the attempt in general is severely handicapped, I believe, by a failure to recognize the importance of a recovery of metaphysics to such attempt. We have at least, however, restored ethics—even morality—to some degree of respectability in the intellectual community. It may even be possible to escape the closed cosmology breeding untenable myths about earth as Gaia in that new paganism abroad, the sociobiological reductionism of the universe as a whole as represented in E. O. Wilson's "sociobiology."

The thing—not just against creation as a background, and not just as integral to a self-justifying closed system, but as a part of a whole cause—is not simply itself. That is the vision toward which intellect tends whenever it inclines to an openness to existence. For openness is a gesture of piety whereby intellect moves toward its own potential perfection, within the limits of its gifts of being through grace, toward a simplicity of spirit, whereby the soul becomes comfortable in creation but not interred by creation. It is a simplicity of deportment toward being, whose difficulty for intellect is the necessity of the understanding's incorporation of knowledge. When knowledge is properly possessed by intellect, it becomes possible to maintain a spiritual deportment toward both the knowledge and the things known. That is the deportment we call wisdom. It is a simplicity which is always inadequately spoken to by sign or concept or knowledge possessed. Or even as known in the limited understanding vouchsafed intellect when it is open to the complexity of existence in pursuit of a vision of existence as transcendently simple—that is, as held in existence by the grace of God. And so perhaps I am well advised, from such reflections, to be cautious with metaphor, lest it prove merely attributive. As I must be cautious with terms, lest they prove but a pin or scalpel murdering when I but intend by a dissection of the thing through terms to pay tribute to the thing as itself.

One may not refuse the danger. *Concept* as a consequence to *experience* requires *consequent* terms, such is the weak nature of discursive intellect, though it desire strength beyond discursive necessities. It is in and through terms that the intellect battles its way in an attempt to recover that simplicity beyond the necessity of any term, and in that battle not the least victim may be truth itself. One's

hope, in response to one's desire, is that at last one may be graced
with vision such as that St. Thomas came to, leading him in his last
days to declare that all his things made with terms were but straw
before a visionary fire. Through that fire uncertain truth is refined to
certainty as a glass from which the darkness is expelled, allowing a
vision of the Beauty-Truth-Good that is Absolute Perfection.

And so I find as my own first necessity, waiting the destroying
grace of such a fire, a renewal of terms, lest they merely hack at the
body of being. One refines a term by discovering its origin as precedent even to a concept itself, in the existential experience of oneself
as person within the grace of being. And an important direction of
recovery is of that experience as memorialized, even memorized, in
poetry and philosophy and science and history, which we encounter
in our world under the rubric of a recently popular discipline, "the
history of ideas." But I believe the most significant recovery, without
which the "history of ideas" is but a whistling in a dark world from
which truth seems fled, lies in those still points in which my own
most particular mind meets another particular mind as a presence,
not as a residue of history. In that encounter of mind and mind, the
burden of time implicit in such terms as *history* or *poetry* or *philosophy* or *science* or *idea* or *image* or *concept* falls away. I shall have proved
only able to make this point as the poet might, and so the point is
likely ambiguous at best. But then, I must do what I am able to do,
here and now.

I do not think of myself so much as a Thomist but as a companion to St. Thomas in matters intellectual—albeit a lesser hanger-on,
one who would witness to the poet's suitable presence in that intellectual company gathered about St. Thomas. I carry with me from
St. Thomas not so much his highly formal arguments, which fascinate me, as rather an awareness of his *presence* in those arguments, a
sense that in these words I share a present vision with him as himself
a present intellect, though vaunting History would declare him dead
these six hundred years and more. My seeing may or may not be
soundly of the truth of things, and it is assuredly not so in every
particular. But what is assured as continuous is his own steady devotion to the truth. I recall often those specific words, steadying in the

presence of complicated or heated argument, that the end of intellectual action in this world is the "truth of how things stand." These kindly words do not in the least say that it is not important that I both know and understand him and others, as if by his authority intellect were granted a continuous holiday. His is a capacious, considerate, respectful mind, to whose presence any other mind is made welcome, but only on the condition that the welcomed mind be devoted through piety to the truth of things. This is to say he is a considerate host, requiring the intellectual manners of a considerate guest. St. Thomas would have little patience with the Sophist, of course. But he would be intolerant to any mind that would, through an unearned deference to him at the expense of truth, ignore difficulties in his words. Such is St. Thomas, the great teacher. But what is more central to him at last is that he is foremost the great student of *being*.

And so, though there is an endless comfort to me in St. Thomas as teacher, there is an even greater comfort to me in my recognition of him as the great student, for it helps recover to me something of my own prospects as student, encouraging me toward a liveliness of intellect beyond the formalities sometimes spoken of as "Thomism." It is also cautionary to me, for when one has lived through many years or even many academic degrees, the burdens—not inappropriate burdens, but burdens to be ordinately assumed—the burdens of being a teacher become inescapable. One hopes to maintain in the circumstances of age or of academic certification—or at least I hope to maintain in myself—that balance of self-awareness, wherein I continue old enough not to be embarrassed by what I do not know and young enough to be hungry to know it. That, I think, is the characteristic deportment of St. Thomas, and it is this that I would emulate, knowing that we have gifts differing one from another.

It is in this spirit of St. Thomas that Gilson engages him. True to the expectations of his companion St. Thomas in their common being, Gilson examines Thomas himself, as for instance on whether certain problems subsequently develop out of Thomas's assumption (out of Aristotle) that all creation is organic. The question Gilson raises is whether in that assumption medieval Thomism proved unsuited to the explosion of empirical explorations rising in the Renaissance. Thomas would expect no less of Gilson, though I dare say Thomas would expect as well a careful consideration of the question whether Thomism was increasingly rejected, beginning with Occam, on precisely these grounds. Or whether instead these grounds were rather an appropriate, defensible means of rejecting the whole of Thomas. For Thomas's vision of being, his understanding of the structure of existence under the rubric of the principle of proper proportionality, was most inconvenient to the new gnostic spirit a-borning whose passion was for a freedom to manipulate being. I have elsewhere suggested that the "Romantic Age," which I put in quotes, begins at least with Occam in philosophy and Dante in poetry and proceeds apace through an increasing dissociation of sensibilities until intellect at last can declare itself autonomous. That some recognize this separation with spurts of adrenaline stirred by passion in the intellect, whether in defense of *thought* or of *feeling*, seems to me evident. Our century's witness to the separation are frightening figurings of a fundamental heresy against the *person*. We recognize them at once in such figures as Hitler or Stalin or Pol Pot. More subtle and therefore more challenging manifestations may be a Gorbechev. But the most subtle and challenging and at last most disorienting recognition comes when we see that heresy in ourselves, though with the poet's playfulness we might begin a recovery from the terror. That is why Walt Kelley's Pogo proved such a wise possum, among his most telling lessons: "We have met the enemy and he is us."

III

So do the poets remind us, such poets as that country girl from Milledgeville, Georgia, Flannery O'Connor. Or as that impressive intellectual poet T. S. Eliot does. Eliot in one of the "Choruses" from *The Rock* says

> *The great snake lies ever half awake, at the bottom*
> *of the pit of the world, curled . . . .*

Seek not to count the future waves of Time;
But be satisfied that you have light
Enough to take your step and find your foothold.

We must realize that the moment of recovery to reality is always a moment peculiar to the specific, discrete soul. At issue at every moment of that soul, beyond all other consideration, is that discrete soul's destiny, for we are not rescued in groups. That contention suggests another nineteenth-century Romantic poet's discovery of the point and his insistence upon it. From that discovered point it followed for him that he must establish the specific soul in its ordinate relation to the world and to the body of mankind whose head is Christ, without distorting either the world or that body. Yet he must do so without abandoning that most fundamental vision of the soul. I mean here Cardinal Newman, from whom I now treasure a saying: "Vital movements are not born of Committees." It is an aphorism derived from his vision of the discrete soul on its necessary journey through the world and among members one of another. Mankind endured as crowd is to be elevated as a body. But the vision is sharpened by Newman's experience of man's conduct in his social, political, religious institutions. (Newman's aphorism is companionable to a more playful one I have always before me on my desk: "For God so loved the world that he didn't send a Committee.")

As "Romantic," Newman, too, had to order intuition in relation to reason, the speculative intellect in relation to the practical intellect, before he could move beyond the entangling counter-tensions in intellect, becoming that person we now remember as Cardinal Newman. He was from the beginning very much engaged in a struggle with his Romanticism. He even wrote poetry and fiction during this struggle. Those suspicious of the poet may forgive him this excess, however, since he did not write very good poetry or fiction. Nevertheless, he did have to contend with the temptation to intellect of which Eliot reminds us, pinned and wriggling in our "literary criticism," thereby reducing that temptation from its ominous nature as the "dissociation of sensibility." I have argued that Eliot, at the time he appropriates this nineteenth-century phrase to his use, was rather severely limited in his own understanding of his intellectual origins and of his destiny out of those origins as literary critic and poet.   Through agonies that seemed initially intellectual, but which proved to his understanding at last to be spiritual, he discovered the depths of that dissociation and deepened his understanding of what is signified by "sensibilities."

In 1990, a symposium at Rome on John Henry Newman, which included a talk by Cardinal Ratzinger, inquired whether there is a contradiction between Newman's insistence on limited human knowledge on the one hand, and on the other of dogma as decisive in commanding intellectual assent.* Now dogma's proximate origin is necessarily human knowledge, and that is where the problem lies. This question haunting these doctors of the Church is perhaps the same question haunting those recent doctors, Gilson and Maritain, who contended with each other over whether intellect can ever know with certainty, a question not likely to be settled so long as the finitude of human intellect in relation to Absolute Truth constitutes the poles that are tensional to the discrete soul. It is a question to be fully resolved through Beatitude, save for the Saint who is enveloped by grace on his journey through this world. But then in that state of Beatitude, so we pray, we shall be beyond all question of question. Indeed, Newman's epitaph reflects his faith in a happy issue out of the tensional concern: *Ex umbris et imaginibus in veritatem.* We remember the epitaph concludes a long journey, out of shadows and imaginings, the tensional and unsettling contingency in question put to intellect, toward the soul's peaceful abandonment of our world.

At the Rome symposium, John Crosby argued that a resolution of this tensional intellectual dilemma lies in Newman's sense of mystery. Perhaps we may summarize the argument without excessive violence to it, introducing a metaphor of our own to the concern. Revealed truth, certified by dogma, is not transparent to intellect; or perhaps one might put it rather that it is compatible to intellect as

---

*   Tommaso Ricci, "And Consciousness Was No Longer Taboo," *30 Days* (July-August, 1990).

knowledge but not as *understanding* in the soul. Were it transparent, the danger would be that man could take liberty in changing some formulation too peremptorily in an attempt to improve upon it. Put another way, human intellectual finitude cannot plumb revealed truth under its own power alone, though supported by the truth of its own nature. That is so since that nature is, insofar as it *is*, a part of complex existence, of the whole of creation. The danger, metaphorically put, is its presumption to plumb existence deeply by intellect, as if independent of that diving bell, dogma. Intellect risks the bends, if not a drowning, by such presumptions of indifference to dogma. It is when intellect loses the sense of mystery that supports dogma, as it also supports the discrete intellect in its independence—those deep and mysterious waters of being—that a subjective dissolution occurs.

The necessary oxygen to intellect, provided by dogma, is derived at the very beginning from those mysterious waters of being which intellect would explore. So the necessity to discrete intellect is an accommodation to the diving bell, rather than an insistence on its own jerry-built diving bell. But the accommodation requires that the bell of dogma not become intellect's end, rather than the means it indeed is. It is a means made possible for the particular intellect through a continuous response of dogma to the pressures of reality upon it: the pressure of the truth of how all things stand—the bell, the waters of the world, and the discrete intellect in its given nature which must accommodate to reality. That is the recognition T. S. Eliot comes to in his controversial *After Strange Gods*, in which in a reflective digesting of his personal experience he sets Tradition down lower at Intellect's table, turning to Orthodoxy as honored guest. And it is Orthodoxy that will accompany him in his subsequent journeying out of that moment's pause.

It is in the interest of our theme that we consider that in the Romantic intellect—that is, intellect as intuitively moved toward the Good—such an intellect so moved may succumb to the deceptions of subjectivism. It may do so in a passion for immediacy, whereby it revolts either against tradition or against orthodoxy or against both. Thus an intellect may respond excessively to the intimations of mystery in being itself as encountered intuitively and denigrate the gifts of rational intellect through an excessive dependence upon the intuitive. Such an excessive response becomes an intellectual act of reductionism whose effect on the person is his arrested intellectual and spiritual growth, on the inadequate authority of "feeling." That reduction through subjectivism has often been seen as rather peculiar to the poet. The Romantic poet resists dogma, or so he is likely to insist. But over the past two hundred years that has increasingly meant he rather resists a false dogma—not the Church's but science's. An examination of the poet's resistance, as exemplified by significant English and American poets, will show them conspicuously in revolt, but it is a revolt against dogma as evolved from Enlightenment dislocations of the sensibilities, through which the *ratio* is established as absolute in respect to the truth of things. That dogma reflects the *intellectus* as at best a vestigial intellectual presence, the "appendix" of intellect no longer required, left over from the "Dark Ages." It, indeed, is a threatening source of intellectual discomfort to the rationalist. A preemptive appendectomy is always in order from that rationalist perspective. For the continuing presence of the *intellectus* troubles rationalism, as we may observe in the development of that new science of intellect, psychology. It accommodates the intuitive to the rationalist position, serving as midwife to a still-birth of the intuitive, to a damaged, handicapped issue of the intuitive. The instrument used is deterministic Darwinism which sees the physiology of intellect as registered through the nerves to the mind from events past, and to be explained fully by past events. Such at least is the evolution of psychology in Freudian and kindred psychologies.

In retrospect, we might consider that Enlightenment rationalism could establish its power only after first having carefully divorced the *ratio* from the *intellectus*. In the complementary offices of the *ratio* and *intellectus*, intellect continues anchored in mystery, and is so anchored by St. Thomas in *Questiones disputate de veritate*: "Although the knowledge which is most characteristic of the human soul occurs in the mode of *ratio*, nevertheless there is in it a sort of participation in the simple knowledge which is proper to higher beings, of whom it is therefore said that they possess the faculty of spiritual vision."

How desperate, then, that Romantic poet who is unskilled in rational disputation over the nature of truth. Wordsworth, for instance, protests passionately:

> *One impulse from a vernal wood*
> *May teach you more of man,*
> *Of moral evil and of good,*
> *Than all the sages can.*

And he concludes his protest against a too-rational friend bent by his studies:

> *Enough of Science and of Art;*
> *Close up those barren leaves;*
> *Come forth, and bring with you a heart*
> *That watches and receives.*

There is here, we may argue, an intuitive recognition of the need to recover the services of the *intellectus*, and it is very much to the point to remember that the poet, almost from the beginning of Western literature, has recognized both modes of intellect. Heraclitus remarks the mystery of "seeing" into the nature of things, as distinct from the rational explication of that vision. Eliot, in *The Waste Land*, a poet most notorious for his intellectual commitment to the *ratio*, speaks in the conclusion of that poem of the necessity of recovering the "heart," traditionally associated with the mode of the *intellectus*, in complement to the head, the *ratio*: "My friend, blood shaking my heart." Such is that dimension of consciousness spoken to in the recognition that the "heart" leads to a giving, sympathizing, controlling of consciousness in its response to the mystery of existence, most especially the existence of consciousness itself.

Not that there does not accompany that recognition a sense of danger, an intimation that subjective dissolution is a possible consequence of surrender to impulse from a vernal wood. Coleridge struggles with this Eliotic "dissociation of sensibility" which endangers intellect, whether it surrender to rationalism or to subjectivism through its intuitive knowledge of mystery. The most commonly remembered of Coleridge's arguments about the mind of the poet is his attempt to distinguish *imagination* and *fancy*, attempting to anchor imagination in the great I AM against the chaotic confusions of fancy.

One might be given pause who considers the dissociation of sensibility and the poet's attempt to recover "feeling" to "thought"—this Romantic Agony as it has been called—in relation to philosophical concerns, such as Gerald A. McColl in his exploration of Neo-Scholasticism, *From Unity to Pluralism: The Internal Evolution* of *Thomism*. And one considering Cardinal Newman's reconciliation through the presence to intellect of mystery transcending the known and the understood might credit a reassociation of those sensibilities desired intuitively by the Romantic poet, however unsuccessfully that poet may have attempted the recovery. And one might suspect that the nineteenth century's Neo-Scholasticism is rather more indebted to an Enlightenment emphasis upon the *ratio* than to St. Thomas. In this sense, its emphasis does not accord to the mystery in intellectual act itself as sufficiently grounded in the truth of things—that present actual reality in which grace is operative even as intellect attempts to deal with its own reality. That, indeed, is in part why Cardinal Newman was sometimes held suspect by his contemporary intellectual peers within and on the fringes of the Church. One might even suggest that the tension between our own new theologians, growing out of *Concilium*—Rahner, Küng, Schillebeeckx—as *Concilium* increasingly sets itself against the Magisterium, reflects this continuing tension. The presumption among the radical theologians of the primacy of the *ratio*, is perhaps rather more influenced by a subjective rationalism inherited from the Enlightenment than usually credited. For Enlightenment rationalism has as its closed end an autonomy of the *ratio*, inevitably destined thereby to a radical subjectivism in its independent plumbing of mystery.

IV

A gathering of radical subjectivists will result in a new Babel, no matter whether worshipful of the *ratio* exclusive of *intellectus*, or of *intellectus* exclusive of *ratio*, no matter whether radical theologians or radical poets. From Babel ensues the necessity, even to radicals, of establishing its own Magisterium, whether in a "new" poetics or a new theology, though in such radicalism the term new usually presumes an intellectually decreed essence in itself. The irony at this juncture of our dissociation lies in the defense of mystery through a defense of dogma by the Magisterium itself, whose parallel among our poets is Eliot's own defense, after his many years spent recovering a position of orthodoxy against mere subjective traditionalism. And yet this is not quite irony, since the authority of dogma intends most particularly to protect one against rejecting mystery, to establish the limits of the *ratio* against presumptions of intellectual autonomy that become easily transmuted to subjective absolutism. Dogma intends to conserve that which is known but not fully understood. And revolts against dogmas, we notice in our history, are always undertaken in the name of new *knowledge* more resolutely than in the name of understanding. Even Shelley takes the position that his is the true rationality in defense of "Intellectual Beauty."

Professor Crosby, at the Newman symposium, argued that the sense of mystery in Newman protects the "individual" (I would prefer the term *person*) from the dissolving acid of rationalism, whose catalyst is the assumption of autonomy. It does so by counseling prudence in recognition of intellectual finitude in the presence of the mystery of complex being itself. It will follow that dogma is the ground in which a limited certitude of a limited, discrete intellect may best engage mystery. Dogma is the most potent protection to the only subjectivism admissible, namely that recognition by discrete awareness of itself as discrete—as a *personal* and *specific* human existence, and therefore a finite existence.

That is why Newman is so emphatic about conscience in the discrete person as the ground in which God and the soul encounter each other. It is a recognition of a mystery out of which must grow— not *individualism*—a *personalism* accommodating conscience to its finitudes. It is here that the soul is initiated upon its particular journey which, as Cardinal Ratzinger observes in relation to Newman's concern for conscience, involves a constancy of conversion. The striving for constancy is the very nature of the soul's journey, which in its immediacy is always contingent *in* but not dependent *upon* the accidents of the temporal and spacial conditions of the soul. Again, it is a matter of proportional response to the complexity of finite existence, in which one as person repeatedly discovers himself in a context contributing to, but not determinate of, the end of its journey. In those circumstances, given the poet's gifts of response to immediate particularities, his attention to the temporal world which is the burden of language itself, it is no wonder that the Romantic poet turns his attention to the immediate, to the local, to an impulse from a vernal wood as impressive upon consciousness through the body and somehow speaking thereby to conscience and to its intuitive hunger for being. In rejecting the deracinated intent of Enlightenment intellect, the poet turns to this time and this place seeking a recovery, to the banks of the Wye near Tintern Abbey or to this English garden in which a nightingale has just sung. Such a turning all too easily becomes arrested as a seeming end, when it is properly a means toward that final perfection of the soul beyond time which is spoken of as Beatitude: the self fully inhabiting itself in the larger habiliment of its potentiality. Given this danger of the immediate as if an end—the increasing fragmentation of community in the world—it is little wonder that self-awareness begins to take precedence over conscience. Consciousness comes to seem the most likely victim at risk, despite Cartesian reassurances, leading a poet like Wordsworth to actually seize a flower in hand to certify his senses as mediate to a reality larger than consciousness. There is a haunting confusion of consciousness and conscience in the nineteenth century, a century much troubled by multiplying causes in conflict with each other. But the problem is not localized, is not made discrete by Hegelian history. The spiritual journey of the discrete soul is always the crucial issue, however much complicated by all the contingencies of its being. Contingency allows the soul to move toward a community that is both here and hereafter. Certainly Hopkins, Eliot, Newman, and St. Thomas would insist as much.

That late Romantic poet Eliot came to see most insistently that conversion is a continuous journey, a continuous turning from mediate ends to a final end. The constant journeying is through the limits of those mediate ends which circumscribe the soul's finite existence. The nature of that journey, in its intellectual aspect, is the constancy of conscience, prevented always from its desire for unchanging constancy because it must move constantly within circumstance. Conscience contends with dogma inescapably in that struggle, attempting to reconcile itself to the truth of things, a reconciliation which is beyond both the discrete conscience in its limited power as intellect and beyond the communal ground of conscience in the world, dogma. Each needs each, as each struggles with each. And in that tensional condition, the soul is sustained sufficient to the journey, through the largesse of grace. It is this realization that the Romantic poet may at last come to. Eliot put it effectively, in the conclusion of his last significant poem:

> *Every phrase and every sentence is an end and a beginning,*
> *Every poem an epitaph. And any action*
> *Is a step to the block, to the fire, down the sea's throat*
> *Or to an illegible stone: and that is where we start.*

We start, he affirms, "With the drawing of this Love and the voice of this Calling," heard through out finitudes, beckoning us beyond an entrapment by our finitudes. Eliot's then, is a larger and fuller recognition of what Wordsworth spoke of, without an adequate recognition through his intuitive seeing, as "one impulse from a vernal wood," of a gift to intellect through which in still moments it sees "into the life of things."

We may, I believe, from such recognitions as the poet brings us to in support of the philosopher, find hope in this very dark—intellectually dark—age. Meanwhile, the academy continues in disarray, embroiled in factional contentions rising among those who have lost the limits of, and so the proper uses of intellect, the responsibility with which they have been charged by the larger community. We have suffered a gradual, and then an accelerating, loss of intellectual virtues as properly established by steadying intellectual habits—the acquiring of knowledge toward understanding, and of understanding so that intellect may arrive at last at wisdom within the context of reality, within the light of the truth of how things stand. With that loss, the academy in disarray becomes hostage to the latest intellectual barbarism, whose atheologist preaches a doctrine most tempting to our Faustian nature turned sentimental. His is that new doctrine of the "politically correct," his argument wielded like an angelic sword to keep out all who will not submit to an Eden dreamed into a shadowy future existence by his intellect self-evaluated to Godhead. The autonomous intellect of the barbarian gnostic alone would judge what is acceptable. The pursuit of the true, the good, the beautiful, collapses under the rubric of the "politically correct." And intellect becomes slave to the whims of power, transfixed it would seem by the cloudy magic of the formula of salvation, PC.

The academy in our moment rapidly succumbs to an anarchist subjectivism, whose principal dogma is that one must in all matters be "politically correct." The effects are anarchist, the symptoms those of a radical subjectivism, but it is a strategy of anarchist subjectivism manipulated by wily intellect bent on gnostic ends. A word to that point in closing. In the interest of gathering a power sufficient to establish its own authority, this gnostic intellect must attract supporting intellects, manipulative so long as such intellects suppose themselves moved by intuitive recognitions of the intellectually correct. That is, the would-be lords of this accumulated power must seduce a support in the name of intuitive recognitions of the true, renamed the "correct" and reduced to the limited arena of the "political." The instrumental mode is through the intuitive, the mode of intellect St. Thomas calls the *intellectus*, but it is a mode suited to manipulation only as divorced from its complementary *ratio*. Intuition not rationally accommodated makes intellect easy victim to a sentimentality which can rest only in the accidents of reality, in the passing moment—in this present manipuilation—that is, the passing moment of the "politically correct."

But what must be said is that such a dislocation of intellect from its proper ordering is energized by the manipulation of the intuitive intellect, while the manipulation is managed by a rationalism disdainful of the intuitive, insofar as the intuitive orients intellect toward the truly good and beautiful. That is, the gnostic strategist has separated himself as autonomous intellect through the manipulative powers of the rational intellect divorced from the intuitive. This is to say that it is a mistake to suppose that rational intellect is not the principle engine dismantling intellect, operating within the academy in conspicuously spectacular manifestations such as those detailed by Dinesh D'Souza in his *Illiberal Education*. At the level of spectacle, one encounters the irrational, the illogical. If we attempt a defense against these new intellectual barbarians only at the level of the irrational and illogical, the destruction will continue inexorably. For to throw water on smoke may miss the deep destructive fire. *Ad hoc* defenses are never good for long.

I am suggesting that there is a Machiavellian strategy operative, which at once recognizes and takes advantage of the disintegration of our intellectual community. It is a decay, I would argue, consequent to Occam's dislocation through Nominalism, which principle separates sign from the reality that sign would signify and so becomes empowered to manipulate sign. Sign in such a strategy, since removed from controlling reality, can be shifted about the intellectual landscape. Smoke can be made illusionally apparent as if far removed from the actuality of the fire, the burning presence of being. Intellect as autonomous authority thus emerges, whose magic practice in the manipulations of reality is through a usurped command of "name" in the interest of power over the thing. Not Adam under the guiding presence of God in the naming of things, but the arbitrary naming by gnostic intellect. And the magic to which dislocated intuitive intellect becomes susceptible is that illusion of a new substantiality whose cause is purportedly the action of naming by the autonomous, rational intellect. Thus, if "I" say x is y, it damn well is. The threatening *damn* awaits any intellect denying the proposition. If I say Western civilization is racist and chauvinistic, it damn well is, and if you deny my assertion, you are not "politically correct," and have earned purging from the courts of intellect.

What is important to the pragmatic success of this intellectual barbarism is our refusal of an intellectual engagement of the principles barbarically assumed in the interest of power over the truth of things. The assertion that what I say is true when supported by the power of my assertion as justified by the acquiescence of the frightened, inadequate, hungry, lost intellects, is decisive. What is required is that the question be called in relation to the truth of things in themselves, the reality of existence as known and experienced by the discrete intellect, in opposition to the presumptuous principle that by a dogmatic assertion of the truth of things, things thus exist, not in themselves, but in myself as the moment's god of being. It becomes evident, given the assumption of such supreme authority, that in calling the question—in standing against such manipulators of intellectual integrity—the manipulator himself must be put in the dock, to borrow a metaphor from C. S. Lewis. To do so is at once to be charged with an *ad hominem* attack, the response to which is that it is humanity that is at risk, the purveyor of the gnostic position bent upon the abolition of man. One cannot overcome tyranny without having at the tyrant, whose position cannot be declared sacrosanct since no tyrant values the sacred in itself. The effects of diabolical usurpation are not to be remedied without naming the devil, however cleverly disguised in a self-protecting array of Nominalistic words such as the currently popular stalking horse used against the true nature of human existence, the "politically correct," a term which is the dying gasp of a dying ideology, Marxism.

That the question is difficult to call needs only the evidence of the symptoms of assent to false principle, nowhere more evident than in the fearful acquiescence of academic authority as vested in academic administrations, whose fear is not of being wide of truth's mark as properly orienting the academy, but a fear of media attention that is nominalistically called *bad publicity.* For the shibboleth of bad publicity is seldom sufficiently anchored in the reality of truth itself. If it were, we should find the media freed of the necessity of sensationalism, which feeds on the symptoms of disease, on the spectacles of our dislocations from the truth of things. If we could find the courage to call the question in the true name of truth itself, this present magic gnostic formula would dissolve. The "politically correct" wand would become evidently but a random stick with which the arrogant gnostic intellect attempts to beat other intellects into submission. Such a gnostic manipulator of being would himself, as intellect, collapse into dust, as the body of Agamemnon did when his tomb was opened. We should then, as academic intellects, find ourselves once more in the vicinity of reality, sustained by the sun and light of abiding reality in this present moment and once more come to recognize that our proper intellectual concern is to know the truth of how things stand, beyond our finite presumptuous intellects. That is, we should move beyond *understanding* into a *wisdom*, into an ordinate estate of intellect within the context of reality itself. We should then begin to serve, as is our proper office, the common good of humanity in its worldly nature as a community of souls.

6

The First and Last Best Hope
for "Higher Education"

WHAT WE DISCOVER at this moment of our history, and virtually in any place, is a chaos of thought and action disturbing to "higher education" as never before, clamoring for a careful attention. What I hold to be vital to our response in this necessity, if we are to recover intellect from chaos, is not that we establish Thomism *per se*, though we are likely to do worse. Rather, what is required is our Thomas-like deportment to this present moment of intellectual confusions. We need not possess his peculiar gifts, though would that we did. But we may commit ourselves to his openness to the truth of things, and may do so through our callings as theologian or philosopher or poet or scientist or administrator—whatever our particular calling. That necessary engagement of the present moment cries out to be made from deep within intellect itself. I see that necessity, and hear that cry, given my circumstances, most directly in relation to our literature. But that cry we must hear in every circumstance, requiring of each soul according to its gifts. The diversity of gift, St. Thomas points out, answers to the diversity of the truth of things, which are themselves diverse actualities. Having gifts differing, as St. Paul says, "according to the grace that is given us," if philosophers, we must philosophize; if scientists, analyze; if poets, declaim; if husbandmen, plant and tend and harvest. In respect to the diversity of gifts, there attends no significance of virtue in the calling, only in the answer we give by our action. Within complex reality, the truth suited to our gift is to be found, and seeking that truth becomes our calling. That is, it is "becoming to" our office as proper to it.

And in the discrete soul's exercise of the gift of its calling, it is that soul's intellect which most immediately answers the calling, out of the depths of the soul. That alone makes *intelligence* the true soul-food on the soul's journeying. By *intelligence* here I mean truth possessed by intellect, in which respect St. Thomas says of it that truth is the "good of the intellect." I have just had reported to me by that complacent guardian of the popular mind, *Time*, the promise of a new homunculus such as must make human intellect outmoded in the very next moment. "Artificial Intelligence," popularly recognized as AI, is now a sign as common to us as E=MC² or DNA. But AI is now so advanced, *Time* reports with excitement, as to require a new term: "Artificial Life." Now, largely because the term *life* is so indecisive a term in our decade that no one seems to know what it means, the attempts at definition are increasingly debated, but less often with words than through radical physical actions and counter actions under various banners such as *abortion* or *euthanasia*. As for this artificial life, first advanced as artificial intelligence, I take some comfort, though not much, from Roger Penrose's book, *The Emperor's New Mind*, subtitled *Concerning Computers, Minds, and the Laws of Physics*. Penrose calls into question presumptions about artificial life, and he does so from his authority as physicist. I am not at last comfortable with the position from which he questions, but he poses the right questions. (I suggest, with mischief intent, but not malice prepense, that he might profit from "three or four books on metaphysics" as Keats realized he might possibly do.*) Penrose's own

---

* Keats, leaving London for Margate, wrote back to a city friend, expressing in his confused state the necessity of a metaphysical position and asking for three or four books that might lead him out of the difficulty. It is of interest that another Romantic poet, T. S. Eliot retreated to Margate at a point in his own journey: "On Margate sands" he can "connect nothing with nothing" either.

premise is his acceptance on faith of evolutionist theory as the central truth about being, as revealed by finite intellect, though he recognizes a degree of confusion in that theory, which confusion he takes to be occasioned by its use of "Anthropomorphic terms." Still, he is willing to accept them metaphorically, he says. We must observe that his reading of metaphor as analogy is that of attribution, which is to say: an assignment of likeness in unlike things made by finite intellect, and not seen as intrinsic to the things compared. One might even suppose that Penrose, like some modernist poets—for instance Ezra Pound or William Carlos Williams—intuitively recognizes the anthropomorphic language he holds suspect is suspect precisely because it is attributive, though often supposed by unwary poets to be merely descriptive of reality.* Both Pound and Williams are cautious about metaphor.

Using attributive metaphor, the scientist flirts with fancy, as Penrose fears he may be doing, escaping the inherent difficulty by asserting it "merely metaphor" and so not to be taken too seriously by rational intellect. But even Penrose's argument depends, under analysis, upon attributive analogy in support of his faith in evolutionary determinism, an analogy whose ultimate source is finite intellect. One may well conclude, therefore, that his faith is quintessentially founded in anthropomorphism, whether expressed metaphorically or not. Indeed, how could it be otherwise?† In that intellectual position, metaphor aside, what is supposed is that the

---

* My use of the term *attributive metaphor* is anchored in the meaning of analogy—that is of *proportion*. When attributive, the value of proportion is assigned by intellect itself, as it were, and may fail to be governed by the actuality of proportion in things to that being in which things are inherently dependent—I AM THAT I AM, Being Itself, God. Analogy properly used must be so anchored, in relation to the creature's *participation* in being. The articulation of this proportionality in being St. Thomas calls the "principle of proper proportionality." In this concern, see St. Thomas's treatise *On Being and Essence*. There is a helpful explication of the principle by Fr. Gerald B. Phelan, "St. Thomas and Analogy," the Aquinas Lecture for 1941.

† Lest we continue in an intellectual fear of "anthropomorphism," we might consider Gilson on the subject. Rightly understood, he says, anthropomor-

actuality of that being which St. Thomas defends—man as intellectual creature—is only the actuality of a machine—a body-mind—the
cause of which is ambiguous at best. For at the heart of Penrose's
faith is his commitment to existence as mechanistic, though it is evident he is uncomfortable in that faith. It is also out of this same
anthropomorphic faith, however, that the definition of life is made
to fit the term *artificial intelligence,* whose promise to the popular
mind seems to be our final release from the residue in our thought
associated with the "Puritan work ethic." What a happy slave!—this
Artificial Life! And our possessing this Artificial Life absolves us of
guilt over our possessiveness. I say *guilt,* a more acceptable term because anchored, in the history of mankind, in the errors of our immediate fathers and not in our nature as fallen persons. Historical
error bears psychological effect, suited to expiation by the therapy of
action. By such good work one expiates himself, with a little help
from his friendly therapist. Sin, on the other hand, suggests circumstances to the soul beyond self expiation. Above all, we must set
aside Original Sin. That is what less enlightened ages spoke of, not
being so advanced as we in psychological intricacies.

So, then, what a happy slave this artificial life will make, justifying us as happy master over nature. It is obviously not really a *person,*
even that term an outmoded concept, though it still haunts us because entangled in historical guilt. It is rather a mere mechanism.

---

phism may prove the indispensible element in our understanding of existence
itself. "Since I am a part of nature, and my experience of self in virtue of its
immediacy is a privileged case, why should I not interpret what I know only
from without in function of the sole reality that I know from within? In man,
and in man alone, nature attains to consciousness of itself. That is the foundation of *all* legitimate anthropomorphism. . . ." (*The Spirit of Mediaeval Philosophy,* 88) The convolutions of intellect in its attempt to occupy a purely
"objective" position deny the very reality of intellect itself, and in extremity
even deny the existence of intellect itself. That has been the gradual tendency
of science when misunderstood in its own nature, in which tendency authority
comes to be rested in mechanics. The elevation of the intellectually-made
machine as the determiner of "reality" has been the consequence. In this drift
away from reality, the sanctuary of human spirit, the Church, is replaced by the
laboratory, in which alone it is supposed that any "Absolute" is to be found.

Therefore we may, without guilt, take pleasure in lording it over this new slave, toward accomplishing what the president of a state university recently charged his faculty to pursue: "We must," he said, "find a way to reprogram nature." Since this new species of "life" is freed of personhood, we may exercise a tyranny over it, and through it, and at the same time be freed of any sense of guilt, let alone of sin. Still, it is at least an artificial *life*, for who could take pleasure in lording it over a mere mechanism? Not even the old discarded Christian God would be content with that relationship to man. Such is the tempting mode of our Modernist conduct toward existence by Gnostic intellect self-transformed beyond reality. Until a recognition comes: in such an arrogant power through pride, the fundamental effect of this Gnostic intellectual action is to reduce man himself, even the man commanding the new homunculus. Such is the consequence foretold by C. S. Lewis in *The Abolition of Man*, and *Time* celebrates our having virtually accomplished that abolition.

Whether we subscribe to Penrose's assumption of our nature as evolved or that of the advocates of "artificial life" whom he questions—whose arguments are out of the same assumption—the presumption puts actual life in jeopardy by their submission of the mystery of life to the limits of mechanistic thought. Modernist thought, perhaps at a level of sophistication where biological mechanism is admissible, is so weakly founded in the mystery of life as each person knows it, because each experiences it, that abortion and euthanasia must be acceptable, if that gnostic erector of public opinion triumphs and in that triumph engineers the final fillip in the abolition of man. I have made a serious, even apocalyptic assertion, and in doing so intend to underline the point central to our recovery of ordered thought. For *ordered thought in relation to truth* is the principal responsibility of higher education. What we here recognize, then, is that the *meaning* that our words assert is the turning point of intellectual action. And that must take us at last back to our responsibility as intellectual creatures, whose governance the popular mind conceded long ago to institutions of higher education, after which progressively that community abandoned its responsibility. Let the academics teach; we the community will do: theirs the *words*, ours the *action*. A dangerous concession, because words prove always the most decisive action of intellect.

I

Modern linguistics, as Gilson shows us in his *Linguistics and Philosophy*, assumes an authority as a science, but it is able to do so only by denying meaning to our assertions—to our signs, our words. It is thus, through this late manifestation of Nominalism, that modernist linguistics serves as handmaiden—whether knowingly or not—to the advocates of artificial life. Artificial life becomes established, not simply as our slave, but becomes the means whereby we ourselves become enslaved to gnostic ideology. For it is posited as the ultimate image of man, an idol of man as a perfection of mechanistic being, to which we are commanded to turn in worship. As idol, artificial life is a dead sign, but the death it reflects is the spiritual death of its perpetrator and its patrons. But such is the reality of actual creation, including even that of wayward man himself that the *meaning* in sign (even this meaning of death in that idol of artificial life), like *life* in animate creatures, persists. And in persisting, it contradicts the meaninglessness asserted by Nominalist linguistics, which asserts emphatically its own signs that signs have no meaning. Such is the entrapment of Nominalism by reality, though the consequences of this self-entrapment often takes long to recognize, let alone remedy.

It is the remedying of this nonsense with sense, this meaninglessness paraded as meaning, that becomes the first elementary task to those intellects whose calling is a service to the community of mankind through offices of higher education. For the question is not whether signs bear meaning—they do so inescapably—but whether the meaning they bear signifies reality, whether they speak a truth held in the thought of the sign-bearer. The sign is always a present witness, either to a truth or to a falsehood. The steadying point of departure for that mind which loves and seeks truth is to realize this truth about our words first of all. For if we bear false witness, the consequence of that false witness is likely to be unfortunate to community, whether as false witness we are a scoundrel or only a fool. To this point Gilson says "it is truly from the meaning that all difficulties in linguistics are born, just as in biology the most serious difficulties come from the obtrusive idea of life, which does not explain anything, but calls attention to that without which the biologist would have nothing to explain." The poet, intent on the same discovery about the relation of the word to the reality, puts this continuing struggle of "life" in man as a struggling continuum of thought engaging signs:

> *Every phrase and every sentence is an end and a beginning,*
> *Every poem an epitaph. And any action*
> *Is a step to the block, to the fire, down the sea's throat*
> *Or to an illegible stone: and that is where we start.*

For awhile yet, the shock possible through extremes of attributive analogy, attributive metaphor, may stay that process of the erosion of meaning somewhat. One at least aborts flawed design if one is to succeed on the assembly line, even the assembling of a throwaway "lifestyle" which at this moment is strangling the social body with the waste of "life's" technological processes. Still, a focus on this problem of attributive analogy as destructive of reality we witnessed recently: our attention upon artificial hearts, which was an attention at once disturbed and fascinated. The whole of that evolutionary faith, which is actually a fundamentalist faith supporting most of our intellectual community, turns necessarily upon a limited anthropomorphic metaphor. The problem with such metaphor is that obtrusive truth, out of existence itself, is deeper than the shallow level of such anthropomorphism. The artificial heart is not a heart, and we know it. Nor do we need a degree in biology to recognize the disparity. Truth is both persistently and insistently abiding, as deep as being itself, so that thought may not in the end avoid engaging that which it knows, the truth it possesses intellectually, though it may deny the possession—a fatal refusal. Being is fundamental to discrete existences, whose recognition has been progressively denied through attributive manipulations of the accidents of being in an attempt by gnostic intellect to dominate being itself. I speak here of the residual subversiveness of Nominalism in popular thought.

In its most immediate aspect, intentionality as the gnostic's way of energizing intellect to action is effected by his will, whose precise object, as Eric Voegelin says, is to establish power over being. But the justification of this intentionality requires a reductionist faith in other actual intellects as separate from the reductionist's. The irony is that such an intellect does not recognize the larger mystery of its own existence, which deterministic evolution cannot explain. Such, however, is the deportment of the activist gnostic intellect. And it would impose its reductionist account of the mystery of life upon the whole of creation, excepting itself, as if creation were itself immanently intentional. It imposes a pseudo-paganism, which hovers at the moment about the latest holy of holies: the gene. Genes are somehow most magically committed as intentional in this new faith, having succeeded Pan and Artemis and Venus and Mars. We have proposed by such science that genes are somehow concerned about their own propagation, desperate to maintain their own immortality, even at the expense of their environmental habitat, the discrete body of this person. One needs no Sartre as theologian for the gene's justification. The gene will serve itself well enough as explicated by the latest laboratory tests.

Attributive anthropomorphism, refined as genetic ideology, is increasingly pervasive of our new collective thought, namely Environmentalism, in which "Nature" becomes its own self-realizing god. Increasingly, man is concluded an infection of that god's body, an infection of the Environment. Except for man, that world would still be an Eden. One notices how often the myth of Eden creeps back into television's "nature" programs in which the infection-bearer himself explores remote corners of the earth where an Eden still is perceived to linger, at least until the arrival of the camera.* To

---

* On the day of this lecture, November 21, 1991, *USA Today* carried a review in anticipation of the PBS series about to "air," *Land of the Eagles.* Under the title "Covering the 'Nature' Beat: A Reporter Makes Wildlife His Story," George Page of PBS's *Nature* tells of the thirty "Nature" cinematographers spending three years "scouring national parks and remote areas," searching for "unmarred vistas." Page remarks that "It became very clear that the social, human history and the natural history of North America were inextricably linked." A

point to such sentimentality as an extension of "science" is at once to be misunderstood, as if to point to this falseness in a new species of intellectual ideology (which is now largely supported by popular sentiment) were to become thereby an advocate of ravenous exploitation of the world's body. As if one were thereby sworn enemy to reality itself, a confused response which more than any underlines the task waiting upon Thomistic realism. For if I declare this new ideology to be only partial and not an inclusive vision, and so insufficiently a vision of all of reality, I risk either the wrath or the ridicule of embarrassed emperors in the kingdom of genes.

Such companions of St. Thomas as remain are challenged to a mutual concern for the truth of how things stand in this present moment, buffeted as that necessity is by conflicting notions that yield false visions of reality when not anchored by our intellectual responsibility to the fullness of reality. At this moment, a casual righteousness pervades the secular intellectual community. Its faith rests in a new deterministic evolutionism whose mystery is the gene and whose method is Artificial Intelligence, in concert leading to "Artificial Life." The difficulty for the companion to Thomas will be his ordinate regard for mechanisms, genetic or electronic. For the central problem lies not in the knowledge afforded by such discoveries as those which every day multiply out of the virtues exercised by genetic scientists or computer whizzes. These provide fruits suited to sustain intellect on its journey, depending upon our intellects digestive powers. The central problem lies rather in what is made of such knowledge in an age when *knowledge* is mistaken as *understanding*, and a partial understanding is extrapolated as if it were *wisdom*.

II

There lies as the immediate task to the companions of Thomas, then, the making of such distinctions; which is to say, the task requires a

---

late date for such discovery, and the naïveté in such a remark, if that is the proper word for it, tempts one to sarcasm—to remarking that, yes, and if one looks up on a clear day the sky appears blue, and trees at certain seasons and certain places appear green or multicolored or brown or even bare.

rescue of metaphysics to the laborious pursuit of wisdom. The intellect which mistakes knowledge as understanding and understanding as wisdom, by that very miss-taking at least bears witness to a continuing desire for understanding and wisdom. It is a sign justifying hope. One sees certain attempts already made toward such recovery. There is the continuing work of Stanley L. Jaki in several books such as his *Road of Science and the Ways of God* and *The Origin of Science and the Science of Origin.* There are Gilson's works, especially two late ones recently made available in English translation by John Lyon: *Linguistics and Philosophy: An Essay on the Philosophical Constants of Language* and his *From Aristotle to Darwin and Back Again: A Journey in Final Causality, Species, and Evolution.* One could compile a considerable bibliography reflecting recent concern to recover a metaphysical view of reality.

What such thinkers have in common, and powerful thinkers more numerous than I have named are among us, is the recognition that we must recover metaphysics to restore intellect to its proper offices. We must do so, if we are to come to terms with such abiding challenges to intellect as that of *meaning* in words and life in *bodies.* I submit once more Gilson as witness to the necessity. The gist of his argument, meticulously presented by this responsible philosopher, is that we know, and know that we know, that life and *meaning* have real existence, though science cannot substantiate that reality because the reality at issue lies in a dimension of immateriality. Such knowledge baffles "pure" science. "All that is physically real," Gilson says, "is material and particular." But to the contrary, the universal, "whose nature we are seeking to understand, is immaterial by definition. It is necessary therefore that that which produces it ought to be equally immaterial if one does not wish its production to be quasi-miraculous. But the order of the immaterial, of the nonphysical, is precisely that of the metaphysical. Language, therefore, involves the reality of the metaphysical by the very fact that it involves an element of universality." Gilson's is a recognition, let us add, which requires our understanding that language is not fully explicable through any science. As Gilson says at another point, "whether the linguist wishes it or not, [even] grammar is philosophy."

This order of the immaterial reality which concerns Gilson is inescapably the arena within which those concerned with higher education are resident by their calling. One cannot even deny the immaterial without speaking, Gilson says, and that act of speaking itself attests to the reality of the immaterial. That inescapable condition of intellect, he adds "is the witness in us of the reality of metaphysics. Although entirely legitimate in itself, the existence of general linguistics raises the most serious philosophical difficulties. These result precisely from the fact that one cannot make the physics of language correspond to the metaphysics of thought. . . . The *Nous* [the mind or intellect] creates distinction through language and is itself neither distinct nor confused, but anterior." And from that recognition, the mystery of language itself devolves. For though there is a materiality to speech which may be measured, so that we speak the word in decibels, even as we speak of the *word* which is an immaterial but actual thing. The "meaning of the word escapes servitude to space, for it is an act of thought, and thought exists, but in a literal sense it has no place." He adds, "[E]very truth is such. And so it proves inevitable that language should lead us back once more to the threshold of the immaterial and of the metaphysical. Everything leads to it: biology as soon as it admits that there are living forms; noetics and epistemology as soon as they reflect upon the conditions required, by the object known as well as by the subject knowing, in order that science might be possible; linguistics itself as soon as one accepts language in its relations with the understanding, of which it is at one and the same time the body and the means of exchange." "It is difficult not to recognize," Gilson concludes, "the presence of metaphysics, even if one refuses to engage it."

Such is the context of intellectual action in those strange reservations set aside by the social body to be devoted to higher education, the academies, even if we refuse to engage it. It is so, whether one's special responsibility is defined in relation to the atomic table or biotechnology or grammar and logic and rhetoric. I recall a remark by that great teacher Donald Davidson, made many years ago. We begin with a class of green students, he said, attempting to teach them the agreement of subject and verb, the importance of clear pronoun reference. And then pretty soon we find ourselves wrestling with them to save their very souls. So suspect is that term *soul* to our secular age that it may be necessary for us to recast the point. Let us at least say that as patrons of intellect, which is the fundamental justification of institutions of higher education, in teaching grammar or physics or chemistry or biology, we are wrestling to recover to the student his potential as intellectual creature. It is this primary responsibility that the academy has abandoned, whose effect is everywhere inescapable, and nowhere more patently than in the collapse of the intellectual community, however much we may rationalize it through a sentimentality in favor of pluralism.

The responsibility of intellect in community: how easily we escape it through pseudo-rationalizations justifying a plurality of intellect by denying the reality of truth itself. We have systematized the justification, as in most of the current arguments for "multiculturalism" or for a "politically correct" deportment as a legalistic substitute for good manners. In doing so we but establish the mechanisms of alienation as the required principle of higher education. The clamor for the right to "do one's own thing" which rose in the 1960s becomes now, not a revolt against the establishment, but the new establishment itself, against which intellect is increasingly required to make a radical revolt. The alternative, alas, is the prospect of community itself as constituted only of an individual, isolated intellect. One is left to commune with oneself.

The dream of such an absolute freedom, put in traditional terms, is the dream of becoming like the gods, as the old serpent encouraged Eve to dream. The consequence must be that isolation which we have lamented for a century now under the title of "alienation." The accidents attending the disintegration of community, whether in the family, or the community, or in educational institutions, increasingly terrify us. That the terrors are justified needs only our recalling the fundamental cause, which John Milton caught in telling lines that I contend well serve as the motto of our political state as representative of a secular civilization in rapid decline:

The mind is its own place and of itself
Can make a heaven of hell, a hell of heaven.

As philosophers, we must divide those words in quest of the simple truth. With Gilson we say that, indeed, the mind is its own place—or rather let us say that the mind has no place. For that is a more nearly accurate putting of the truth, whereby we avoid the presumption of a declaration, as if the placelessness of mind were determined by our own "creative" assertion through the "being" verb. Given the truth of this mystery whereby man is—that is to say exists by nature as intellectual creature—the very freedom of placeless, timeless mind becomes mind's greatest temptation. We know, from experience, that mind is a reality, despite its being immaterial. It exists, though undifferentiated by time or space whereby it might be sensually perceived, leaving us with only the brain as a temporal, spacial organ closest to our struggle to perceive mind sensually. But if it is an immaterial reality, its immateriality does not therefore make it infinite, nor are its powers over time and place sufficient for its full comprehension of, and justification of, existential reality, either that of its own or that of other existences whether material or immaterial. Therefore it cannot *make* a heaven of hell nor hell of heaven, despite all the utopian attempts strewn through our history, especially those recent ones from Robespierre to Joseph Stalin and Adolf Hitler. (Since the time of these two utopians, most of our utopian dreams seem to proceed out of Washington, D.C., one is tempted to say.)

Mind, then, is always—this side worldly death—in an in-between state, a tensional context of being. But that we presume otherwise as intellectual community is inescapable. Eric Voegelin names this presumption of mind as self-empowered to a transcendence by its own will: it is "Modern Gnosticism." What we presume, in this Gnostic stance, explicitly or tacitly, is that mind transcends reality by its own action, rather than being included in reality despite this illusion of transcendence by its own will. But reality, both material and immaterial, depends from an enveloping, causal Love—from I AM THAT I AM, from Being Itself. Modern Gnosticism is, from my point of view, but a recent version of a most ancient heretical act, which is why I recall Milton's lines from *Paradise Lost* to characterize it. Those lines, we should remember, are spoken in the poem by Satan, just after God has flung him into Hell.

III

The recovery of intellect from its Gnostic delusions about reality: that is the pressing task for the academic mind, and the task is first of all the recovery of *my own intellect* from such inclinations. So formidable the task that it may seem an impossible one—until we remember that it was ever thus. We only think the task more pressing upon us, think ourselves exceptional in history, because it is *we* who must *now* deal with a responsibility, in this present moment. Our first recovery is to realize that by the accidents of existence it *happens* to be our moment, by the grace of our existing at all. Otherwise we shall conclude the circumstances determinate. We shall declare all history concentrated in this moment—as if our intellectual nature were a determined point on history's continuum. That would be to lose our purchase as created souls in that country of the immaterial which Gilson reminds us of, without which neither life nor thought has meaning. But in consequence of the loss of those concepts of life and thought as beyond material existence, neither would such a concept as history or community have meaning, nor will any of those attempts to name high concerns once signifying realities—truths possessed by intellect and given meaning through our words out of that held truth. We must then, at best, be left with pragmatic—though deterministically inevitable—ethics, but with no moral virtues oriented by the possibility of Beatitude, which term bespeaks our hope of a perfection of our being beyond our finite dream but not beyond our realistic hope.

To say that this is our moment by the accidents of our existence is to be reminded that what we call the historical context to our intellectual quest for the truth of things is the proximate occasion of confusion to our thoughts about ultimate things. Through such confusion, we mistake mediate for ultimate ends of intellectual actions. We become divided, such is our limit as created intellect, be-

tween actions relative to mediate and ultimate ends. Which means
we have, as the most decisive concern to our intellectual action as full
person, the task of coming to terms with, and then to an acceptance
of, a relativism anchored in our own given nature. It is a relativism
consequent upon our finitude, which means that we are limited toward truth as existing in its absolute source—in that I AM, which is
Being Itself.

I emphasize the point, since for some centuries now we have
been increasingly given to another sort of relativism. I mean that
gnostic species of which we spoke, whereby truth is supposed as par-
celled out relatively from the "absolute" position of finite intellect
itself. Such an address is possible only from the assumption of finite
intellect's transcendence of truth itself, as opposed to that address
proper to finite intellect, through which truth becomes the good of
that intellect but in a measure suited to its limits as finite. The distinction at issue is most important, though most difficult to make
clear through words bearing truth. For mind depends upon—depends *from*—truth, not truth from mind. It is important because, as
we understand the distinction, we are at last enabled to address mediate and final ends proportionately, without refusing either or ne-
glecting either. The point recognized requires a prayerful vigilance,
which T. S. Eliot dramatizes in "Ash Wednesday" in his prayer "teach
us to care and not to care." Teach us to engage the mediate circumstances, our contingency to earthly existence without concluding
them, by the action of our own engagement, our final end.

The present context to our existential life, then, imposes a certain necessity but a limit to that necessity, for we are called to engage
mediating circumstances. We are created free, but existence itself
implies limited freedom. We are called to engage existence in this
present moment, while we must at the same time not suppose it our
ultimate calling. This is to say, by way of recovering hope in a dark
moment, that our present moment as history is not ours to redeem.
That is not the final, nor the proper, end to our intellectual action,
though we may not be indifferent to circumstantial necessities. Our
ultimate end is our own discrete specific soul saved in a fulfillment of
its potential being. We must care, and we must do what we are both

able and enabled to do *in the circumstances.* As I say this, I remember one of the most moving and high epitaphs I have ever encountered, put on the tomb of a beloved wife, in a cemetery in Crawford, Georgia: "She done what she could." That is what we may pray will be our own epitaph at last even if caught in flawed verb, after our sojourn in the academy, over whose doors there seems at the moment to be engraved a most formidable message: "Abandon hope, all ye who enter here."

It will have begun to appear that I have long since abandoned my topic and gone to preaching, which perhaps I have. But my concern is to justify a recovered hope to us, without which we are not likely to care about the academy as we ought, such is the pressure of circumstance upon our caring. Hope abides so long as we remember that our true country lies always by implication in an immaterial dimension of our created existence, even as through that immaterial dimension we become threatened in our own actions with an entrapment in history. The uncertainty of our necessary deportment as relativists of the truth, our deportment through which we both care very much and do not care too much, attends inescapably our recognition of that timeless, placeless dimension of our being through our openness to truth beyond the accidents of our history— those accidents recorded by dates and perhaps the words, "He (or she) done what he could." The high cause of higher education is never a lost cause, anymore than it is ever a won cause. But within our acceptance of these conditions to the relative nature of our intellectual gifts, we will find that our good is always supplied at the level of how things stand in truth, and that signifies the highest cause as gained at the last. That is what we mean by *circumstantial*: the *standing* of the *thing* in itself, within an encircling, enveloping reality of existential creation. So it is that we thus recognize the hopeful within those otherwise disturbing words that speak always to our present moment: "Sufficient unto the day are the evils thereof."

Now, lest it seem we conclude on too solemn a note, as if hope were to be left with the worldly shadow of a forlorn countenance, insofar as we live and breathe and have our being for a time in the circumstantial world, let us recall a joyful poet. Not Eliot this time, though he speaks to our point, which is that we must be always returning to the point from which we set out, at which place, when the journey is truly made, we are enabled to see that place "for the first time." I have rather in mind Gerard Manley Hopkins. He is the poet who immediately supports us as academic intellectuals called to witness to the truth of things in this present moment of the world. He celebrates them through poems whose mediate end is his catching an *inscape* of things in words, he says. That attempt in words to catch the truth of a thing is out of his response to his own vision of the *instress* of things. And that instress always speaks beyond material manifestations of a thing, speaks toward the immaterial reality whereby that thing which is, is in its first place. For Hopkins knows that "There lives the dearest freshness deep down things," despite our seeing with our sensual natures that these are "dappled things," such things as "rose-moles all in stiple upon trout" or "Fresh-firecoal chestnut-falls," or for that matter the flashing recalcitrance of eyes in a confused defense against a shared light from the boy or girl or man or woman on the back row of this morning's class, challenging and so bespeaking an intellect and a soul not yet dead. We wrestle for the beauty possible in things, not only in that "sheer plod" that "makes plough down sillion," but in the sheer plod that makes us try to reveal that when we say a verb is a word expressing action, being, or a state of being, we are dealing with a reality spoken to through our words which the words must respectfully attend. In this instance of the *verb* St. Thomas's *being* itself is at issue, or Hopkin's "dearest freshness deep down things." That is why grammar is philosophy. It is also, ultimately, theology. Donald Davidson is right, then, about our circumstances in the teaching of even elementary grammar.

Such is the love of wisdom we must support, whose ultimate end is a love of that Creating and Sustaining Love. That is, if higher education is to be rescued to more viable circumstances for the sake of community, we must care, though not too much. And we must accept without despair that we are always on the edge of being lost in a dark wood, a circumstance requiring of us that virtue of humility which saves us from a presumption that the whole of that wood in which we are lost is dependent upon us in an absolute way for its light, at each moment of our encounter with things, in our quest for the truth of things. Eliot says of this moment that it finds us always in the middle, for we are always in the middle. We are

> *not only in the middle of the way*
> *But all the way, in a dark wood, in a bramble,*
> *On the edge of a grimpen, where is no secure foothold.*

That is the *abiding* moment which abides because all existing things, ourselves included, are momently held, as Dame Julian of Norwich says of the chestnut she holds on her open palm—a chestnut whose fellows are Hopkins's seen as "Fresh-firecoal chestnut-falls." And because thus momentarily held by Love, they do not cease to be. That small fruit because of Love, a thing in the circumstantial world, will be sustained. For as Dame Julian says in her moment of vision, it "lasteth and ever shall for that God loveth it."

Her words alone are sufficient reason why we must exercise the special office of our varied callings in the academy, whether we be called biologist or theologian, chemist or poet, or even philosopher. Only this reminder, once more: in answering that call we may not rest hope in effecting a present and permanent restoration of the world, for that is to prepare ourselves as victim of despair. Our primary obligation, inherent in the gift of our being—in our life as discrete person, whatever the gift whereby we may be praised by the world as *specialist* or *expert*—is to accept our discrete intellectual gifts in their limits. The gifts, in reality, are suited only to a portion of the largesse of creation, and so they are always only a relative gift, for though easily tempted to presume otherwise, we are not God. What we make of our gift in the world, at last, is not the world, but ourselves, through grace. By our ordinate care, leavened by our not caring in the light of eternity, we will be bouyed by a hope sprung of vision, which vision made Dame Julian cry out to us those words that Eliot chooses in ending the lifetime of his poetry:

> *All manner of thing shall be well.*
> *And all manner of thing shall be well.*

7

In Pursuit of the Multifoliate Rose

Within its depths I marked how by the might
of love the leaves, through all creation strowed,
bound in a single volume, there unite.

Dante, Paradiso, Canto 33, 85-87

L ET ME SUGGEST at the outset that our nation's has been a civil
religion, though regularly declared practiced in the name of
God, signified on our coins.* It is a religion emerging out of
Puritanism and dominating our civil consent for some hundred and
fifty years now. At the close of the twentieth century, its inadequacies become depressingly apparent in symptoms of civil collapse,

---

* In making such a bold statement, I am aware of the impressive arguments
made that the Founding Fathers were firmly anchored in both Western philosophy precedent to the Renaissance and in Christianity as derived from the
Apostles and the Fathers of the Church. On this dimension of the intellectual
climate at the founding, see M. E. Bradford's *A Worthy Company: Brief Lives of
the Framers of the United* States *Constitution* (Marlborough, N.H.: Plymouth
Rock Foundation, Inc., 1982), and especially Ellis Sandoz's *A Government of
Laws: Political Theory, Religion, and the American Founding* (Baton Rouge:
Louisiana State University Press, 1990). But my point is that to be only re-
sidually affected by that thought, to which is added Enlightenment thought,

whether one explores that collapse in economic or social terms, whether in ecological terms signified by the plight of the spotted owl or crime in the streets of our glowing, neon-lit cities. We are increasingly the children of fathers devoted to a god that failed, no longer able to localize that god of "materialism" in the Kremlin or the capitals of Eastern Europe. Solzhenitsyn warned us, in his famous (or infamous) Harvard Commencement address in 1974, that the rivalry of East and West was more nearly a struggle over the manner of worship of a false god than a contention between the forces of right and wrong. On one occasion I suggested the irony in the circumstances of Solzhenitsyn's warning—at Harvard University, the home of ideological pragmatism, itself grown out of Emersonian solopsistic "transcendentalism," which was itself out of that Puritan Gnostic intent to conquer the natural world as the enemy of its god in order to build a shining city on a hill as the soul's launching pad into the transcendent. This abbreviated genealogy of our civic religion I have explored more widely in *Why Hawthorne Was Melancholy*, my defense of this present description of our civil religion. That religion has long since lost its orientation to the God of being, and to being itself as the created context of existential natures, so that we are left not only philosophically, but theologically, with the moment's *ad hoc* necessity of dealing with a continuing collapse of the fabric of society.

Even at a symptomatic level, as opposed to analytical exploration of the disease—the spiritual *dis*-ease of our common experience of our inherited world—we may take my point. If we speak of our-

---

especially such as that of John Locke, is quite different from that thought actively advanced as primary to recent political history of Western Europe and England. It is the primary concern I think missing. The Great Awakening in New England in the late eighteenth century signals an alarmed concern for a recovery of that older tradition to intellect, then being recognized as severely threatened. But it is an alarm registered more conspicuously in the general populace than in the elected or established political leadership, as seems evident from the New England Brahmin reaction to the Great Awakening. That early disparity between a popular consensus in the general public and the position actively established through its elected representatives haunts the American political arena from the beginning.

selves in the international community as Yankees, it is with a pride in our pragmatic "track-record" as we might put it, as if human existence in community were a race and not properly a dance, as Chesterton once suggested. We feel relieved at the moment by the general economic collapse of the East. We are inclined to charitable gestures to those now enduring the realities of a defeat of their ideological reductions of reality. We are quite eager to discover to the Russian or Hungarian or Polish entrepreneur just how it ought to be done, to the general benefit of all—an attitude in which there is a dangerous mixture of genuine charity of persons toward persons and the continuing ideological bifurcation whereby that charity does not extend adequately to the conditions of stewardship toward all creation, inclusive of persons. Hence the present alarm over ecological problems.

Solzhenitsyn, now long silent, must in that silence shake his head in pained disappointment at having been apparently heard, but not understood. One trusts that he finds some comfort in that kindred voice raised to counter our difficulties in the name of a recovery of community health, Pope John Paul II. Consider the encyclical *Centesimus Annus*, issued on the centennial of Pope Leo XIII's *Rerum Novarum*. Pope Leo's was a critical examination of the dead end into which secular liberalism was leading the world, and its collapse occasions Pope John Paul's reflection upon the spiritual drift of the West this intervening hundred years. As Gerhart Niemeyer remarks, in his own reflections on *Centesimus Annus*, the Pope's warning is that we "must realize that 'totalitarianism in reform' is not just 'their' problem but ours, too," the "their" being the Eastern European nations whose spectacular collapse focuses our attention away from our own companion weaknesses. Says Niemeyer, in our relation to Eastern Europe in collapse there is "a meeting of one kind of poverty with another. If they lack productive property, as well as capital and managerial skills, our poverty is [in Pope John Paul's phrase] 'the loss of the authentic meaning of life.'" What is required, Niemeyer concludes, echoing *Centesimus Annus*, is "a great effort to move toward the freedom of truth."

In the light of the long history of warnings to us that we must not neglect the freedom of truth, one feels never more disquieted than when we seem most victorious as a nation on the international stage. As Yankees in that international community, we speak pragmatic virtues, rather than the virtues of truth about the complexity of existence itself, confident still that we can restructure that complexity under the moment's pressures, whatever those pressures may be. We do what needs doing or can be done, whether that be winning a desert war in a few days or capping oil well fires in a slightly longer period of time than was needed to set them going. We are efficient makers of things, executioners of programs toward structuring or restructuring current conditions of social existence. Clichés are ready to mind, sharing as common a tribute to our national character as doers of our own word, the emphasis always upon *doing* over *being*. If but in brief, then, such is the ambience of feeling in regard to our national destiny, *feeling* dominant over considered *thought*. And it is in the larger context of such feelings that the difficulties of our educational institutions must be thoughtfully addressed, with some recovery of the importance of *being* as precedent to that address if it is to be effective.

I

It has become acceptable to the intellectual community of late to view Jean-Paul Sartre skeptically. He formulates, justifies, and attempts to exercise the primacy of doing over being. But my concern is that though we recognize difficulties at an analytical level with that philosophy called "Existentialism," we have drifted into a consent to a governance by that very ideology, elevating doing over being. We name it with some pride "Yankee ingenuity." He who can, does, we say. He who cannot, teaches. That was a position assumed by that confused and confusing "romantic" writer who was—or so he thought—in revolt against "romanticism." I mean Mark Twain, who had little sympathy for Hawthorne's concerns for the nature of sin in the conduct of human nature toward itself and creation in general. At first assuming such romanticism a residue of history, Twain was merciless in his excoriation of romantic writers. The notorious instance is his treatment of Sir Walter Scott's influence on American "feeling" in Huck Finn's encounter of it in the Grangerford episode of his best book. Twain treats the same concern more nearly in his own person in another work, unable to quite achieve that detachment that had been possible through the mask of an adolescent protagoinst in the *Adventures of Huckleberry Finn*. His Connecticut Yankee, translated to King Arthur's court, proves quite superior to the medieval man, it at first appears, precisely because of the ingenuity of his doing over medieval bumbling attempts to recover an ordinate being.

What is remarkable about Twain's account of this encounter of Modernism with Medievalism, however—presented with wicked hilarity at the expense of the medieval world—is the very dark conclusion of that work. For if Hawthorne is threatened by melancholy as he considers the spirit of Modernism, we discover Twain overwhelmed by despair, not only in his *Connecticut Yankee at King Arthur's Court*, which follows next after his one great work, but especially in that late volume called *The Man Who Corrupted Hadleyburg and Other Stories and Essays* (1900). Language as doing—the gifts of outrageous spectacle in words—was increasingly insufficient to still his despair, and it was a despair, I suggest, out of his inability to order and so reconcile the relation of doing and being to the health of intellect.

One significant, near success, differing quite markedly from his *Connecticut Yankee*, we might note in passing, is his *Personal Recollections of Joan of Arc* (1896). As historical determinist, Twain understands that *being* is naturalistically determined, that *doing* is the necessary revolt against that determination by historical and biological *being*. One may hold either nature or God responsible for *being's* entrapment of the will from its freedom of determination. In that conception of existential reality, therefore, one may see either nature or God as malevolent antagonist to the individual spirit which would will its own being. But there is the strange presence of Joan of Arc, of whom Twain says in an essay, "There is no blemish in that rounded and beautiful character." In presenting that character fictionally, Twain employs two masks through which to ponder the mystery of a person whose being and doing are so mysteriously one: namely, the purported author of a first hand account of Joan, Sieur Louis de Conte, and the translator-editor of the account, one Jean François Alden. There is quite a shift in Twain's own perspective thus effected: the octogenarian de Conte, aristocrat by origin and a devout Roman Catholic, is sympathetically projected. The "translator" Alden, is scholarly, objective, direct in his commentaries on the text in his "Preface" and footnotes. Strange authorities, these, since they are used sympathetically to establish Twain's own view of Joan as a "rounded and beautiful character" without "blemish."

The point is that Twain in this work attempts to reconcile himself to Joan, seeing in her a witness to the accommodation in this most singular presence in history, Joan of Arc, of being and doing. The only possible reference to that accommodation is a transcendent author of all being and doing, God, with whom Twain in his own person is always most uncomfortable. The shift in Twain is from Hank, the emerging "Boss" of technology at Arthur's court, to Joan, the "Saint" despite history.* Twain's inability to reconcile the dilemma himself leads to those dark, last works: "The Man Who Corrupted Hadleyburg" and "The Mysterious Stranger." But he is able, for the moment of his fascination with Saint Joan, to defend ignorant, naïve innocence against all else, and so his own position is not lost. He need not submit to the God of creation. Joan is remarkable "by reason of the unfellowed fact that in the things wherein she was great [as general, lawyer in her own defense, and so on] she was so without shade or suggestion of help from preparatory teaching, practice, environment, or experience." Unlike the other great persons of history, she does not grow toward her high place through years of experience. She is great on the instant, a seventeen-year-old peasant

---

* It is revealing to juxtapose Twain's comic encounter between Modernist and the medieval mind in his novel, that work of an aging adolescent skeptic, to a similar reflection on the medieval and Modernist mind by a sophisticated historian, Henry Adams, in his *Mont St. Michel and Chartres*. Both Adams and Twain reveal themselves unable to resolve the disparity between the two, and both men are increasingly inclined to a despair of spirit in consequence of the speculative juxtaposition of the two minds.

girl who is suddenly general to the first army ever she saw, leading it in victories, never once defeated in the field. She is confronted by Twain's usual antagonists, those with every "advantage that learning has over ignorance, age over youth, experience over inexperience, chicane over artlessness," and so on. For instance, she proves conqueror of that assemblage of judges who condemn her, those "ablest minds in France," dying still a girl, a child, and so remaining "the most extraordinary person the human race has ever produced."

Such are Twain's praise-full words of Joan in his essay on her, open and direct in his own person. She triumphs in death, but Twain's reflections seem to suggest she triumphs because she meets death as a girl, as if, like Huck, she "lit out" for a fabulous West before it could appear to her but fable, as only a fiction as it is to the aging Twain. As for the long-lived Twain himself, there is that seemingly inevitable darkness as his romantic attachment to youth and innocence, equated with ignorance and inexperience in his portrait of Saint Joan, dissolves. In "The Mysterious Stranger" it is Satan, not God, who possesses the truth, the concluding lines revealing the dark valley into which Twain descended and from which he found no exit. Satan tells the youthful protagonist, who is slowly waking from his innocence, "*Nothing exists save empty space—and you!* ... It is true, that which I have revealed to you: there is no God, no universe, no human race, no earthly life, no heaven, no hell. It is all a dream—a grotesque and foolish dream. Nothing exists but you. And you are but a *thought*—a vagrant thought, a useless thought, a homeless thought, wandering forlorn among the empty eternities!" The awakened protagonist concludes that "all he had said was true." Such is one of the ends of Cartesian separations of thought from reality, dooming Twain's fitfully romantic version of ignorant youth.*

---

*   In "The Mysterious Stranger," Twain's central complaint is against existence itself, though focused in the term "God." The protest is against the necessity to intellectual creatures of dealing with the mystery of good and evil, a necessity which Christian theology orients by the reality of evil in relation to Original Sin. Twain's Satan delivers a scathing indictment of "God," who "could make good children as easily as bad." The complaint is an ancient one, of course, a famous instance of which, in the thought of T. S. Eliot, leads Eliot to

These then, are the ambiguous clouds in which our thought attempts to resolve itself from feeling, and, alas, increasingly with little help from the American academy whose principal responsibility to our civic nature is precisely and centrally such help.

In that climate of feeling as a people there continues dominant the inclination to a goal, temporal but clothed by the rhetoric of feeling, as if feeling alone were a proper transcendent end: to build some shining city on a hill in this world, to build a "Great Society," to structure a "New World Order" in the wake of Marxism's collapse, whereby the whole world becomes peopled by a kindlier and gentler race, an inclusive humanity rescued by its own good intentions. Out of such ambiguities emerge our attitudes toward education itself, attitudes which turn more and more programmatic, as if some process could effect moral character in the peoples of the world. At the heart of this assumption lies that continuing inherited assumption that doing effects being, an assumption that in effect divides and externalizes from human nature its own doing. But in truth, *doing*, in respect to human nature, is always and necessarily a movement out of *being* toward the fulfillment of that potential being intrinsic—the gift of discrete being itself: the *being* of this specific creature, this *intellectual* creature, this particular *person* named John or Mary, or Maria or

become reconciled to his own nature as created soul. Dame Julian of Norwich makes the same objection, only to understand at last that sin is "behovely" and that "all manner of thing shall be well" beyond the reaches of evil. Twain's Satan indicts God, "who preferred to make bad children," and charges God as one "who mouths justice and invented hell—mouths mercy and invented hell. . . . who mouths morals to other people and has none himself," and so on.

What is curious about this indictment, making it quite different, for instance, from the indictment of God by Dostoyevsky's Grand Inquisitor, is the nature of an execution of judgment against God subsequent to the indictment. That action is to deny all being, through which denial alone it seems possible to be revenged upon God. It is curious, in that *being* is thus willed to be an illusion which, before it may be an illusion, must *be*. Thus the counter-assertion by willful intellect: nothing is—neither man nor nature nor God nor Satan himself, the assertion put into Satan's mouth. By this great denial, both man's conscience and his consciousness are obliterated. Consciousness—awareness—is devoured by willed doubt in its dissipation of existence, thus attempting to solve the abiding mystery of good and evil in the contingencies

Carlos, or Gretchen or Karl, or Dmitry or Annushka. Meanwhile, the attempt at process applied to mind, in a mechanics of mind-tuning, so dominates our attitude toward education that even where there are advocates of liberal arts education, the arguments dissolve almost at once to the practicalities of programs.

There are, of course, practicalities required in the interest of developing intellect. In the older and sounder concept of liberal education, these were first addressed at the level called *grammar*. There are those necessities of subject-verb agreement, even perhaps an acceptable system of punctuation of sentences, that at least helps orient us in common to the signs we would use. (Twain expresses envy of Adam, who had no worry over the proper use of commas.) Those elementary virtues of grammar, now assumed the responsibility of higher education, seem more likely to be established in our educational "product," if he or she has been "processed" in junior college disciplines at the level of grammar by courses assumed "liberal arts" education. Remedial English, remedial math, remedial science have become the imposed responsibility of undergraduate education, and the more insistently imposed, the more education degenerates. Alarmed, would-be employers, out of their practical experience of college graduates, demand that the colleges at least assure a grammar school education.

---

of intellectual action through the shell-game played with words divorced from reality. The affirmation of this dark proposition by the novella's protagonist is as dark an assertion of willed oblivion of the self as it seems possible to make with language, since language is anchored, *a fortiori*, in the actual existence of discrete intellect. It is not that Twain is unaware of this logical impasse in his willed perversion, but that in his desperate despair he wills the non-existence of intellect itself, to be accomplished only by the self-contradiction of blasphemy. For, as Flannery O'Connor's Haze Motes realizes at last, you can't blaspheme against something that doesn't exist. If one cannot arrest oneself in that state of a perpetual innocence such as possessed by a Huck Finn or a Joan of Arc, then there seems to remain for Twain only this suicide of self-denial. God could have made "good children," Twain's Satan complains. The orthodox rejoinder is that he chose to make free children and not windup toys, one consequence of which is a duration in time and nature beyond perpetual childhood, which was always Twain's version of Eden.

The pragmatic concern for efficiency and a dependable product of the educational system enters decisively into higher education with Charles Eliot's elective curriculum at Harvard in the late 1860s, though the principle intellectual assumptions about the nature of and end of education is already operative in Puritanism from the outset. That was a spiritual pragmatism addressing the created world in a manipulative, Gnostic way. Once the transcendent end of that Gnosticism is discredited by the new Darwinian assumptions, out of which assumptions Twain for instance inherits his deterministic view of nature and society, the shift of the gnostic end from the transcendent to the immanent is no great problem. Subsequently, pragmatism as a national philosophy grows out of Charles S. Peirce's attempt to recover to philosophy the medieval virtues of Scholasticism. It is presented to us through William James's appropriations and adaptations of Peirce's thought. But that pragmatism establishes in the end only a secularized version of intellect, furthered as the new secular theology by the growing dominance of Darwinian speculations in the sciences. Little wonder that Peirce's intuitive recognition of a dislocation of intellect led him back to Duns Scotus in his attempt to recover reality to intellect. But the attempt leaves Peirce himself in that valley of despair inhabited by Twain in his last days, which are, significantly, contemporary to Peirce's own last days.

Thomas Henry Huxley, as patron intellect to Charles Eliot's dream of Harvard, a dream complemented by the muddled thought of Ralph Waldo Emerson, establishes that degenerative dream of the ends of higher education, whose consequences we experience in our day as the collapse of the academy. By the end of the nineteenth century, the dying gasps of liberal arts education grow fainter and fainter, in spite of those last minute attempts to resuscitate intellect at Harvard, made by such men as Santayana and Babbitt. From the turn into our century, however, *doing* becomes the dominant virtue to be established in the student by formal education. Being is less and less an acceptable deportment of intellect. He who can, does. He who can't, teaches. Even our poets turn increasingly activist, shuttling here and there, increasingly engaging in political and economic activities as necessary justification of their office as poet.

II

I am, of course, speaking both cryptically and in a most summary fashion, as if teaching a survey course in Western intellectual history from Scotus and Aquinas and Occam to Deconstruction—from Beowolf to Virginia Woolf—under the pressure of the ten-week academic quarter. But perhaps I might refer you once more to my more extended exploration of this rapid transit from Puritanism to Pragmatism—at least to that segment of our space-age journey—in *Why Hawthorne Was Melancholy* and in my essays on such diverse participants in the recent drama of Western intellect as Emerson or Solzhenitsyn or Voegelin. Our confounding loss of an ordered perspective upon the virtues of being, to which doing is subordinate, is surely one of the sources of Hawthorne's tendency to despair, as it is Twain's succumbing to despair. That is a point about Hawthorne at last understood by that distant cousin of President Eliot of Harvard, the poet T. S. Eliot. The poet Eliot came to see Hawthorne as something more than merely our first "psychological" poet, as he at first describes him. At that first taking, the poet was rather under the influence of William James, to speak nothing of the influence of William's brother, Henry. The novelist Henry, considering himself an intellectual "realist" and opposing the dominant literary "romanticism," was himself much embarrassed by Hawthorne as fiction writer, since Hawthorne kept returning to this problem of sin. But the question of "sin" was at last made more intellectually tolerable at the turn of the nineteenth into the twentieth century by the new science of psychology. It became tolerable as a concept because removed from the reality of sin in the orthodox understanding of the term. Indeed, one of President Eliot's concerns as educationist was to rid education of such concepts, declared antiquated and unreal. One might well read President Eliot's lecture to the Harvard Divinity School on his retirement, the proposal he entitles the "Religion of the Future." There he presents his version of a secular use of the religious impulse from which all religion has been removed in order to establish merely pragmatic intellectual programs.

I am attempting, you see, to avoid reductionism in these intricate but central concerns to higher education, though lacking world enough and time it is impossible not to be reductive. Let me suggest, then, even though in a reductionist way, that we must recover an educational vitality, recover a vision of the nature of our intellectual being, from the distortions of our intellectual nature which have been underway in the West since the Renaissance, and most especially since the deliberate dismantling of that reality by our Puritan fathers. It matters little, in the end, whether the deconstructors of intellectual reality believed in God or did not believe in God— whether they were divines such as the Mathers or Jonathan Edwards, or secularists such as Emerson or Charles Eliot. Both species of the Gnostic deconstructionists are causes of the present academic chaos. What we, here and now, are responsible for is a recovery of an educational vitality founded in the true nature of intellect, a recovery of a vision of our intellectual being, as opposed to the merely pragmatic extensions and distortions of intellectual being through endless doing, whether such doing be done in the name of God or against the name of God—whether in furtherance of the so-called Puritan "work ethic" or its secularized version, whose end is that proliferation of things divorced from both art and understanding that overwhelm us as a nation.

Everywhere, at all levels of our social and political structure as a people, there are calls to recover that vitality of being, and everywhere our schools are being charged with the loss of that vitality. The alarm is, unfortunately, very like that raised not so long ago after the Russians launched their Sputnik. But in our current ringing the bells backward—that old alarm warning of barbarian invasion—we find our alarm unpersuasive to those most at risk, for we too long neglected the necessary defenses, defenses resident in the virtues of being. In the ensuing panic among alarmists, we call again and again for some immediate restoration of *being*, having long since lost that music of the bells when they are orderly and ordinately rung, to which the counterpointed cacophony and disorder could therefore be a recognized signal of threat in the old dispensations of orderly community. Now the confusion of *ad hoc* alarms and defenses, momentarily obsolete, have become the only music we know. And in this present moment, the 1990s, not Sputnik, but economic pressures from Japan in one hemisphere and from the European Common Market in the other, times the music of our distress. Increasingly our public chants toward higher education appeal for an immediate effective program. Education must do something about the present threat of the budget deficit.

What is most likely to be lost, in an attempt to recover intellectual order under such pressures, is any possibility of an abiding health in the body civic. For *ad hoc* programs in answer to an emergency can only be a temporary delay, since the cause of emergency has grown over long centuries and with accelerating destructiveness. The *ad hoc* responses made will only touch the decay, the accidents of the enveloping intellectual disease I call, as do others, *Modernism*. Our deepest concern seems to be for the body economic at the moment, and that is not concern deep enough. It is not that I discount the importance of economic concerns to the health of our community body. Rather, I fear a divisionary reduction of that body, in which action the possibilities of its essential being—as opposed to its merely multiple hierarchical *doings*—should be lost. The structures of society, if seen in a merely mechanistic—that is, structural—light, without recognition of the depths of order that alone make the social body organic and alive, doom us to breakdowns in those structural mechanisms and lead to despair over the failure of mechanistic order as salvific of spiritual being. It is this level of attention to existence seen in a mechanistic way that is the so-called materialistic obsession of Western thought, in which our own view of social structure is akin to the collapsing Eastern version of that same secualirized thought. Material existence when used with gnostic intent, I keep insisting, violates the reality of material existence, which in itself bears the virtues of being because it constitutes the complex of creatures created. Again, materialism is not our problem, but a gnostic address by intellect to material existence, an address that dooms us to *ad hoc* attempts to rescue intellect from a chaos of its own creation. Not materialism but abstractionism is the problem: our reduction of actual, material, existing things by intellect's Gnostic disjunction from those things.

Now the educational vitality to be recovered lies in our recovering to orderly thoughtfulness the nature of intellect itself, a known but forgotten understanding which Charles Peirce saw slipping away as we turned into the twentieth century. I summon Peirce to the present concern in part because the late Walker Percy found in Peirce some possibility of rescue from our intellectual confusions, though Percy turned to Peirce only late in his own thought. It is a notable coincidence that both Percy and Peirce turn to the scholastics for orientation, Percy to St. Thomas, Peirce to Duns Scotus. But this is more than rare coincidence. We may multiply instances of similar turnings in this century by notable intellects, turnings which are considered a sign of "romanticism" by a careless evaluation. In pursuit of a recovery of realism, not only Percy and Peirce, but T. S. Eliot, Jacques Maritain, Allan Tate—and so on and on. Such minds turn to those ancient doctors of intellect. If theirs is a species of "romanticism," it is a quite different sort from that of Sir Walter Scott in his novels or John Keats in his "Eve of St. Agnes." Duns Scotus or Thomas Aquinas hardly appeal to *feelings* in that generally accepted, but misunderstood characterization of romanticism.*

We might well remember another son of Harvard in revolt, a son President Eliot persuaded to teach history there for a while. I mean Henry Adams, who when he recognized the dislocation of intellect in his world turned toward the medieval world to discover the sources of that dislocation. Thus he comes to consider, to ponder, the relative virtues of "The Virgin and the Dynamo" in his account of his own education. And in his celebrated *Mont St. Michel and Chartres*, he juxtaposed two great churches, considering in his exploration of architectural analogy the growing presence of a Modernist spirit in the one as opposed to the other. This last of the Adamses turns to that late medieval world out of which there had been a Modernist turning toward the secular pragmatism that left

---

* I have explored the relation of the "romantic" poet to existential reality as revealed by the poet in *Romantic Confusions of the Good: Beauty as Truth, Truth Beauty*, and in *Intellectual Philandering: Poets and Philosophers, Priests and Politicians*.

him unsatisfied. Henry Adams, uncomfortable in the world, but with nowhere to turn, recognizes his own family's role in that disjunction, reflected still in our civic and political thought.*

I contend that, in the late medieval period of Western intellectual history, we too eagerly abandoned a metaphysical vision. The abandonment has been progressive as we more and more have pursued a substitute god, Progress. The consequence to intellectual authority, whether in or out of the academy, has been that without a metaphysical vision which anchors those questions proper to intellect itself in a present reality, we come to address those questions unavoidably in a merely *ad hoc* manner. For having lost orientation by intellectual principles soundly established and held out of metaphysical vision, we are doomed to *ad hoc* responses to any crisis of circumstances, the only virtue in that response being our recognition of crisis itself. With the overwhelming advances of technology, the stepchild of Modernist intellectuals that everywhere disturbs the modern world, this unleashed technology presses relentlessly upon our intellectual responsibility. Mary Shelley's parable of Modernism was popular at our own mid-century. Now, however, we find to our increasing panic that adjusting our relation to the latest technologi-

---

* If we read *The Education of Henry Adams* against St. Augustine's *Confessions*, the memoirs are instructive. St. Augustine's recollections show intellect issuing from despair. Adams's reveal an intellect descending deeper into despair as he struggles to recover vision lost. Adams's ironic detachment through the literary device of a memoir written in the third person gives rise to a sardonic presence of Adams at the time of his remembering as he looks upon himself on the journey up to the point of his present remembering. He is detached from himself by irony, and so is still present. He talks not as "I" past and present, but of "he" past. More than literary convention is involved, and we begin to discover something of intellect's loss of reality since St. Augustine in reading *The Education* in this light. Or one might compare to the same point Dante's point of view in the *Divine Comedy*. Both Dante and St. Augustine begin from a way-station along the journey, arrived at with some confidence in the rightness of the way taken. Both are an immediate presence less protected by irony than Adams feels necessary, the two older works taking as a point of departure, to adapt Dante's opening to the work, the same moment of arrest: "In the middle of *my* life *I* came to *myself* in a dark wood."

cal homunculus by *ad hoc* address is futile. Thus Dr. Frankenstein's monster suits our situation only in an antiquated way at the close of this century. Earlier, the monster as mechanism was at least in the semblance of an actual person. Now, however, the new monster is as distantly abstracted from reality as the gnostic intellect itself has become. The silicon chips and the programs encoded on them dominate our lives, and they hint darkly that we have lost touch with both body and spirit.

We seem to exist as beings ourselves rather in that state which Twain's Satan describes: we ourselves seem but "vagrant thought, a useless thought, a homeless thought, wandering forlorn among the empty eternities." That is a quite effective characterization of our perceptions of the modernist malaise spoken of as "Alienation." Still, a sign of hope remains, for signs signifying the loss of the virtues of intellect, though encountered again and again without relief, are signs of loss, and so they are hints toward possible recovery. The revolt of the young against present conditions—revolts that are *ad hoc* undertakings by intellectual Luddites—direct destruction against, not actual machines, but against an unacceptable intellectual machinery. Insofar as one takes the revolt as an intuitive recognition of their own intellectual dislocation, there is at least the hope remaining that after a general destruction some intellectual rebuilding may commence, out of stones from the rubble they cannot obliterate, try as they may. As for us older survivors of the intellectual chaos of this century, we stand often arrested, regretting that we cannot somehow adjust the computer to a healthfully ordinate relation to humanity, the way we could once repair Henry Ford's T-Model with a piece of bailing wire. And so we continue with awkward futility our *ad hoc* solutions to educational problems out of an intellectual nostalgia. We propose a program of some sort, which we advance to its inevitable failure. And all along, the lingering nostalgia cannot locate the thing it regrets. What that thing is, I suggest once more, is the ordinate relation of intellect to reality, the intuitive desire in intellect for its community with being beyond the restlessness of doing, whose spiritual nature, for all its agitated nature, is properly described as the sin of *acedia*.

III

I am suggesting that what has been lost is the spiritual dimension in human existence which our intellectual natures properly serve. Since the introduction of Nominalism by William of Occam, there gradually emerges an attitude toward existence itself which comes to a completion, or rather to a dead end, in secular pragmatism, leading intellect toward an end as a whimper such as that dramatized in the final paragraphs of Twain's "Mysterious Stranger." When our version of higher education begins to rise out of medieval metaphysics, and gradually in opposition to it, the reflective deportment of intellect toward being, upon which active responses to creation are properly founded, begins to disappear. The term "monastic" is applied to such a reflective concern, increasingly in a pejorative sense. A concern for orientation through *being* yields to the exigencies of *doing*, whereby being becomes subject to a restructuring through an intellectual activism that sees intellect itself as autonomous, as independent of the metaphysical *being* which reflection cannot help but encounter as the ground of reality itself. In that movement away from the medieval sense of reality, it was for a while still understood that intellect is a special gift which requires a maturing toward the fulfillment of the discrete intellect's peculiar gifts: namely those gifts as a singular, specific spiritual creature. But in time, that self-liberated intellect will reject its own existence as a gift in favor of itself as its own cause. "I think, therefore I am" is the shibboleth of that rejection in favor of autonomy, though Descartes formulates an already pervasive attitude, pervasive of intellect long before that famous formulation.

Now if intellect is a gift consequent upon existence itself as a prime gift, it follows that an intellect's capacity for knowledge, always unique to the particular intellect, must be encouraged toward the end of *understanding*, not being content with its power derived from simply *knowing*. In the formalities of knowing, though we make pretense to the contrary, there is no egalitarian commonality. It is only insofar as the knowing creature advances toward understanding, and perhaps even to wisdom, that it enters into that dimenision of commonality whereby wisdom accommodates intellect to its own limits as finite and thus justifies it in its communal nature. In that accommodation operative humility makes a brotherhood of intellectual creatures, a body in whom the members, though differing one from another, are yet united in a singleness of community through virtues practiced, as they may only be practiced through humility.

Put yet again, for such is the importance of the point: to *know* within the limits of our specific, discrete intellectual personhood as knowing creature, should properly lead to *understanding*. Thus in the long growth of the singular intellect, it may come at last, through understanding the limits of its being, to wisdom. In this view of the nature of intellect, the purpose of education must be addressed, but not by a process whereby intellect is individually programmed on an assembly line to the service of the social body, itself conceived of as a mechanism. Service to mechanism as ultimate end will lead to intellect's ever wilder and wilder revolt against pretenses to order. That is nevertheless our inheritance from Charles Eliot's "elective" system, this concept of intellect programmed to social utility. That elective system, operating upon a self-evident principle—the recognition of the discrete limits of varying intellects—appropriates that limited truth about our existence as intellectual creatures to its mechanistic ends. Our distress over the inadequacy of such ends is much lamented in our day as a failure of our intellectual "products." It is through the specialization of their intellect, a specialization which takes a part as a whole and extrapolates what may be true of the part as inclusively true of the whole. Thus we derive a false governing principle for all education. In that older, sounder view of education—sounder because more closely attuned to the reality of our natures as intellectual creature—the movement from *knowledge* to *understanding* to *wisdom* is seen as a development more like a metamorphosis than an imposed process. This is in Dante's mind, for instance, when he speaks figuratively of his journey as that of a lowly worm seeking transformation into angelic butterfly. Instead, we modernists would adjust the raw material of *person* by abstracted systems with a variety of wrenches, adjusting that intellect on that assembly line of knowledge, the academy. For Dante the end is unique to the unique soul: to grow into a fullness of a discrete spiritual nature as proper to the singular creature. We rather reduce *person* to *individual*, thus making individuals suitable to an accounting within the social body as conceived mechanically.

Still governed by such false assumptions about the proper principles of education, we appear distraught and harried as our systems fail, and little wonder. Ours becomes a state not unlike that of the frantic parent on Christmas Eve attempting to assemble a toy from garbled instructions, using inappropriate tools. Such a figure characterizes our repeated, shifting *ad hoc* attempts to re-assemble the academy, with dawn far advanced toward daylight and the restless children waking, stirring with their intuitive wonder in the new day. They will only be disappointed by our shoddy toy awkwardly assembled and waiting under an artificial tree in a climate-controlled, "materialistically" comfortable living room in which *living* seems rather far removed.

My figure of the desperate parent fumbling to assemble an imported toy on Christmas Eve intends to recall a common experience, with the imported toy from an emerging nation no doubt located in the fabulous and mysterious Far East beyond our lost Christmas. Perhaps it may arrest metaphorically our sense of confused panic experience at this moment in which the academy is everywhere in collapse before the restless expectations of our green youth. If only we had metric wrenches, or perhaps even a power-driven screwdriver, we could assemble a shining toy that would delight the restive children in the new strange light of this new day! But there will come inescapably, mutually inevitable both to parent and child, the moment when the actual, the *real* nature of mind itself in the world must be acknowledged by parent and child alike, by student and teacher alike. The restless expectation at the coming of the light— that wonder is never recovered through understanding to wisdom's deepest awe before the mystery of being itself: that is the end lost in our educational "programs." It is an end which those suffering its loss may not be prepared to name, such is the failure of our "education system." But the intuitive recognition that something ultimate has been denied by the system itself will trouble the body social, making mechanistic orderings of society tenuous at best. What is lacking lacks its true name. But the culprit responsible for that loss will not lack epithet. The young in the 1960s, suffering deracination, a desire for substantial *being* where it found only an aimless *doing*— called the culprit the "establishment" and rejected that establishment's "system." They insisted on "doing" their own "thing," an awkward attempt to speak to the necessity of *being*.

IV

Such has been our intellectual conditioning by the advocates of Modern Gnosticism, in philosophy and political science and in natural sciences and theology, that right words attempting the truth of things do not come easily to the tongue. For, while we are quite adept at counting things, possessing a multitude of discrete technical vocabularies out of the specialized disciplines devoted to a reckoning of existential reality, we have lost that richer language which orients intellect to the complexity of reality as that reality impinges upon mystery beyond mere reckonings by the instruments of science. In that larger orientation, the thing being named is recognized as always exceeding the limits of all our naming by the fullness of its actualization, so that only a language resonating out of the mystery of existence itself is capable of keeping intellect opened by its acceptance of its own limits. By that deportment, intellect responds to the ineffable through its own enlargements. Put another way, in that deportment of intellect which is open to the mystery of being, intellect discovers itself encompassed by being, rather than presuming itself to encompass being by its actions. The language of mere denotation, upon which there is a necessary dependence, tends nevertheless to sterilize sign of all resonance when it denies that being itself encompasses any sign. Weary of its labor, intellect would rather presume that sign encompasses being. The openness I am describing in opposition to this intellectual presumption of the authority of sign over being is the deportment of the intellect in its piety toward being.

Lacking both that openness and a faith that through words as oriented by piety we may approach the mystery of existence—especially the mystery of our own existence—we reduce language to the level of accountancy. Language thus reduced will serve only reductionist ends in a narrowing of intellectual vision. That narrowed vision is necessary to intellect if it is to be effective in the manipulation of existent things, and is especially important as a method of managing those things called individuals, persons in whom mediate ends are taken or imposed as ultimate ends. Such a reductionism, however, if it is to command devotion of this recruited "individualism" to a common acceptance of mediate ends as ultimate, must give an illusion that it is a full vision of existence. Unless it seems convincingly to posit its ends as ultimate, the intruding mystery of existence through our actual experience will stir us. Reductionism requires a persuasive management of our consent to signs that are declared common, a language dictatorially controlled by the reductionist mind. There has been a very considerable critique of the once common language which has decayed over the past two hundred years, critiques coming to the level of alarmist warnings in this century. One remembers such diverse alarmists as Ezra Pound, who insists on a recovery of viable names of things, Confucius his mentor. There is George Orwell's satiric treatment of "doublespeak." One recalls the searching revelations of that decay by C. S. Lewis at a theological level; by Richard Weaver, in respect to rhetoric; by Eric Voegelin in his recovery of Plato and in his analysis of Modern Gnosticism as the agent of obfuscation of our signs.

In relation to the concerns of these minds, consider the fate of our language in its "connotative" dimension. With the impetus of rationalistic science, ambiguity is concluded intellectual ignorance, its proper cure lying in the restrictiveness of language as denotative. Fact's long tyranny is out of this very insistence, though there is a connotative dimension even to the language of fact, namely the tacit implication that fact is the essence of the thing from which it derives. Not that such a reductionist perspective upon complex reality does not admit ignorance; there are facts not yet known perhaps, but these formulaic namings of essence of things though not yet in mind are destined to be possessed by mind, such is the modernist's faith in his own autonomy over being. It is not a matter of any mystery beyond our capacity to know, but rather a matter of time before we possess by knowing, time itself accelerated by computer technology. Thus the piety proper in the intellectual address to reality which I advocate, impossible to completely exorcise from intellectual action, is turned toward a worshipful attention to intellect itself. Intellect becomes its own idol. What I insist upon is a presence in intellect, in its very nature, of a teleological necessity to pious action. The gnostic recognizes that this necessity to intellectual action, this piety which alone contents intellect in its hunger, is not to be obliterated. He will nevertheless see that it can be seriously inhibited, and so the Gnostic manager of intellect—the Gnostic eroder of being—will shift attention and intention to a lesser end. And often with a degree of success, for a time. Consider here the famous remark of Marx that religion is an opiate of the people. In formalizing the aphorism, he calls in question the old "religious" end, dominant in Western thought since the Greeks, intellect's pursuit of a transcendent end. But Marx engineers a shift of the religious hunger to immanent end. The religion of the state becomes the opiate necessary to the structure he would impose upon society itself. The teleological necessity intrinsic to intellect is not denied. It is manipulated to a Gnostic end in the state.

Such is the necessary manipulation of our intuitive intellect if we are to be made to serve a strictly rationalistic science. That is, if we are to be made to serve the principle of autonomous intellect as itself the Prime Cause of systematic structures to be imposed and by the imposition declared ultimate reality. The extension of rationalistic science in such Gnostic operations is revealed variously in the specialized restrictions of intellect, and a principal one is now called "political science." Through political science, the state emerges as the centering symbol of all temporal ends, and those temporal ends concluded ultimate. Thereby all temporal ends congregate in an ambiance about that symbol, the state, requiring our worshipful obeisance. If that Gnostic intellect fails to establish the virtues of loyalty, patriotism, hero worship as under the auspices of a common symbol like the state, which still carries vaguely transcendent aspects, our intuitive hungers (native to the soul in its hunger for its ultimate, proper end) will prove disjunctive from the Gnostic ends intended by the manipulators of human nature. The utopian dream will crumble. At this moment, we are both puzzled and concerned to see the collapse of discrete "states" in the Eastern block, following the collapse of the Marxist religion of the state. Ethnic antagonisms erupt in ugly events, as in the encounters between Croatians and Serbs and Muslims. Those events in turn are colored by a residual Marxism fitfully relocated in multiple instances of "nationalistic" desire. There is a conspicuous intellectual fumbling to recover order out of history, leading to merely historical justifications of the particular violence of the moment.

In one sense, the political turmoil we are currently witnessing is an effect of a desire to recover reality from its ideological dislocations. But it is a struggle conducted by a language too far decayed by ideological manipulations of language, by separations of intellect from the complexity of existence—from reality—resulting when words are dislocated from true signification. In the desperateness of the political attempts to *reasonably* seize what are but vaguely intuited necessities to community, what wonder that the old violence to words finds its immediate effect in the violence of the gun? Ideological language is always, in its pretension to truth, insistently denotative. It names the thing with the authority of intentional intellect, convinced of its control of truth by its control of language. Ambiguity is denied by idealistic dogma, so that intellect, though pietistic in appearance, lacks that piety I urge, a piety to which humility is a significant virtue which recovers a self-love beyond selfishness, in an acceptance of the limits of gift in the explicit, discrete intellect—its limited capacity to act at the practical level of encounter between its own reality and the inclusive reality of creation. It is, then, at this most fundamental level of the person as person that a recovery of reality is first necessary, if there is to be a significant recovery of community, as distinct from the conveniences of merely aggregate bodies of individuals bent on political power and so doomed to endless contention.

We have suggested that whatever is connotative in language is disturbing to the particular intellect when it is not governed by piety. It is desirably disturbing, we add, though adamantly resisted by any intellect bent upon reductionist ends. For, whatever is strictly denotative through sign is reassuring to willful intellect. Willful intellect supposes the denotative the direct means to operational power. "Just the facts, ma'am," the television detective is famous for insisting. But facts alone are insufficient to the crime of intellect's revolt against reality, a revolt in which the denotative is posited as the only absolute appropriate to language. Here is the locus of the old, sometimes bitter, quarrel between the "Poet" and the "Scientist" since the eighteenth century. Having introduced this quarrel as conspicuous in recent Western intellectual history, however, let us rather consider it as common within the experience of each discrete intellect. We may discover it so through some memory of a personal encounter, each of his own intellect with a particular, actual thing separate from intellect. In doing so, we shall discover the quarrel of "Poet" and "Scientist" peculiar to any given intellect, the discrete intellect itself being the arena in which some "poet" encounters some "scientist." For the point is that the historical battle, recruiting legions of persons to one side or the other, reflects a battle which in its fundamental nature is always first encountered within each distinct intellect. It is operative there in each encounter of that intellect with anything separate from itself.

Now the specific "facts" appropriately descriptive of personal encounter will differ from person to person, but there is common to the experiences, separate from those factual differentiations, a common dimension: there is a common *sense of encounter*, which our "common sense" tells us has been actual. By virtue of encounter, we know that we are. And we know as well that there is in us an emotional effect from that encounter with which we must come to terms. It is an effect signifying the encounter as prior to effect. Such a proposition, we should recall, is denied by Cartesian Idealism, which denies the reality of encounter, as independent of intentional intellect. Idealism desires a recovery of encounter as real, a contradictory circumstance to its articulated position, ambiguously present in Idealism's exposition of experience. Thus occurs the entrapment by Idealism when it refuses the evidence of precedent encounter and an effect of knowing by that encounter that is prior to its deliberate rejection of that knowing as prior. And so with Descartes, intellect asserts that I am because I think. While true in one sense, the formulation is insufficient evidence of an existential *I*. In the view of realistic philosophy: I think because I am, and I think in consequence of an encounter of my "amness" with an other. It is this distinction that leads Gilson to observe, in *Methodical Realism*: "*Res sunt, ergo cognosco, ergo sum res cognoscens.* What distinguishes the realist from the idealist is not that one refuses to undertake this analysis whereas the other is willing to, but that the realist refuses to take the final term of his analysis for a principle generating the thing being analyzed. . . . Idealism derives its whole strength from the consistency with which it develops the consequences of its initial error." And again, "The illusion . . . is that one can extract ontology from an epistemology, and . . . discover in thought anything apart from thought."

William Wordsworth, no Cartesean Idealist, though troubled by that temptation, thought that encounter was the initiating event from which poetry rises. He called poetry, in a tribute to the experience of encounter itself, "emotion recollected in tranquility." It is the nature of that "tranquility" that we move toward in our argument, a tranquility which is a sign in intellect itself of its reconciliation to its own initial, disturbed response to an actual, specific encounter with reality. For in this initiating encounter, there is a moment of emotional disquiet which threatens to disorient awareness, so that it may hardly be said to find itself tranquil in response to the immediacy of encounter. It is this disquiet, incidentally, which leads the Cartesean to his own attempted rescue by Descartes's famous formulation. But in that rescue, what is effected is not a recovery of reality to intellect but a disjunction from it which Cartesean thought cannot bridge. On this point, Gilson has presented the Idealist impass clearly, showing the impossibility of intellectual recovery from the Cartesean premise.

Let us agree that a disquiet of some degree is effected by encounter. But the cause of that disquiet is not simply attributable to the peculiar nature of the particular thing which intellect encounters, as the Cartesean Idealist is quite rightly aware. This is not to deny that a range of actual *things* which intellect may encounter is such that the emotional effect of our encountering is itself quite various. Encounter is various in the degree of disturbed tranquility. But what we are concerned with is the nature of encounter itself: the experience by intellect of some other in a complex that binds intellect and thing in some degree of disturbed response. There is a considerable difference between an encounter with a tiger and a beautiful lady, as the mischievous story writer knows. There is a difference between an encounter with a stone seen as if separate from complex reality and an encounter with a stone in a stream or in a wall, where it is apparently multiplied in its own existential nature. There is a difference in our encounter of a voice that is new and one that is familiar. Or with a known poem—known to be arresting because one has been arrested by it many times—and with a new poem which one knows at once will be endlessly arresting. Or there is the experience of encounter with a poem regrettable in its inadequacies, for some poems are better than others. Or with voices grating upon the ear for reasons more various than the physics of sound. There is the experience of the stone fallen in a wall's decay, or a voice fallen in the decay of age. And so on and on, the complex of which experiences web us more or less in complex reality, in relation to our actions of intellect as affected by disparate experiences. But what is of importance here is that the desperateness, insofar as the intellect's *engagement* to reality (the phrase intended metaphorically) is that they differ in degree but not in kind.

This is experience at what we might speak of as a primitive level. It is the *beginning* of the *coming-to-be* of intellect as it were, consciously or unconsciously known. But then, our *consciously* and *unconsciously* (or *subconsciously*) are terms too heavily laden with modern psychology's uses of the terms. We set them aside in our attempt to express the simple nature of encounter. We say, rather, *intuitively* or *rationally* known. Two points are of interest here in our consideration of the "primitive" encounter as a beginning of the

coming-to-be of intellect. The first is that we are not speaking of a
linear progression from primitive to sophisticated. That is, experience has the nature of beginning but anew in each instance of encounter, life being a complex of encounter and not linear as
measured by instrumentalities of various "clocks." That is what T. S.
Eliot comes to say as a final conclusion to his own exploration of
encounter in relation to his calling as poet. "East Coker" opens with
"In my beginning is my end," a thematic statement explored in that,
as in all of the *Four Quartets*. But the summary recapitulation of the
theme is near the end of "Little Gidding," in arresting lines:

> *Every phrase and every sentence is an end and a beginning,*
> *Every poem an epitaph. And any action*
> *Is a step to the block, to the fire, down the sea's throat*
> *Or to an illegible stone: and that is where we start.*

The *starting* is in each moment of intellectual action, and in each
moment there is always a return to that "primitive" dimension of encounter.

The second point of interest in relation to this "primitive" dimension of encounter is that it always proves already ripe with a
resonance beyond that elemental dimension. Intellect recognizes
that aspect of experience intuitively, though it is only through the
aid of rational intellect that the recognition is brought to intellect as
understanding. That intuitively perceived resonance of encounter, as
we revisit it at the merely primitive level reflectively, affects intellect
according to its response *as intellect*. That is, according to whether
intellect in both the immediacy of encounter and in reflective response to that immediacy, engages experience as suited to its own
given nature. But let us take a parabolic instance of experience
which may perhaps make the distinction clearer.

On a May morning, in a garden, a rose. At once an arrest which
we might call the arrest of awe. There is in this awe a suspension
between terror and delight, a moment the critic would categorize as
"aesthetic" response, though such an accounting of the experience
seems always inadequate to the experience. What has happened
seems quite beyond the limit of sign, though we turn to the poet for

support. (It is the poet who requires of sign that it press its limit.) And what an anthology of poems and fictions in which the common experience of encounter with a rose centers this tension of terror and delight. Burn's love is like a red, red rose. Blake's rose is "sick," for an invisible worm is destroying it with a "dark secret love." Keats goes to the morning rose to find origin of his unshakable melancholy. One could extend instances of such arresting encounter before and after the turning of years into the nineteenth century, the most remarkable instance being Dante's multifoliate rose of that visionary moment in the *Paradiso* that resolves the whole of the *Divine Comedy*. That turning point under the shadow of linear time helps our argument: we wish to move beyond any arrest by history at any point or span of time. In using these "Romantic" poets—romantic in different ways in response to their experiencing the rose—I underline the point of awe as initially operative in their experience, of which the particular poems are more or less recollections of personal encounter, remembered more or less in tranquility.*

Of the experience, we might put it that in the moment of encounter we are responding in awe as if to a beauty thus encountered, whether morning-fresh as in Burns, or midnight sick as in Blake, or

---

* We might well introduce as counterpoint to these "Romantic" instances Gertrude Stein, famous for her rejection of reality by the exorcism of the word's attachment to reality. There is the notorious instance, much quoted, of her "a rose is a rose is a rose," *ad infinitum*. Her word strategy intends a disengagement of intellect from reality by the instrumentality of the word dislocated from any reality. Here then there is no rose of which the term *rose* is a signal. What one has in such a use of language is a sly adolescent intellect, self-preserved by intention from the intrusions of reality upon intellect. In this respect, where Descartes strives desperately to bridge intellect's separation from reality by sign, Stein rejects the very desire in intellect that such a bridge exist. It becomes, then, an active denial of the actuality of experience, a denial possible only so long as the empty words "a rose" can be extended by vacuuming the sign of any signified thing. I suggest it is adolescent by analogy to the child who threatens the adult by holding his breath. He will, of course, either breathe because those realities of existence, particularly those of his own body, will not be denied, or he will cease to exist, his non-breathing becoming his willed non-being.

midnight sick at its morning freshness as in Keats. It is the ambiguity of beauty that troubles the poet, who is in some degree ourselves always. For what I am suggesting is that the troubling is not by any poet *per se* through signs only, but of any intellect by its nature in encountering being. What the "poet" knows, though he may not understand what he knows, is that "beauty" is an inadequate concept for the resonances experienced in the encounter, resonances always beyond any attempted reduction by analysis of the experienced encounter. How futile to set an encounter's "parts" in a pattern: the time, the place, the thing, the intellect, and so on and on. The reality of an experience is larger than the summing of its parts. But this is not a knowledge peculiar to the poet as poet. It is common to each intellect's experience of reality by virtue of the gift of intellect in its very nature. And therefore there is a *common* in the potential response to experience by disparate intellects, though the experiences are not explicitly common in existential details. We do not all experience the same rose at the same time.

Moved by awe, which I suggest is the emotional effect of intuitive intellect in its response to an encounter of reality, what action of intellect follows? For will intercedes upon an initial arrest. Will intrudes upon that moment which Wordsworth called a "spot of time" and Eliot called a "still point." The most probable move by intellect is toward reducing the experience to its parts. Thus one plucks the rose, smells it, crushes it, sketches it, dissects it to see what "makes" it at the level of its cells. If one doubt this is the probable action following an initial encounter whose effect is awe, let him walk with a three-year-old child through a public garden on a spring morning and watch the child seize a rose, thorns and all.

The response that is likely, following the effect of the awe of encounter of a thing, is toward a denotative possession of what we recognize as an existent thing, whose very existence is so disturbingly connotative as to stir us to possessive reduction. I have elsewhere suggested that this is the moment of the Little Fall, a moment echoing that paradigmatic action of intellect in relation to existence which Genesis's garden speaks of. "In Adam's Fall," said the New England primer, "we sin all." The conditions allowing our "sinning"

I am attempting to locate within our own very local, very particular, very present experience of existential reality. Out of a present encounter, there is a falling away toward a denotative self-rescue through language. We acknowledge the "language of the senses," but in the acknowledgment make senses central and not mediate, as they are in the initial encounter. Little wonder, then, that we so easily conclude a separation of intellect and body, of soul and body, in violation of a simplicity of our own existence which only grace restores. But perhaps we must emphasize here that such a falling away is in one sense a necessity, given that our intellect in its finitudes is discursive by nature. It cannot sustain the intuitive encounter of things in themselves at an intuitive level. Still, intellect perishes if it does not recover the validity of intuitive encounter. For if it attempts to make an absolute virtue of its falling away, it denies its own nature. That is the danger of a rigidly unyielding rational response to experience—intellect purged of intuitive knowledge. The only yield is the purely rationalistic inadequacy to reality in its complexities, a denigration of intellect itself. And that is the danger in intellect's inescapable descent from awe. Awe is the emotional climate of intellect in its primary, mysterious union to a thing, by degree abandoned through the limited, rational, denotative level of deliberated knowledge. In that descent, the danger is that intellect will be insistent in resting knowledge as "real" only at the level of the denotative.

When such an insistent intellect carries with it a general consent of diverse intellects at a moment of intellectual history, "fact" becomes the only transcendent, with autonomous intellect easily posited as fact's first cause. But in this reductionism of reality, we said, the "thing" actually reduced is in the end only the particular intellect itself. It is a reduction of a "self," a self-willed prohibition of the fullness of a discrete soul in which intellect is operative through the will. What has occurred is a refusal to recover the conditions whose effect is awe. Now awe recovered I would term *wonder*, and describe wonder as the emotional effect of rational intellect conjoined with intuitive intellect in a recovery of the truth of encounter. In this recovery lies that intellectual estate of *understanding*. In respect to our rose, we *understand* the flower without a presumption of having encompassed the flower, either by our intuitive knowing or our rational knowing.

Wonder reflects a movement whereby reason explores that encounter of being whose first effect in us is awe. Wonder reflects a controlled response to an encounter of being resident in particular things. By cultivating the intellectual climate of wonder we maintain an intellectual manner of coming into what St. Thomas calls our proper "habit of being" as intellectual creatures. And through the habit of intellectual being, in which we rise beyond mere knowledge to understanding, we prepare the way for the effect of grace on intellectual action, which we call wisdom. Through wisdom, in which the mode of intellection tends to the reflective and then to the contemplative and so toward visionary union, there is less likelihood of a dominant habit of reductionism, that continual falling away into the merely denotative uses of existence itself by intellect, those uses which Wordsworth laments as our "murdering to dissect." It is this falling away that I have spoken of as reductionism, whereby finite intellect, if it take the falling away as ultimate, presumes an infinite authority in its relation to existences other than itself. That, alas, includes other intellectual existences.

I have used an experience with a rose, supposing such an experience either actually common to diverse persons or significantly available through analogy to anyone's encounter with existing things other than roses. For surely what I have described here is common, whether in details as might be rationally articulated by the chemist at his trade or by a mathematician or particle physicist or political scientist or literary critic. To say nothing of those callings to a direct encounter of the world's body of things in which rests the mystery of existence: the physician in his knowing this particular wayward body; the farmer this particular field. Experience is intellectually disquieting, whatever its special (as opposed to common) calling. But whatever one's special use of signs—the plow in earth, the chemist's formula, the physician's remedy, the poet's poem—a use of sign properly engaged intends reconciling denotative and connotative experiences of our encounter with explicitly existing things. They are actions toward fullness, toward wholeness. That is why, for instance, the great poet's capturing of this common rightness of intellectual action will be arresting to diverse intellects, turning them meditative. To borrow Hopkins, though "worlds of wanwood leafmeal lie" out of our experiences, we shall (through an awe recovered to wonder by intellectual action) weep for the morning rose, but "know why." Thus the prophetic poet puts it. Only in this way of the intellect may one move beyond that "carrion comfort," Despair, discontent to feast on it. Vague melancholy is, for Keats, the emotional effect of despair. And despair is the inevitable state of the soul when intellect fails its responsibility to wonder.

v

There is present to our experience of a thing—say a beautiful stone or a rose or a person—a sense of disquiet as the effect upon us of our encounter with the thing. We know not whether to name it terror or delight, such is the ambiguity of the effect. It requires both terms, and yet more terms, in our attempt to find an adequate connotative name, as the poet among us knows well. And one of those naming terms, which turns us from the effect *in* us, yet carries acknowledgment of that effect, is to call the thing that so stirs intellect the "Beloved." Dante explores this mystery of encounter through that long pursuit of the Beloved Beatrice in the *Divine Comedy*. Martin Buber speaks of the complex of encounter as an "I-Thou" relationship of intellect to thing, as opposed to the "I-It" relationship of intellect as divorced from the thing with manipulative intent. And nearer to us, a "Romantic" poet recovering that ancient truth about intellect's proper relation to some other, Gerard Manley Hopkins, catches at the wonder possible in us through his words. In response to existent thing or things he names the "dapple-dawn-drawn Falcon" as borne up by "the rolling level underneath him steady air," till the falcon's stoop which has our "heart in hiding" as a startled prey; or he speaks of many "dappled" things, including Felix Randal the farrier, dead but yet Felix beyond death: Felix, at his "random grim forge" fitting "the great grey drayhorse his bright and battering sandal" in his own recovered devotion to things emerges bright beyond death's own

grim fettling of life, rising in his "heavenlier heart" beyond
dappleness. Such is the compactness of signs that is required if we
are to speak toward the mystery of existence itself, for the denotative
is inadequate to the reality of the existence to which the poet's signs
would speak. Exposition falls short of the captured or touched presence in the words. Thus words may at least prove an opening of
intellect upon presence. That is what great poetry gives us.

Hopkins as poet, we are trying to say, moves us from our remembered awe to a present steadiness of wonder in response to existence.
For wonder floods an intellect which is open to the mystery of existence itself. And we discover reflectively that this openness is jointly
effected by rational and intuitive intellect under the consent of will.
In advocating that openness and its pursuit as the desirable habit of
our intellectual being, we have been severe in judging its obverse:
that action of willful intellect which refuses its own recovery. It is a
perverse action in which the Beloved is reduced, first in an "I-It"
relation to intellect, whereupon intellect withdraws even more from
that binding reflected in the term *wonder*, in a sort of self-induced
transcendence of intellect over being. From that position, it seems
that being itself can be manipulated. That is the intellect we describe, as denotationally as we may, as rationalistic, Gnostic, and reductionist. And we have concluded that this perverse intellectual
habit is successful, not in its reductions of being, but only of its reduction of its own intellectual being.

Though our summary here tends to the anonymous, to the representative, in respect to the reductionist intellect, we need only recall
the growing struggle of the particular poet or painter or composer to
recover wonder through an openness to existing things as that
struggle was intensified from the late eighteenth century down to a
crucial, wider confrontation by increasingly disoriented opponents
of reductionism at the close of our own century. Under the pressures
of a rationalistic dominance of social affairs (in which are included
economic, political, religious affairs), the poet responds intuitively,
increasingly suspicious of rationality itself. If Matthew Arnold
could look at the nineteenth-century encounter of the new science

with the old religion and see ignorant armies clashing by night, that clash has become very nearly Armageddon in our century, as night has intensified on the battlefield. That is why we are attempting to recover some light to the reordering of the lines of battle. And though the poet may often lack the light which sound philosophy might supply, he has nevertheless, though most variously, recognized the necessity to resist rationalistic reductions of being. He opposes that established fear of submission to being, that habit of fear in response to which the denotative alone is given credence as signifying reality. Thus the denotative is purged of ambiguity for the sake of an insistent intellectual accountancy whereby intellect as I is safely removed from existential reality which is at best taken as an It. By such reduction of reality, it appears a suitable prime matter as it were, for its indifferent uses in building future dream gardens for the new Adam; intellect as its own creator.

The poet's intuitive concern for this past two hundred years is of great importance to us if we hope to recover intellectual virtues as the principal concern to "higher education." His attempts last century seem seldom associated with the academy. Such "Romantics," as they tend to be denotatively described (which term becomes pejorative in its uses by the Modernist Gnostic mind), found themselves on the fringes of the academy, as of other parts of the social body— the political or economic or religious. This century, especially from mid-century to its close, the poet has moved to the academy, becoming increasingly a "revolutionary" presence. Increasingly, then, he is a problem for the order of the academy. That his invasion has been a mixed blessing seems certain to me. Indeed, it has been often the poet who exacerbates the conflicts of intellect, more often than not deepening the darkness settling upon the academy.

Perhaps it may be briefly put that the poet, moved intuitively to oppose reductionism, in the end makes an ideology of openness itself, whereby the openness becomes the *end*, and not the *condition*, of the intellect's fulfillment. To "do one's own thing" becomes a slogan for a devotion to "one's own self," no less than the reductionist position. In the issue, as engaged on the grounds of the academy at our century's close, random openness for its own sake engages deliberate closedness for its own sake, though the *it* here must at last be translated as the isolated "self's" sake, whether we speak of the poet or the scientist. In the larger vision of the present dark battle, we must conclude the confrontation one between the pseudo-poet and the pseudo-scientist. Between them, and out of their confused encounter, the chaotic ground is marked in which barbarian intellect emerges triumphant, sometimes in the person of the pseudo-poet, sometimes in the person of the pseudo-scientist.

I would not side with the pseudo-poet in this conflict when he refuses the support of rational intellect to his intuitive deportment. For in the refusal, that deportment becomes an end in itself and not a gift of means toward a larger end. This false deportment by indirection underlines in his opponent those actions which, equally destructive of the academy, make it possible for both to flourish for a moment, just before the pending general collapse. What I mean is this: The decline of "liberal arts" in the academy is directly related to specialization, which has become a dominant principle in the academic community. Sir C. P. Snow has lamented our division into "Two Cultures"—those of arts and those of science. And so the failures of academic intellectuals, in respect to the liberal arts, have been first their failure to maintain an open vision upon "arts and sciences." In that vision, those devoted to the arts do not succumb to the intuitive habit as exclusive, or those to science of the denotative habit as exclusive. This is the failure in "specializations," the failure which prepares the way for intellectual barbarism now so erosive of the academy.

The new intellectual barbarian tends to dominate art in the interest of "culture," demanding curricula suited to "Multiculturalism." What that means is an education reduced, through pluralism declared a virtue, to an anarchy in which each person is his own culture. On the other hand, the opponent of the intellectual barbarian is rhetorically defeated and forced back upon a defense of higher education in pragmatic, materialistic terms. His ultimate defense becomes the general good of society, but his *good* is limited in the end to merely pragmatic immediacy of convenience, whether in respect to "miracle" drugs or economic programs or the like.* Though briefly put here, such is the sad spectacle of the failure of intellect in the academy. The result of this failure is that where there still linger remnants of colleges of "arts and sciences," one is hard pressed to find either the one or the other developing intellect to the fullness which such titles pretend to encompass.

It was in recognition of the complementary gifts of intuitive and rational intellect that liberal arts as a discipline was established in the Middle Ages. And once we began to disjoin "arts" from "sciences" as separate disciplines the process comes to such a stage by the close of the nineteenth century that the disintegration of intellect as the effect of "formal" education was generally assured. And since the pragmatic access to power rests more and more in rational science through its denotative productiveness, the ravaging of being becomes the established habit of our social existence and is displayed in the variety of commodities, whether in entertainment media or on store shelves, of which we are everywhere encouraged to be insa-

---

* There is an irony here: the "hard" sciences as established dominant in the academy continue less concerned with the invasion of that barbarian intellect which is moving at the moment under the banner of "Political Correctness." But what is left of our common sense, whether in the barbarian or scientific intellect, knows that particle physics is indifferent to cultural requirements, as are salmonella bacteria. Whatever the ascending complexities of our concern for H_2O, water, at that elementary denotated level is asocial and apolitical, and to this reduction of things the hard sciences hold with tenacity. It is among the remnants in the academy who are fighting over the residue of "arts" that the conflict rages most conspicuously, the hard sciences proceeding rather serenely on their denotative way. What these intellects do not realize is that when the connotative language decays to the anarchy of that extreme subjectivism which is unordered by rational intellect, their own days are numbered. Already they are becoming divided in the emerging battle on the flank of the academy, that between the "environmentalist" and "developer" of nature, recruits to those contending forces increasingly sought among the "hard" sciences. The point of their vulnerability is that they are dependent upon financial largesse, the flowing springs of which are in the control of political forces. Such is the comedy, one most depressing, which is now before us in institutions of "higher learning."

tiable "consumers." Indeed intellectual decay in the academy is a
principal route to our having become a "Consuming Society," the
latest degree of our self-reduction as society, beyond our having been
declared earlier merely a "Materialistic Society." Through a consumerism disjoined from stewardship in creation, we become the
strangest of creatures. Where Dante saw a figure of man as a lowly
worm in the chrysalis of the world but destined through grace to
develop toward angelic butterfly, we rather intensify our chrysalistic
defense against openness. We are alienated at last from becoming a
communal body enlarged toward the possible fulfillment of the participating member. Consider only our emphasis upon youth, upon
adolescence, whether in relation to pragmatic science's products that
promise eternal youth—cereals, soaps, medications, wrinkle-remov-
ers of all sorts—or those social, political, even religious, promises of
eternal youth as rationalized by the intellectual community itself.
For most central to these dislocations, leading to the disquiet of a
chrysalistic alienation, has been the academy bent upon justifying
regressive appetites, as opposed to its responsibility to make possible
the *spoudaioi*, the "mature" persons once valued in the ancient academy of Plato's day, and even into the early Renaissance, but not decisively beyond the time of John Milton.

Given on the one hand a serenity resting in a faith in the denotative, a serenity easily disturbed of course by intrusion of mystery with
its connotative dislocations of signs, and on the other the wild distortions of the connotative by a desperate intellect committed to dis-
locating itself from reality, it is little wonder that epithets are
inadequate. For the effective epithet, when effective because true to
the complexity of the reality it would name, always opens upon complexities of existence. The poet often reminds us of this necessity to
epithet, and it is of some importance to note the barbarian intellect's
pretense to the offices of poet, in which the prophetic nature of true
poetry—its power to call us back to known but forgotten things and
to the wonder of existence itself—is excluded. Thus those old resonant epithets, from Homer's "rosy-fingered Dawn" or "Odysseus, the
man of many devices," are supplanted by a Jesse Jackson as Odysseus,
chanting "Hey hey! Ho, ho! Western culture's got to go."

That we have made such perversion possible through intellectual decay of language is a point made succinctly by Michael Platt, who observes that the term *teenager* is not to be found in Webster's Dictionary in the 1930s but is a conspicuous entry after World War II. His ironic remark: "There were no teenagers before World War II. . . . The youths of that earlier time and all previous times wanted to grow up, to become men and women, fathers and mothers . . . . The Teenager [post-World War II] does not want to grow up; his heroes are other Teenagers, rock-stars of whatever age."* What needs adding is that such inclinations are not themselves new to adolescent experience. What is new is the general indulgence of these inclinations by the adult world. Thus Platt's characterization of the teenager is a characterization of an ideal we have established against reality, which he very aptly expresses: "The Teenager wants to live in the present as much as possible; his food is fast, his music is ephemeral, attention short, and his life nomadic. . . . Of all the lives a man can choose, the life of the Teenager is the one most conducive to conflating Being and Time. The Last Man, American style, is the Teenager."

Platt's teenager is not simply the young person between thirteen years old and twenty. He is rather the provincial intellect for whom being is an enemy and time a handicap to any victory over being. He is the intellectual Gnostic, and the teenage culture is itself a Disneyland established by that Gnostic intellect for its occasional relief from its losing battle with reality. But the illusion of an eternal youth, through Gnostic power, has consequential effect in our social world, evidenced by youth itself as now considered a toy for "adult" desire. Thus we have a culture in which we have programs elevating teenage desire by scientific satisfactions of it. In one formulation, as one perceptive critic puts it, we have a "culture" oriented by "sex without babies and babies without sex." Such is the never-neverland of adolescence.

In the present conditions of intellectual disorientation, it is an almost overwhelming task to recover language to the reality of expe-

---

* "Souls Without Longing," *Interpretation*, Spring 1991.

rience. Once we spoke of *pregnancy* in speaking of a woman "with child," or of her being "in a family way." Now pregnancy is reduced to a "sexually transmitted disease," as advocates of abortion put it. The mother is herself spoken of as an "incubator" by the advocates of birth through biotechnology. Little wonder that any epithet proves inadequate. If we have come to this pass, or impasse, between generations, localized in the words we use, we have done so in part because we do not recognize in the emerging teenager his intuitive recognition of a growing dislocation from reality. In the 1960s our "youth" contended with what they called the "establishment" and against what they called "the system." But those epithets were themselves most immediately derived from the abstractionism of the intellectual reductionists, which the young intuitively opposed. What they knew, but did not know the name of, was the denial of reality by such intellectual machinations. In their attempt to recover reality, lacking ordered intellectual actions, they could only imitate the error they opposed. When ignorant intellects clash, disorder is the only possible issue. Thus in our concern to recover reality through intellect, as oriented to reality by signifying words, it is the abstractionists themselves as discrete intellectual actors who must be confronted. They are the most immediate obstacle to recovery. And they are *particular* intellects, given in varying degrees to violations of intellectual virtues. It is they who must be forced to rethink their own natures if we are at last to engage reality to their health and to our general health as a community of creatures.

And so it is they who must be directly and explicitly engaged by our recovered language. It is continuingly futile to protest a *system* or an *establishment*. For in doing so, we will have lost by imitating those whom we confront. *Establishments*, like *social bodies*, exist as secondary formulations. The primary reality is that those otherwise vague phenomena exist only insofar as they are constituted by *persons*. The particular establishment exists by virtue of the real existence of the persons who constitute it. Any *system*, when that term intends to name ordered structures of social or physical or intellectual elements in concourse, is always a term imposed upon that named thing by our intellectual action. If the thing named is a reality at a secondary level of existence—a *system*, an *establishment*—and if we fail to recognize the primary ground in which it is established, we shall be able to deal with reality only at a secondary level. Failing this distinction, we shall fail to realize a crucial truth about such secondarily existent "things": neither an *establishment* nor a *system* in and of itself is the cause of evil, though our failure in the distinction may easily lead to evil consequences.

The difficulty lies not in the secondary dimensions of reality attributable to intellect, but in the primary dimension of reality, here specifically in the active address of discrete intellects to reality itself. We are speaking, then, of specific *persons* as agents of disorder, however systematic the pretense to ordering reality may be. One might, for instance, consider whether our long endeavor to come to terms with the philosophy of Hobbes or Hegel or Descartes has been such a considerable task to us precisely because we fail to make this very distinction, a distinction their thought must deny in the end, lest their "system" collapse. On this point, I recommend once more the little book by Gilson, *Methodical Realism*, which effectively engages Descartes and his successive Cartesean Idealists, for Gilson demonstrates the validity of my argument most persuasively. What we must recognize is that such thinkers, whose ideas have disturbing consequences to our late desire to recover legitimate order after these past three hundred years and more of wandering, are the mediate cause of our wandering. Through a gradual process, developed by their followers, the implicit consequence of their systematically willful separation from reality, through imposed intellectual systems which ignore common sense as common sense, requires that we bring actual experience to bear upon those systems. Such thinkers have (however well-meaning) bequeathed us false intellectual address to the complexity of existence, a complexity which cries out to us in our personal encounters with it in the present moment of our conscious life in this world. To approach such persons in this perspective is to discover that they suffer a decay of their bonding of intellect to reality, a bonding discovered to intellectual awareness through the instrumentality of signs rightly taken, of words oriented to truth and measured by the truth of things themselves, rather than presumed in themselves to be the ultimate measure of the truth of things.

Words suited to a concept, when concept is suited to reality, are what I mean by *true* words. Concepts willfully decreed as the cause of reality, simply by a willful act of attribution, are doubly removed from reality, in that they are empty in themselves and derive their emptiness from false concept, and empty of substantial referents in the signs employed. Intellect so acting inevitably decrees words innocent of the truth of things. But these words can be used only to answer emptiness with emptiness, leaving each intellect isolated in its own echo chamber. Thus intellect discovers itself entrapped, as for instance the Cartesean Idealist finds himself to be. Our words, to adapt famous lines of T. S. Eliot, will only maintain an illusion of the "streets"—of reality—which the streets cannot understand, given such entrapment.

It is only with the difficulty of intellectual labor that specific persons recover their own specificity from the purview of broad categories of ideas to which they have been reduced by manipulative uses of signs, of words, directed against their own nature as created intellectual creatures. That is why it becomes important to the recovery to engage specific intellectual creatures who manipulate others by that impiety. This is the necessary level of confrontation, a direct, local, immediate struggle with specific persons for the recovery of signs to proper relations to reality. The significant battle is precisely that: the battle over authority in signification. That is why the word is important, why it must be reestablished as anchored by our experience of reality at the most local level of our existence. The Gnostic intellect recognizes this as the issue at once, since it is upon the immediate local level of the specific person's being that he must apply force to sever that person from reality. His most formidable danger in the attempt is the specific person's common sense. Through common sense, one recognizes his dependence in reality, and one recognizes it always at the most local level. It is at that level, as actual person, that one engages actual contextual creation, in this place and at this present time. Only signs estranged from such an anchor of intellectual experience are suited to the process of distancing, of alienating, a particular intellectual creature from reality to his condition as "free" agent. By that disjoining in the name of freedom, one is made malleable by the illusion.

VI

The principle task of education—higher or lower—is to recover our words to their proper service in the fulfillment of discrete personhood, the proper end of our existential nature as intellectual creatures. It is a recovery possible only through the word's orientation to reality. Words thus understood anchor intellect, without which anchor intellect floats free in the vague currents of political and social winds, dragging the "freed" person along. It is thus that a person becomes content to be, not person, but *individual*, a redesignation which denies that the fulfillment of each creature's potentiality as person is the elementary ground in which alone community is viable. For the primary end of man is precisely that fulfillment of personhood, and the secondary ends he serves must be acknowledged as properly secondary. That is the point Jacques Maritain is making when he says: "The common good of the city implies an intrinsic ordination to something which transcends it . . . because it requires, by its very essence and within its proper sphere, communication or redistribution to the persons who constitute society. . . . To say . . . that society is a whole composed of persons is to say that society is a whole composed of wholes."

This is the paradox of the specific person's relation to community, leading Maritain to add to his argument, "It is the human *person* who enters society; as an individual, it enters society as a part whose proper good is inferior to the good of the whole [that is, of that whole society constituted of persons]. Because of the highest requirements of personality as such, the human person, as a spiritual totality referred to the transcendent whole, surpasses and is superior to all temporal societies. . . . With respect to the eternal destiny of the soul, society exists for each person and is subordinate to it." Maritain's "eternal destiny" is what I intend as the fulfillment of personhood, the justifying end of our community participation. It is in recognizing this truth about our personhood that the Gnostic thinker realizes the necessity of a persuasive substitute for the "transcendent whole" in reorienting the person. It is in this recognition that Marx, for instance, attempts a secular metaphysics of the "state."

In the light of this understanding of man in society, developed in Maritain's *The Person and the Common Good*, we realize the importance of recovering words as measured by reality, rather than supposing that words themselves measure reality. And that is why we must begin with the recognition that community is viable to the extent that it serves the fulfillment of its discrete members' personhood. Thus it becomes important to confront directly, by intellectual force, those who abuse words by divorcing them from reality in the interest of their dreams of reconstituting reality by abstract structure, in "systems" as ultimate ends. For such willful persons, the fulfillment of what I see as illusional desire is the only reality admissible, and since such an end makes of the dreamer a parasite upon reality itself, it is as intellectual parasite that he must be treated. Nowhere is this battle more decisively joined than in the academy, but nowhere is it more conspicuous as a problem for our social health than in the media's disorientations of sign through the appetite for spectacle— the academy and media "each making the other for to win," as Chaucer says of the shady relation of his Doctor and Apothecary. The recent demonstrations of media personnel as "liberal" for instance, while arresting in factual particularities, leave us still dealing only with symptoms. We have by the recognition of symptoms yet failed to penetrate to the root cause of the disease. That cause is disoriented intellect. If the root cause is to be exposed to the healing light of reality, it is to the root that we must descend.

Intellectual abstractionism, intent on restructuring reality to conform to willful desire, can be made to appear real only through such spectacle as the technologically sophisticated media supplies. The media's first necessity for success, then, is to put common sense to flight. And that is most likely to be accomplished if the superficial is made essential. In turn, that may be accomplished perhaps if the media gain our consent to the superficial as if it were the sophisticated, a substitution by association. For who would not be "up on the latest?" Who would not choose to be at the "cutting edge of Progress?" Who would not wish to be socially and politically and theologically "correct?" And so spectacle, the accident of the complexity of reality, becomes the simplified object of our intellect. In the process, common sense is pushed aside in favor of whatever large or startling figures are made available for further enlargement through advanced technology. Thus the media supply a "romantic" fare for our progressive appetite.

Recall, in this regard, the destructive effect in the social community of media spectacle when television brings us the latest public demonstration, whether an anti-war or pro-war, an anti-life or pro-life gathering. The destruction by false signs of the essential realities in such events has reached the point that community confidence in the validity of any purported community sign is dissipated, an effect in us which nevertheless argues that common sense will not long remain in exile. Slogans used in fighting advertising wars, whether to sell one candidate or one automobile or cereal or feminine hygenic product over another, erode signs. Signs attached to causes, whichever contentional side attached to them, raise a cynical response. From Vietnam to Desert Storm, we have been subjected to signs hurled at us like water-filled balloons, to the delight of the media in its concerns for Nielson ratings.

A retreat into cynicism, the tendency of our citizenry at this moment, is a retreat from the emptiness of sign, accompanied by an embittered sense of betrayal, but with no clear recognition of just who has betrayed us. It is that specific *who* that we must confront, a confrontation effective only when signs are recovered to an order of intellect relative to reality itself. Meanwhile, we fumble with emptied words. There is, for instance, a smothering presence upon community, named as abhorrent by all, including the purveyors of that vacuous presence: the Dread Bureaucracy. But always behind and beneath that dragon are particular minds, some of them ancient but still operative out of history upon the present, and some the present disciples of such minds. The "bureaucratic mind" either explicitly or tacitly operates on the presumption of autonomy in relation to complex reality. And it is upon that presumption that such minds erect depersonalized, mechanistically conceived abstractions such as *bureaucracy* or *establishment*, or such less pejorative abstractions as *individual* or *democracy*. Any word sufficiently emptied of relation to existential reality will serve, requiring only our consent to the peculiar coloring given the word by the abstracting mind. And so when the word embraced in its emptiness proves false, our inclination to use it pejoratively proves ineffective. Thus epithet removed from the communal recognition of any anchor in reality proves inadequate to exorcise the vaporous dragon. Again and again, we decry bureaucracy or the establishment or some such, but when we succeed in overcoming the thing decried we discover that we have only succeeded in substituting a species of the same abstractionism. Currently, for instance, the academy suffers from an "establishment" which overthrew the old academic "establishment" in the 1960s and 1970s. That is why this establishment, advocating "political correctness," has been so effective in establishing intellectual chaos as the intellectual principle of higher education.

Now to oppose presumptuous abstractionism by direct confrontation of persons holding or advancing such presumption at first earns one the complaint of an *ad hominem* irreverence, even unto declaring that the confronted person's "civil rights" are thereby threatened. For to insist, as is necessary, that untenable abstraction as intellectual principle has immanent origin in a person bearing a particular name is a most disquieting experience to such a person, in proportion to his long comfort in the sanctuary of his abstractionism. But immanent intellectual actions are identified properly with *me* in my name always and are inescapably personal in relation both to their effect on my own personhood and their effect on other persons. It is this first effect, upon myself as actor, that is most difficult to make clear. False intellectual action dislocates the actor's own possible actuality as an intellectual creature. The potential of a fullness of being is prevented if that particular being takes refuge within abstraction, as thieves on occasion used to take sanctuary in the local church.

That analogy is most pertinent. For having removed our belief in the consequential effect of sin upon the sinning person, through presumptions establishing intellectual autonomy, abstraction becomes the only rescuing paraclete. Sin, we used to insist, is a failure of intellectual action through willfulness. But we circumvent acknowledgment if we first declare the act of sinful intellect separate from effect, so that effect becomes lamentable. Thus the act itself is supposed understandable and so acceptable by intellect itself. Sin is thus reduced to mere error, to be corrected by a newly revised abstract system, so that the social machinery will run the more smoothly. Little wonder that, given two hundred years of such dislocation, it becomes impossible to teach today's students Dante's central issue in the *Inferno:* what is most destroyed by sin is the soul of the sinner. Even as a merely speculative idea the point proves evasive for the student raised on modernist fare. There is incredulity when, in Purgatory, one finds repentant souls, the effects of whose sins in their earthly lives have been murder or treachery. When told that in Dante's vision these are destined for Heaven through their confession and amendment and submission to grace, the children of our permissive age are disturbed because "justice is not done."

The particular person wielding abstractionism against reality, or cacooned from reality by abstractionism, is not easily persuaded that the potential of his own discrete nature is thus willfully held hostage—that he is divided against himself. That is at worst merely an "error" awaiting final issue beyond the immediate existential arena of the world in which he operates and within which he distorts reality to the detriment of others no less than of himself. He holds his position resolutely by denaturing not only himself, but insofar as his power in that arena allows, by denaturing others. The saint or martyr, and to a lesser degree the hero, resist and overcome that attempt in the final reckoning of intellectual actions. But meanwhile the continuing disturbances of dislocation affect the social or political or educational dimensions of community. It is in this more limited dimension of our existence that the dislocator must be confronted directly.

That is why such confrontation seems so "personal," leading to an initial defense instinctively based in rejected but still remembered principles of civilized conduct among intellects in quest of truth.

Thus the objection that such confrontation is *ad hominem*. And so we need to put the necessity of confrontation more clearly, if symbolically and at an extreme, in reference to our common knowledge of this century. A Hitler or Stalin, a Pol Pot or Saddam, require our direct and "personal" confrontation, which from their point of view will at once be considered *ad hominem*. Always the intellectual tyrant acts in the name of *humanity*, an emptied word, of course. So that hard pressed, he will plead his own humanity. It is easier to confront such deconstructors of being as Stalin or Saddam, given the spectacle they afford, than to confront the less conspicuous tyrants busily deconstructing reality in the name of humanity. That is why Solzhenitsyn was taken as such a rude intruder into the intellectual sanctuary of abstractionism when he insisted that he sees "the same stones in the foundations of a despiritualized humanism" pervasive in Western society and "any type of socialism," including communism, which is but another species of "naturalized humanism."

VII

Earlier, we quoted Michael Platt on the American teenager: "The Teenager wants to live in the present as much as possible; his food is fast, his music ephemeral, attention short, and his life nomadic. . . . Of all the lives a man can choose, the life of the Teenager is the one most conducive to conflating Being and Time. The Last Man, American style, is the Teenager." He is, as we then argued, the provincial intellect. To see him in operation we need only consider his destructive manipulations of connotative terms as if simply denotative and as if justified fully by denotative science. Our illustration is from a conspicuous battle currently raging over a specific social, political, but ultimately religious issue, but it could be paralleled by similar battles in which the attempt to establish the truth of things is opposed by the desire for the comfort of intellect in declaring truth rather than discovering truth. My instance is the battle between the "pro-life" forces and the "pro-choice" forces over the question of abortion. What I emphasize here is the manipulation of language to ends submerged in their actualities by language itself. I take departure in two carefully analytical works by Donald DeMarco, *Biotech-nology and the Assault on Parenthood* (1991) and *In My Mother's Womb* (1987). As the battle intensifies over this particular question, what is increasingly evident is that the "pro-life" side of the argument discovers itself ill-equipped to maintain its position (which is my own, if that were not already evident) precisely because it has been ill-prepared to marshal rational intellect to the support of its intuitive recognition of what is at issue. Professor DeMarco's books are intended to support that recovery, and he is particularly perceptive in revealing the pretension to rationality by the forces defending "choice."

In doing so, he shows that at the bottom of the issue lies a perversion of love itself in the interest of the convenience of "lifestyle." What we discover, if we look closely, is a sentimentality focused on the intellect as disjoined from complex reality. The ploy is that man is the ultimate consumer of reality by intention, leading to a personal consumerism whereby one may have "sex without babies and babies without sex," as Professor DeMarco puts it in relating the companionable ideas of abortion and surrogacy: "In abortion, the child is depersonalized while the mother is praised for her courage to choose. By contrast in surrogacy, the child is elevated to the status of 'tenant' (orphaned at conception from its parents) while the mother depreciates to the status of an 'incubator.'" The child as intellectually manipulated in its declared nature, whether reduced to nonperson in the interest of an abortion or elevated to consumer product by surrogacy, has the sanction of our reductionist science. Thus Dr. Elizabeth Connell, a president of the Association of Planned Parenthood Physicians, assures her colleagues that "pregnancy is a kind of nasty communicable disease" and therefore abortion is to be justified.

At that same conference (cited by DeMarco in *In My Mother's Womb*) three employees of the Center for Disease Control in Atlanta give a paper called "Unwanted pregnancy: a sexually transmitted disease"—thus an implicit sanction from the Federal Government itself. In that argument, pregnancy is established as an evil out of which the man of science can bring a good—either by abortion or transference of the disease to a surrogate incubator, depending upon the desire of the woman, who is little aware of the degree to which she is under the power of science as the god answering her vague desire. Thus it is established that the woman as absolute individual in command of her "body" determines whether the creature conceived shall live or die. The moral responsibility is shifted from the manipulator by that slight of logic. With that absolutist position established, Magda Denes as "pro-choice" advocate can declare that "Abortion is murder of a most necessary sort," made necessary to the convenience of the erstwhile incubator.

What is easily overlooked, in the illusion of such absolute freedom of a woman with her body, is the possibility of her intellectual enslavement to a gnostic power greater than her own. We need only remember what seems already forgotten: the prospect of a Super Race through the manipulations justified by established law under the Nazi's utopian dreams, balanced on the other hand by the mass exterminations. There is the large and startling representation which we deny at our peril, the intellectual position justified in relation to the individual woman writ large in its consequences: on the one hand, the gas chamber; on the other, the managed incubation of a true "Aryan" race—on the one hand, private abortion; on the other, private surrogacy. The reduction here is of the spectacle, not of the essence, of the action. The degree to which this intellectual position has become embroiled in the confusions of the law already removes it from the pretense that the issue is merely one of individual privacy.

The agitated battle over abortion and biotechnologies, now so intrusive upon the mystery of parenthood, centers in the mystery of *being* in its human dimension. It has led to abrupt and violent encounters, whose stresses upon social legalities cause disturbances to the intuitions of our community deeper than legal or scientific letters of the law can resolve. A mother who bears her daughter's children, becoming thereby both mother and grandmother to newborn twins, fascinates us by the novelty of the terms, which as terms do not correspond to the strange reality they attempt to characterize. It is the term's inadequacy which arrests us. Meanwhile, organized protestors besiege abortion clinics and are carried away to jail, to judgments of incarceration and fines. That both these events involve violence centering in the mystery of being will be seen only through words restored to reality. But that such violence grows out of a conflict of intellectual principles concerning the nature of being, that old "medieval" concern we have thought ourselves escaped from, is already significant beyond those spectacles of violence in which the media seems to take profitable delight. They present one event in the "Lifestyle" section of our family paper, the other in police reports. The phenomena are both significant, however, of the collapse of intellectual discourse, and indeed might be suitable as parables to enlighten the difficulties of "higher education," were it not that the violence centers upon actual human creatures who are defenseless before the gnostic manipulations of their arrested natural being, through the sophisticated tools of technology.

We may at least make the suggestion of analogy, however, for through that suggestion perhaps we may come to consider intellect itself in its own infant nature—its nature as an existing member of the whole body of individual personhood, a member of our "self" whose potential is to be husbanded toward full birth. Our present educational hospitals seem given to effecting either stillbirths or retarded births of intellect, preventing by false science the full life of the mind. They do so through perverse manipulations of intellectual being, in that they violate by reductionism that mystery of existence which is revealed in and through human beings in their discrete personhood. There are many symptoms of our world's systematic violations of being, regularly made explicit in those words and pictures reporting daily events in our dominating media, the media having become the ultimate dictators of sign to the community of mankind. What is to be recovered is the use of words anchored deeply even as the words float on current events—the surface flow of this moment's history.

We must recover that control of the word because the existing world is committed to the stewardship of man because he is an intellectual creature by the gift of his nature. The recovery of responsibility, or so I contend, will be possible only through the intellectual deportment required of man by virtue of that gift, each within the

limits of his own nature. Now, that responsibility is incipiently
known by each of us, out of our inclinations toward at least some
things other than our own isolated selves. That is the inclination in
us called love, governed and ordered by wisdom. What we must recover through "higher education," then, are those virtues of sign—of
words—as properly governing the deportment of our love in our response to the mystery of existence itself—our own person's existence
as well as the largesse given as mediate to our love, a largesse called
the whole of creation. Such is that deportment of intellect in relation to the created soul in its relation to the created world which is
called *philosophy*.

PART III

NOW AND THEN

8

Modern, Modernism, and Modernists

I N HIS *Copius and Critical Latin-English Lexicon* (1850), E. A. Andrewes gave extensive treatment to the term *modus*. The entry gives a fleeting glimpse of Rome's history, of the rise and fall of empire, if one take an imaginative perspective. *Modus* begins with a firm sense of *measure*, as in physics. It moves to metaphorical *way* or manner of conduct. And it comes at last to designate time fleeting: *just now, a moment ago*, or with more hope, *at this very moment*. What might interest us is a similar progressive meaning in that term's cognates as they enter English and American usage by the time of Andrewes's *Lexicon*, that decade in which appeared a theory concerning "The Preservation of Favoured Races in the Struggle for Life," popularly known as *The Origin of Species* (1859).

Modus's history in English begins to gather excitement in its descent to us, as we watch its meaning shifting to reflect the spirit of the age. For Shakespeare, *modern* meant the *everyday*, the *ordinary* or *commonplace*. For us it means *the very latest* and when attached to ideas or things about us carries an undercurrent of meaning: necessity. What is modern, we *must* have. For though we may not have followed the connection analytically, we nevertheless tend to respond to our moment of history from an assumption that he who is most modern is most fit to survive; he who is most fit to survive is blessed with greater happiness. Happiness, therefore, is a natural, political, and social right, a conclusion whose denial reveals the denier himself as Neanderthal. Such is our climate of thought, in which thought itself has increasingly eroded, replaced by the impulse of unexamined desire pretending to be thought. And so we have come to the final decade of our century, pushed and pulled along by desire, only to find ourselves suspecting a precipice of some sort directly ahead, compelled to it by a momentum of survival that now raises very old questions: Survival for what? Survival as what? There begin to stir intellectual misgivings about *Modernism*, a term being gradually replaced by *postmodern*, which suggests our having somehow crossed into an unknown country in which the causes of survival are less surely known than once supposed. If we have not yet tumbled over a precipice, we seem at least to find ourselves on a flat earth, fearing it may end at the near horizon in a collapse into elemental chaos, where once we held the dream of infinite progress: up and away to perfection.

But even within this climate of uncertain thought about existence, about survival beyond the clutches of chaos, *modern* itself survives as a term of consent, one of those "god terms" Richard Weaver explores in *The Ethics of Rhetoric* (1953). It survives in company with other "coterie passwords," though to speak them seems more and more a faint whistling in the dark past the graveyard of ideas: *science, progress, freedom*, even *democracy*. Weaver observes of *modern* as used forty years ago: "To describe anything as 'modern' is to credit it with all the improvements which have been made up to now. Then by a transference the term is applied to realms where valuation is, or ought to be, of a different source. In consequence, we have 'modern living' urged upon us as an ideal; 'the modern mind' is mentioned as something superior to previous minds. . . . It is as if a difference of degree had changed into a difference of kind." But if thought, when we are forced to it, very quickly reveals the dangers of mistaking degree for kind in our everyday, ordinary, commonplace conduct of our existence, it may take a considerable forcing of thought to bring a clarification when we have drifted in the confusion for a very long time, as Weaver believes us to have done.

In this light, we see it no accident, though consequent to accidental intellectual error, that the latest cliché for our current state of confusion over Modernism, issuing in a postmodern world, is spoken of as "the end of history" in some intellectual circles. The cliché is already overtaken by history itself, as witnessed in Eastern Europe and the Middle East. But *something* has happened to us. If not an end of history, we do have an inescapable sense of having somehow crossed a border of some sort.

I

In this moment of confession, feeling our development arrested and so fearful of survival, fit or unfit, we might well wish to recover as we may some dependable bearings in this vague new world which proves increasingly hostile to the remnants of desire still in us. A preliminary exploration of the intellectual history of *Modern, Modernism,* and *Modernist* as that history, since Shakespeare, reflects a loss of a certain innocence: that might prove a suitable beginning to a recovery of thought beyond mere impulse, a recovery of an intellectual orientation to this moment of history that is peculiarly ours. In doing so, what we begin to discover is that since World War II there has appeared a considerable literature exploring our concern in more than a preliminary manner. Much of it is directed upon the most popular religion of the Western world since the Renaissance, Modernism, as our citing Richard Weaver begins to show. Philosophers, historians, and poets of a particular intellectual deportment began to appear in the 1950s, remarking the changes in our "ways" and "manners" as evolved from certain Renaissance principles, often lamenting or rejecting those principles as deep causes of current intellectual and spiritual discomfort.

These thinkers, who constitute a conservative intelligentsia, take as a point of departure our current confusions, whether in the political, social, philosophical, or aesthetic deportment of Modernism. They are concerned with our sense of dislocation, our sense of having lost our way in the world. And in their critiques of that condition, in the analysis of our thought and the exploration of the sources

of that thought—the history of our ideas—they come upon a principal cause of our dislocation, our separation of intellect from reality,
whether they locate a beginning in Joachim of Flora in the twelfth
century, or William of Occam in the fourteenth century, or
Descartes in the seventeenth century. That is, they point to an intellectual defiance of reality through "ways" and "manners" unsupport-
able by experience itself. This Modernist state of mind as it develops
down to us out of the late Middle Ages we speak of variously: *angst*,
alienation, ennui. Such terms intend to name the discrete person's
baffled recognition of his exile from all save his own consciousness,
which he tends to find intolerable as well. He is anything but happy
with that "self," though the pervasive idea of happiness as a right has
seemed to require the elevation of the self. Thus elevated, the self
finds itself *out of this world*, to borrow a modern phrase whose anchor
in old understandings of ecstasy are long since decayed. For what
that condition means in Modernism, at its end, is a severe isolation
of consciousness. Such is the spiritual state often recorded by our
poets, even poets as ancient as the Psalmist. But the Psalmist at the
outset of Western intellectual history still held to a transcendent as
an appeal beyond the limits of his intellectual finitude. The Modernist, however, is burdened by a faith that disallows any reference of
the self as an existence to the transcendent. It is a denial required as
an act of faith, established by a central Modernist principle: intellectual autonomy.

Such, in a partisan brevity, are the mental circumstances of the
individual as projected by much of "modern" art. Paul Johnson, in
his *Modern Times: The World from the Twenties to the Eighties* (1983),
finds Modernism emerging as a common ideology at the turn of this
century, citing Cubism and Surrealism as instances. It underlies the
purportedly new fiction of Proust and Joyce, the new poetry of Eliot
and Pound, and especially that new science which so fascinated the
ideological artist, Freudianism, which science has late in our century
appeared more subjective art that science. One could develop this
point about Freudianism by showing its progress as an influence in
art, first upon the artist as radical, then upon criticism as settled more
or less mechanically into the academy, with Freudianism the instru-

ment used to disassemble all literature from Homer on, but at last gradually rejected by the ever present radical artist, some of whom return to a reality denied by Freudian perspectives. At the moment Freudianism lingers in an antiquated condition in humanistic disciplines in the academy. But instead of such an extended exploration as might be undertaken, let us rather look at Johnson's consideration of Freud as Gnostic. And we might follow the course of this Gnostic psychology in an emerging conservative intellectual poet, T. S. Eliot.

In his initial exploration of Modernism as an intellectual malady permeating the history of our century, Johnson begins with a quotation from a speech made in Paris in 1905. Sergei Diaghilev, of the *Ballets Russe*, speaks "in the name of a new and unknown culture, which will be created by us, and which will also sweep away" the old culture. And so, he says, "I raise my glass to the ruined walls of the beautiful palaces, as well as to the new commandments of a new aesthetics." Such romantic bravado perhaps steadies the artist, but only for a moment, given the nihilistic implications to which he must now supply "new commandments." We observe that, as Dada rises in art to the increasing fascination of the popular media, a debate of devastating consequences rises on the European continent, concerned with the subversion of *Kultur* by *Zivilization*. In that debate, the German intelligentsia prepares the way in the popular mind by which National Socialism enters that mind and establishes a dictatorial kingdom.* The horrors issuing from that consequence of ideas still linger with us, of course.

---

* Gerhart Niemeyer remarks my borrowing from Paul Johnson, suggesting that Johnson probably takes this theme from Spengler. Niemeyer, in Germany at the time, remembers no such debate. My point might perhaps be better made by recourse to a piece by the philosopher and theologian Emil L. Fackenheim in his "German's Worst Enemy" (*Commentary*, October 1990). Professor Fackenheim, responding to the breaching of the Berlin Wall on November 9, 1989, remembers November 9, 1938, and his observations the morning after *Kristallnacht*, walking about Berlin with his friend Karl Rautenberg and observing the destruction. The two dates juxtaposed sets him to thinking of Germany's "worst enemy," herself, and he reflects on the Romantic response to Napoleon's defeat of Prussia at Jena, as represented by Fichte. France, the

But long before this adaptation of Nietzsche to the interests of a closed nationalistic society, Nazi Germany, Western civilization had indeed helped prepare the advent, not only of Hitler but of Stalin also. It had done so by elevating Modernism to the status of secular religion. If *Kultur* proves deceptive, as it does, it is able to do so in part by harnessing an intuitive reaction to this other deceptiveness inbuilt in Western *Zivilization* which feeds a growing, disoriented desperation in the popular spirit. And the Western intelligentsia began building that source of spiritual desperation as a religion, overthrowing Classical and Christian understandings of the relation of intellect to reality, beginning in the early Renaissance. One of our Modernists, who repudiated the position, recognized his own narrow escape from Modernist entrapment just as Hitler emerged triumphant. T. S. Eliot speaks of his contemporaries, in *The Rock* (1934), as a "wretched generation of enlightened men," caught up by dreams "of systems so perfect that no one will need to be good." Ours has become "an age which advances progressively backwards." But Eliot here is not looking at either Germany or Russia, though very much aware of what is going on in those regions. He is speaking to England and America.

II

If one is Richard Weaver, Eric Voegelin, or Leo Strauss, members of that conservative intelligentsia rising in the 1950s, he will have heard

---

hereditary enemy to the West, must be withstood and by a summoning of the medieval German spirit. In that vision of a past greatness, summoned to a present recovery toward future survival, Fichte (says Professor Fackenhein) emphasized that Germany's fission sprang not from a Volk like other Europeans, but from the Urvolk, "alone endowed with a language uncontaminated by alien (i.e., Latin) elements." A German "essence" must be recovered to withstand encroaching corruptions. If the terms *Kultur* and *Zivilization* were not salient in debates in the 1920s and 1930s, a certain ambience of thought compatible to the terms as Johnson uses them seems to have been at work in the public spirit, with a growing suspicion of the "outlandish" represented by France. The preparation of the public spirit, in Professor Fackenheim's version, had been underway at least since the early nineteenth century.

in Sergei Diaghilev's words of "raising" his glass to the "ruined walls of the beautiful palaces" and "to the new commandments of a new aesthetics" an ironic echo of Pico della Mirandola's fifteenth-century *Oration on the Dignity of Man*. Pico speaks to "Man" through his own fictional version of "God": "You shall determine your own nature without constraint from any barrier, by means of the freedom whose power I have entrusted [to] you. . . . I have made you neither heavenly nor earthly, neither mortal nor immortal so that, like a free and sovereign artificer, you might mold and fashion yourself into that form you yourself shall have chosen." Pico's joyful anticipation of a new man is of a new Adam, to be built out of nature as appropriated and transformed by science—by knowledge. In short by a Gnostic manipulation of being itself. Thus a new Adam is to be commanded into existence in a new genesis, by man's own intellect, whereby he may make himself whatever he chooses.

Such is the dream at the heart of Renaissance Humanism. And it is Pico's dream that we find reduced to a somewhat desperate bravado by Diaghilev in the face of existence as it increasingly confronts intellect as a nightmare. The new Adam predicted is just ahead of Diaghilev in that corporal on Germany's eastern front, in that would-be priest in Russia—in Hitler and Stalin. And the Eden anticipated? A general destruction of persons and whole peoples in our century so great that even now we have not reckoned the cost at the material level, let alone at the level of spiritual consequence to the survivors. That is the destruction in the social and natural arena of the new Eden. But we find Pico's man as "sovereign artificer" to be also very much the protagonist in our poetry and fiction, a literature dominated by pathos, whose residual effect in the continuing popular spirit is its justification of the antihero. James Joyce's artificer in his *Portrait of the Artist as a Young Man*, Stephen Dedalus, is in the end reduced to cryptic notes to himself in his self-exile from creation. Eliot's Prufrock writes a self-love song of despair over self-awareness, declaring that he "should have been a pair of ragged claws/ Scuttling across the floors of silent seas." Such is the end to that dream of Pico's promise, whereby man as his own god might mold and fashion himself into whatever form he shall have chosen.

And so we must require of our view of modern times a perspective more inclusive that Johnson's "world from the twenties to the eighties." What we must consider is that Romantic Age of Western history, which is subdivided by scholars in their pursuit of specialties into at least the divisions Renaissance, Enlightenment, Romantic, Modern. That is the span of intellect's elevation of man beyond all barriers in his dream of forming himself as he chooses. Or to put the reality of the attempt, as Voegelin and Weaver and C. S. Lewis and others put it: it is the period in which particular intellects propose forcing other men to do as they choose. Humanism, rising in Italy in the fourteenth century, aimed at establishing rational autonomy as the principle overriding all others, the principle whereby mankind is to be reconstituted, made over, as certain men shall have chosen. Humanism chose, in this interest, to exalt an amorphous idea, freedom, as a means against the "establishment" of the day, that establishment constituted by the empire, the Church, and the feudal social order.

The old establishment was seen, from the humanist's perspective, to be based on an intolerable commitment to a cosmic order overarching both man and nature, and the whole of that order under the purview of the Cause of man and nature, namely a transcendent God. The rationale of that old view had been established by medieval Scholasticism. That metaphysics not only gave rational order to social affairs; it also supplied the artist with his justifications of image. And even when the metaphysical ground of metaphor itself was discarded in the eighteenth and nineteenth centuries, it still had lingering presence in art, as in Joyce's structuring of fiction in relation to the elements: fire, air, water, earth. Nevertheless—the metaphysical grounds of metaphor in decay—the poet found himself increasingly in exile from his fellows following the dominance of empirical science, though it was an exile more as poet than as man—or so it at first seemed to the poet. That is, he felt exiled because of his special calling, rather than because of his special nature in creation as spiritual creature, a nature established and defended by medieval Scholasticism.

Renaissance Humanism entered into religious debate early on, in opposition to the established metaphysics, and it did so over the question of the authority of autonomous intellect in its relation to other intellects and to nature. St. Augustine's distinction between the earthly and the heavenly cities provided terms of a metaphor to be used rhetorically but in a Nominalistic manner. For by this dislocation it becomes possible to persuade a popular support for a new order. In this respect, as Weaver points out, Occam manages a defeat of logical realism, "the crucial event in the history of Western culture" Weaver says. This late scholastic, Occam, then, proves one of the fathers of Humanism, the practical result of his victory (in Weaver's words) the banishment of "the reality which is perceived by the intellect and to posit as reality that which is perceived by the senses." Such a shift turns intellect to the earthly city. In this commandeering of language, whereby universals are denied any real existence, the transcendent itself falls in question. Nevertheless, the convenience of naming the senses' evidence arbitrarily, disregarding metaphysical ground to existence, gives rise to a new science which will find its justification in autonomous intellect, namely philology, the Gnostic tool needed to manipulate being. Philology gains a "universal" authority as a science in the nineteenth century, significantly in a school of religious thought specifically identifying itself as "Modernism," about which more presently. But first, our concern is with a new attention to the earthly city which man is to form as he chooses, the center of a new Eden for this new Adam.

Even if there is here no abiding city, as St. Paul and St. Augustine argue, their understanding of that truth was unacceptable to the emerging Humanism of the fourteenth and fifteenth centuries. With a new emphasis on Progress as the emerging Holy Spirit of Modernism, summoned by autonomous intellect and supported by the marvels of emerging empirical science, the Gnostic intent to power began to transfer the glories of St. Augustine's heavenly city to a potential evolution of the earthly city itself. It is immanent in London or Paris or the city-states of Southern Europe. Thus utopian fantasy gains a persuasive presence in popular thought, supported by the practical manifestations of new things and new wealth out of new science. Though not yet perfect, there was in the new

City promise of perfection, a prospect of a capital Eden to be realized through accumulated riches in the Italian city, or perhaps to be
brought about in a new ground, the New World, as it began to supply
those riches.   One may measure a progress along that road upon
which Western intellect, crowned by its autonomy, set out: from
Bacon's dream of London transformed as *The New Atlantis* (1624) to
T. S. Eliot's nightmare London of *The Waste Land* (1922), Eliot's
"Unreal City" in which intellect, even that of a Tiresias, finds that it
"can connect/Nothing with nothing."

III

We must not forget that Renaissance Humanism and its subsequent
strains as they yet survive are quite "religious." The new philosophy
as propounded by Manetti and Valla emphasized work, as would the
subsequent Puritan "work ethic." For work as residual idea bore a
sense of moral responsibility out of Old Testament teachings, especially as traced to man's fall in the Garden, whereby he is doomed to
make his way through the world "by the sweat of his brow." Josef
Pieper puts this necessity in its proper perspective in that lively decade of our century in his *Leisure: The Basis of Culture* (1952), with an
"Introduction" by T. S. Eliot, and in his *In Tune With the World; A
Theory Of Festival* (1963). Unlike the Puritan adaptation, however,
the Renaissance humanist's appropriation of a work ethic to the expediency of its philosophy shifts the Puritan spiritual end to secular
temporal end, from a means to salvation to a means to pleasure in
this world.* It is as if Epicurus as modified by Marcus Aurelius supplanted St. Augustine as developed by St. Thomas Aquinas in that
new hagiography under construction by Humanism.

---

*   It is necessary to "universalize" the prospects of pleasure if there is to be a
     popular support of the ends, exhibited in a general consent to labor. That
     consent to labor must be general to be effective. A "people" must be devoted to
     a temporal goal, since labor can be measured in relation to that goal—giving
     origin to a variety of "five-year-plans" that emerge from this shift from tran-
     scendent to temporal ends to be pursued with the fervor of labor as man's
     principal virtue. In a sense, we find an end to this species of "work ethic" in

A moral philosophy is necessary to pragmatic actions under-taken in the name of Progress, toward the immanent Eden. And so a morality with the force of a religion is required to order and com-mand the source of power needed to transform the earthly city, whether into a Puritan's "city on a hill" or the humanist's heaven brought to earth in a new vision, Utopia. The source of the power required is that commonality mankind, re-Christened under its own auspices as Humanity, with religious overtones that facilitate the shift of the soul's worship from God to man. In this shift, the active life supercedes the contemplative life for the intellectual. There is a celebrated flowering with that shift, the emergence of the "Renais-sance Man" most variously accomplished. Chaucer's somewhat ten-der if satiric portrait of the Knight's Squire is of such a Renaissance Man in the making, even as a less kindly Chaucer shows also the decay in the old Establishment under humanistic attack in his por-trait of the Monk. The contemplative as "egg head," to use our own metaphor, is the Clerk of Oxenford, who had rather have twenty manuscripts of Aristotle and commentaries on him than the world's riches as coveted and pursued by the Monk. The Clerk, precise in a

---

the disillusionment of Russian and East European "workers" in this decade. Boris Yeltsin in *Against the Grain* (1990) speaks scathingly of the secret privi-leges of the new ruling class, the member of the official Communist Party, who on rising to the top becomes the elect, shopping in private for goods only dreamed of by the worker. As member of that elect body, he experiences "full communism: From each according to his abilities, to each according to his needs." But the principal applies to only "a couple of dozen people" at the top. Meanwhile, in the communist satellites as they collapse, we discover East German Eden at Wandlitz: a compound for the twenty-three members of the Politburo. John D. Rockefeller didn't have it so good, we might say. Similarly in Czechoslovakia, Hungary, Bulgaria, even Poland. In Romania, Ceausecu had eighty private homes maintained year round, where few others had even an opportunity of heating one hovel. He shot one hundred deer on one day, out of season. Bulgaria's Zhivkov had his own version of such excess: this seventh-grade dropout is the great author of fifty ghostwritten books, two of which as translated brought "royalty" the equivalent of fourteen years of salary of the average Bulgarian worker. For a fuller account of these workers' para-dises, see Charles Parmiter, "The Red Aristocrats," *Reader's Digest*, October 1990.

speech which is full of "high sentence," echoes old intellectual virtues now still seldom encountered, even in our academy. For "gladly
wolde he lerne and gladly teche." Prufrock, at his late distance, can
only remark sardonically his own propensity to being "full of high
sentence," adding in marvelous understatement that his are sentences "a bit obtuse."

A subtle but effective shift of intellectual object by Renaissance
Humanism lies precisely here: the contemplative life declared in-
effectual requires that moral philosophy shift its end to humanity,
abandoning the old orientation of the soul to the transcendent. The
tea party Prufrock attends may bear some residual trace of the old
virtue of high sentence, though reduced to "some talk" of
Michelangelo. But it seems possible in our century to justify high
sentence socially if it serves to raise "social consciousness." (Tom
Wolfe gives us a devastating account in his *Radical Chic* and *Mau-
Mauing the Flak Catchers*.) Indeed, moral philosophy, it was suggested early in the evolution of Humanism, is higher than either
physics or metaphysics when one recognizes its new end. St.
Thomas's central sciences—physics and metaphysics—are not
sufficient to the day. And even the new physics, only just beginning
to emerge, is principally a means in a new alchemy whereby, as Pico's
"God" suggests, Gnostic intellect may establish itself as sovereign
artificer. Gerhart Niemeyer remarks, citing the work of Frances
Yates and D. P. Walker, that Pico sets out from Hermes Trismegistus
and the vision of the Renaissance *magus*, who through white magic
anticipated such a reformation that the stellar constellations could
be manipulated in manipulating humanity. By the establishment of
such a power over existence, the Gnostic artificer would make of
mankind whatever he chooses. Where St. Thomas Aquinas had
been interested in Aristotle as physicist and metaphysician, the new
humanist was rather interested in Artistotle's *Politics* and his
Nicomachean Ethics as instruments of a re-naturing of humanity itself. (On this re-naturing, both Eric Voegelin and Leo Strauss had
incisive things to say in the 1950s, as does Etienne Gilson in *From
Aristotle to Darwin and Back Again*, in 1971.)

The medieval view of man's existence in creation prohibited the radical intent buried in such a term as *freedom*, the intent of establishing unrestricted intellectual autonomy. In that old view "intellectual autonomy" is a contradiction in terms under the principle of cosmic order. But the new movement is beginning to call the cosmos in question. Its point of attack: creation's relation to an enveloping Cause. The transcendent, either as belief or as actuality, stands athwart the way of intellectual autonomy. The new Humanism, pursuing intellectual freedom, is of the city born, the largest cosmos admissible to its concerns of the moment. A range of time toward the future is one thing; a larger geographical range quite another. So that insofar as it would extend to empire in a present, those member extensions must be replicas of itself. It is in this sense that nationalism intends to be a universal denying submission to diversity in the local, a cause of internal tension no less than cause of foreign wars putatively territorial; but not territorial in a merely geographical sense. Considering this aspect of nationalism, we recognize as suitable to it the famous *New Yorker* cartoon map of the United States, New York City enlarged like the goose's liver. There is, then, a provincialism built into the emerging community of mind in service to the ideology of intellect as autonomous, a provincialism increasingly dooming intellect to being timebound while increasingly indifferent to the reality of place. For a Gnostic exercise over being requires a reduction of this particular place in order to service the Gnostic intent. This local city, then, becomes an extension of this Gnostic intellect; time future is a way of speaking of an occupation of all place by that intellect, but tomorrow.

Intellect conceived of as autonomous is by that conception bound to an attempt to overthrow the old view of reality. And for all its pretense to champion individual freedom for all intellects, it must establish the authority of particular intellects. That is what is involved at last as a necessity to Pico's prophecy. What the strongest intellect knows, when committed to the principle of intellectual autonomy, is that it is fundamentally committed to its own autonomy over all else. To believe otherwise is to surrender any possibility of establishing what it wishes mankind to be. With the emergence of technology out of empirical science, we shall see a suitable metaphorical representation in something like Frankenstein's monster, but the ground to monstrous versions of mankind which have overwhelmed our century with spectacles of destruction is already present in principle in Pico. The strongest intellect will make other intellects, and through them remake being in general into what he shall have wished the new Adam and Eden to be.

Freedom, insofar as it has meaning for autonomous intellect, centers in intellect itself, not in a universal way, but rather, in a particular way. Freedom is justified in and by this particular intellect. That is the arresting, if disturbing, recognition present in that early version of Mrs. Shelley's *Frankenstein*, namely Machiavelli's *Prince*. As Machiavelli makes clear, the "Prince" is to make himself the activating principle of and center of the "city." He must necessarily be antagonistic to any version of hierarchical order that is not sprung operatively from himself, whether an order championed by the old metaphysics or the new Humanism. The Prince is the pinnacle, the operative vortex of being out of whom order proceeds. This is a new Prince, in contrast to old anointed Kings. He can have no concern for dynasty as related to family or tribal history or to metaphysical vision or order. At issue is a particular autonomy sustained by power gathered to the vortex itself. And at its heart is a new primitivism, which I should be content to call provincialism, since it lacks a vision of the complexity of being beyond its presumptions of its own autonomous complexity.

We have remarked the rise of nationalism with the Renaissance, and we may conclude that in autonomous intellect's operation through the city at hand lies the birth of nationalism. Empire, in this respect, is but nationalism become invasively cancerous of being. As we now observe the emergence of the local as recovered from empire's collapse, foretelling a period of political chaos in Russia and Eastern Europe, we may suspect the "civil" disturbances that result as the delayed breaking out of old realities about social structures in nature, of local traditions against nationalistic supressions of those traditions. Gradually suppressed by nationalism's growth, that diversity is forced to be a singleness of collective mind as the prince turns his "city" into a "nation" and then at the next level into an "empire," whether under the auspices of the East India Company in the nineteenth century or our communist empire. I use *communist* here as analogous to Machiavelli's *Prince*. Marx's ideology requires a vortex of common identity, whether that of race or class. But that is but a convenient idea, since to be successfully operative, not a race nor a class, but a Gnostic dictator is the necessity. We find more in common between Hitler's rise under the banner of National Socialism and Stalin's under the banner of International Communism than is sometimes remarked. For banners make obscure a common ground: the "Prince" as vortex of order becomes the focus of that necessary emotional submission of a people, multiple selves turned to the worship of a symbolic Self, seemingly incarnate in a Hitler or a Stalin.

Not only nationalism but much more is born out of autonomous intellect's operation through the city in the name of Renaissance Humanism. Dante realizes the emergence of this new complication to his own existence, himself in exile from his beloved Florence and coming to himself in "a dark wood." If he is to recover the way, he must first recover the proper manner of deportment in the quest for that way. To a degree, he must become Modern himself, but in a sense far removed from the incipient meaning of that term in Renaissance Humanism. And so he must descend to the heart of the City of Dis, whose Prince is always adaptable to the moment, who is always very "modern." Dante, no less than the Modernist artist like Johnson's Diaghilev, discovers the necessity to himself of becoming a new artist, emerging out of old artistic ways while feeling uncomfortably beholden to those old ways. But unlike the Modernist artist, what Dante discovers is the necessity to that becoming lying in himself, in the limits of intellect prescribed by reality from a presumptuous autonomy. He must reach an accommodation with his finitude. If he must, as Ezra Pound is to declare required of the poet, "make it new," Dante (more than Pound) realized that the *it* was fundamentally abiding. As artisan, he could not make *it* whatever he chose it to be—the *it* here ultimately designating being itself. That is the ground in which he at last knows himself bound beyond his temporal moment. Bound to the past and to the future in a present. And that binding by being, as he recovers to his knowledge as artist in the *Paradiso*, is significant of a higher cause of the orders of being, the bindings of reality whereby each thing is the thing it is, whether Dante or the wood in which he finds himself lost. Pound, as a late Dante, set out to build a "paradiso terrestre," to recover to the poet the powers of Machiavelli's prince, only to fail.

Dante, however, realized, as his contemporaries devoted to the new Humanism did not in his view of them, that new ways, new manners, must be established on the old rock of reality which as artisan he could but depend from. If at the top of Purgatory Mountain he allows praise of himself by a contemporary as the maker of "sweet new song," he knew in deep ways that a new song is never made *ex nihilo*. Dante's other late disciple, and a truer disciple than Pound, T.S. Eliot, has been also much celebrated as a Modernist poet, as one rejecting old aesthetics in the interest of discovering those "new commandments" which Sergei Diaghilev declared must govern "a new aesthetics." But Eliot's own testimony through his new art affirms the rock of reality Dante built upon. Eliot comes to speak of it as the Word in the desert, his moments of transport limited to a "still point of the turning world," rather than the sustained poetic flight of Dante's *Paradiso*. His insistence on the point of transcendence proves confusing to some late survivors of Renaissance Humanism, including Pound. Meanwhile, Eliot shows himself glad as one escaped from our "generation of enlightened men."

It is worth our noting that Eliot at his outset had seemed to himself doomed by intellectual autonomy, at first accepted as intellectually respectable. The doom was of an extreme solipsism by denial of intellect as limited from autonomy. But the denial of intellectual limit, the presumption of intellectual autonomy, left him a little world "revolving" upon the axis of the self "like ancient women/ Gathering fuel in vacant lots." That was a condition of intellect he later characterizes in *The Rock*'s "Choruses" as an effect of intellectual desperation whereby "you find explanations/To satisfy the rational and enlightened mind," a mind caught "Between futile speculation and unconsidered action."

By the late nineteenth century, when Eliot is born, Pico's dream has prepared the super-dreamer who, when in a position of power, becomes what Voegelin called the "Modern Gnostic," or what C. S. Lewis will name the "Innovator" or the "Conditioner." The secret word in Pico's formula for the new Super-Adam, authorized by his ventriloquism as if from God Himself, now stands exposed. The touted freedom is the freedom of *power*, derived by an intellectual manipulation of existences, particularly the existences of other intellects. Thus *power* supersedes love as the banner of community. And power may also be called self-love. But just how much that shiny apple proves ashes Eliot dramatizes in an intellect so possessed, singing its own dying self-love, the Modernist J. Alfred Prufrock.

IV

It becomes evident then that in considering Modernism it is well to consider as well its twin, Humanism, through whose continuous support at a level below reflective thought Modernism becomes the ascendant religion from Pico to our day. The two ideological concepts are melded by intellect through their being separated from complex reality. Together, they establish as acceptable the principle Eric Voegelin calls "Modern Gnosticism." The Renaissance humanist such as Pico initially exhibited a tolerance toward the dominant order of social and political institutions that had been established out of Christianity by medieval Scholasticism. A scholar of these humanists remarks that they were not "anti-religious or anti-Christian." But here we suggest a distinction out of a skepticism which the subsequent history of Humanism into our own day seems to warrant. The early humanists could ill-afford opposition to Christianity. Religion as a means, therefore, trading upon the established religion, found pragmatic virtue in shifting the inclination to worship from its orientation to God to an orientation to man himself. With a cautious sentiment of piety, whose object could remain somewhat obscure, the argument could possibly avoid the wrath of the Establishment and at the same time seduce the intuitive necessity to worship, common in intellect, and center it in a new quarter, especially the intuitive desire in the unsophisticated intellect, which through its common sense tends to bear a proper relation to creation. One may more easily rationalize through common sense a deportment to the world bearing pious overtones than through that piety toward the world which understands its relation to the final object of piety, the worship of a Triune God. Culpable man is susceptible.

Strategy dictated to the new Humanism a careful address to Christian authority, in which lay the dominant power of the day, a power sometimes exercised in most decisive ways. And Humanism, if it was to become a force gathering its own power against established power, required at least the nominal consent of the nominal Christian if it was to enter into the courts of power. The history of the period from Occam to Luther reflects no clear divisions of power contended for by orthodox Christianity on the one hand and the new humanist on the other, or at least no division marked institutionally. Humanism finds presence in the citadel of orthodoxy in instances, which when sufficiently advanced spawns a reactionary withdrawal in the name of a "reformation," a reestablishment of the old authority. The ambiguous division of Roundhead and Cavalier in the English Civil War finds such a humanist as Marvell on the Roundhead side, such a Puritan as Lancelot Andrewes (in respect to a "purified" orthodoxy) on the Cavalier side. The relative roles of Lawes or Milton are sufficiently ambiguous as to make it never quite clear-cut that the one or the other stands clearly for or against traditional authority descended from orthodox principles. That period of our history is, in respect to its intellectual nature, sufficiently confused that one must proceed with caution in naming either hero or villain intellect, for intellectual intent is so often buried in action that one may perhaps at best discover a flow, a tendency, rather than a program on one side or the other.

It is only in the nineteenth century, and then more conspicuously in our century, that the inevitable confrontation between Christianity and Humanism, delayed in the accelerating spectacles of events, is brought to issue. Christian authority, founded in the belief in a cosmic order established under the authority of God, begins only at the end of our century to draw itself together to withstand the ideology of Humanism. And it is of considerable interest, in the light of the history of these two inevitable antagonists, that they confront each other, not the one from within an established church and the other from a stand taken in the secular world, but within segments of the fragmented Church itself. Increasingly, common cause emerges from factions beyond denominational distinctions, with a remnant of that old established orthodoxy appearing in a variety of places, just as does the Modernist-Humanist position find advocates joined across denominational lines.

Our current battle between Humanists and Fundamentalists rises in the decade in which Diaghilev toasted "a new and unknown culture," the worship of a new unknown god. The delayed encounter, inevitable from the beginning, becomes public. The encounter had been prepared for public manifestation in the nineteenth century by contentions between Darwinian theory, renamed as a "science" of evolution, and the remnants of Christianity, which had generally lost the metaphysical defenses of belief. Matthew Arnold characterizes their encounter in "Dover Beach" in lines once famous in the halls of academe. Arnold, near Margate sands—where Keats had longed for a metaphysical rescue and where Eliot, in *The Waste Land*, finds intellect capable of connecting nothing with nothing—declares his age "as on a darkling plain/Swept with confused alarms of struggle and flight,/Where ignorant armies clash by night." Those armies, the new scientists and the old religionists, leave Arnold as a survivor of Renaissance Humanism forlornly isolated. For him the now-fading afterglow of Pico finds no hope in either church or science. Perhaps, he suggests, the rescue lies in poetry. It is a suggestion Yeats will champion, centering his dream of poetry as Paraclete in the "holy city of Byzantium" as it existed at the beginning of Renaissance Humanism. As for the Western condition in the 1920s, the situation seemed desperate, with no heroic manifestation of unaging intellect. Poet, politician, or philosopher: among them all the "best lack all conviction, while the worst/Are full of passionate intensity." One attuned to intellect's dire straits is increasingly victim to an engulfing despair, to a blind hope. Such a person vacillates, as Eliot says in that dark period between the two world wars, between "futile speculation" and "unconsidered action." He is at once victim of and perpetrator of a Modernism to which he has been born and from which he seems incapable of escaping. He is alternately pleased by and confused, by being called by skeptics examining his position, a Modernist.

V

The term *Modernist* enters English usage in 1704, with the joint publication by Jonathan Swift of his *Tale of a Tub* and *Battle of the Books*. Thus a pejorative connotation attaches to it from the beginning. Swift's mordant effect upon the word finds locus in his fragmentary mock epic, *The Battle of the Books*, directed against his contemporary Modernists. He pits upstart modern writers against venerable ancients: Milton, Dryden, Hobbes, against Homer, Plato, Aristotle are the principal warriors he sets against each other. One remembers here T. S. Eliot's famous critical phrase "the dissociation of sensibility." Eliot, too, finds a shift to Modernism occurring at about the time of Milton and Dryden, a change detrimental to English letters in that it separated "thought from feeling." Given his distance, Eliot is more analytic, less irascible in his objection to Modernism than is Swift, whose sense of the immediacy of its danger prompts a scathing denunciation through ridicule. Swift's Moderns have as local presiding deity one Monus, who, fearing the fate of his Modernist minions against what even Monus recognizes as the superiority of the Ancients, rouses a goddess to his support: "a malignant deity, called Criticism. . . . At her right hand sits Ignorance, her father and husband, blind with age; at her left, Pride, her mother." All about her throne swarm her offspring, Swift's caricatured version of the current London intelligentsia. "Noise and Impudence, Dulness and Vanity, Positiveness, Pedantry, and Ill-manners." Thus Swift's characterization of the Modernist.

Such a gambit could, in Swift's own day, have some effect, but only of a passing sort, since Modernism seemed breathlessly persuasive. The reaction to his attack has left him with the reputation of bitter misanthropist, though his principal attack is directed against mankind as an abstraction used to justify dislocations of persons from their proper nature as anciently understood. That is, his objection is to the new humanist's dream of reconstituting mankind as a new Adam. Committed to the weapons of the satirist, Swift does not show forth the dialectical premises of his rejection of the Modernist position. Direct analytical opposition as opposed to satiric indirection would not necessarily have had more immediate effect, but his satiric prophecy has a continuing pertinency. One would be hard pressed to find better presentation of "the closing of the American mind" as accomplished through the present academy than in his presentation of the Grand Academy of Lagado in part three of *Gulliver's Travels*. T. S. Eliot was made aware of the intellectual grounds out of which emerge those clashes of armies, not only through his training as philosopher, but because he had read Swift closely as well, and he too began to cast a jaundiced eye upon Modernism.

Swift and Eliot differ, however, in their uses of irony because of an important difference between their intellectual circumstances. Swift directs his assault of scathing words upon Modernism from a position removed from Modernism as an enveloping ideology. Eliot must speak from within it, and as heavily affected by it. Eliot's irony bears a heavy sardonic edge in consequence. It is this difference that makes us aware that Eliot acts out through his poetry a progress as pilgrim, a journey out of Modernism with a perceptiveness about the psychological and spiritual states of his escape that makes him more immediate ally to those contemporary minds who have effectively examined the malady of Modernism by detached autopsies. Such thinkers as Leo Strauss and Eric Voegelin and Richard Weaver, this is to say, arrive at a position removed from the general Modernist malaise, glad as intellects to have escaped its entrapment. Their position is comparable to Swift's in its detachment. Their concern is comparable to Eliot's, however, in that they must resort to a recovery of common sense to a remnant and in an appeal to those yet entrapped by Modernism. Put another way, they must restore reason to common sense, rather than rely on wit as does the satirist. For the satirist assumes an audience sufficiently removed from the object of his attack that his audience enjoys a recognition of irony's focus upon disparity, upon the distance between reality and the pretense to reality in the ideas or persons under attack. It is a commonplace observation now that our age makes satiric art virtually impossible since absurdity is the norm, allowing none of the exaggeration upon which satire depends. Eliot, as a sort of Everyman emerged from the land of Noman, then, proves more suitable to our own prophets who would recover us from entrapment by Modernism. I note, for instance, Eric Voegelin's high regard for Eliot's *Four Quartets* and his repeated choice of texts from them to make his salient points about Modernism's dislocations of the self into our age's dream kingdoms.

The dislocation of the self, the end effect of Modernism, proved baffling and disturbing to Matthew Arnold in the nineteenth century, as to William Butler Yeats and Eliot after World War I, as we have said. Increasingly, alarm over that dislocation, a growing opposition to the justification by Modernists of that dislocation, calls forth *ad hoc* opposition by Fundamentalists from the beginning of this century, and from a "Moral Majority" and "Christian Coalition" at century's end. Such response has been greeted by both amusement at it for its being benighted, since it very often lacks intellectual sophistication, and by shrill alarm insofar as the Modernist intellectual establishment feels itself threatened by a popular reaction to its sway. Whether maintaining a superiority by ridicule or by alarm, that intellectual establishment managed for half this century to delay a rigorous critique of the intellectual issues involved. But in the 1950s there appears a new intellectual, a mind less easily dismissed, which begins the long-delayed critique, and out of that critique there emerges a loose coalition of forces increasingly aligned against Modernist presumptions, conspicuous in social and political affairs. It is a movement rather loosely designated "conservative," which insofar as such a term embraces ambiguous diversity, has lent itself to caricature by the Modernist objects of that incisive analysis.

It is this analytic work which must be recognized, reconciled, and so digested by conservative thinkers if their attempt to recover social and political institutions built upon Eliot's "permanent things" is to be effective. For even among the more sophisticated conservatives, the immediate necessity of opposition to the enemies of the permanent since World War II has resulted in *ad hoc* responses. Under severe weathers, one may find it necessary to build shelter of stick and straw. But having thus gained some respite, a building upon rock with stone is necessary. What we realize, as "conservatives," at the end of our century is not only how lost to Modernists are those grounds on which we find ourselves embattled, but most immediately how lost they are to ourselves. This is to say that we must more thoroughly recover the intellectual authority of our position. We must reassociate the "thought and feeling" to a viable effect. It is also to emphasize how considerable a beginning has been made already by a conservative intelligentsia, a community of mind, diverse among themselves but united in opposition to the illusions of Modernism. It is upon these works that a successful recovery of those permanent things always depends, since permanently fundamental *thing* is man's given nature as rational creature. As for works by that conservative intelligentsia, we may name some of them as important to what will prove a continuing "battle of the books," remembering as we do so what they have in common, lest their differences exacerbate factionalism in the face of that common necessity: the opposition to Modernist reductionisms.

Richard Weaver published his influential *Ideas Have Consequences* in 1948. He followed it with *The Ethics of Rhetoric* in 1952. In that decade, Eric Voegelin changed the nature of political science as an academic discipline, though not yet fully recognized by the academy, with his *New Science of Politics* (1952) and put arresting questions to Modernism in his *Science, Politics & Gnosticism* (1968, portions of it as early as 1958). Leo Strauss's *Natural Right and History* (1953) was followed by his *Thoughts on Machiavelli* (1958). Russell Kirk published *The Conservative Mind* in 1953 and in 1957 (along with others including Richard Weaver and Henry Regnery) founded the quarterly *Modern Age*, specifically devoted to examining Modernism, its advocates, and its causes and effects in the modern world. Thoroughly grounded in history and philosophy and literature, rigorously disciplined as dialectitians, the new species of intellectual began to call Modernism as an idea, and the Modern Gnostic as its advocate, to account.

There had been important harbingers of this renaissance of conservative thought earlier in the century. In books and essays in the 1920s and 1930s, Etienne Gilson and Jacques Maritain exposed elementary fallacies in the Modernist revolt against metaphysics that had seemed till then to carry all before it out of its Renaissance beginnings. What they began to expose was Modernism's false response, which Gilson called Cartesian Idealism, to the complexity of reality. And Eliot, in his lecture at Harvard, "The Modern Mind" (1933), had characterized the aesthetic dimension of Gnostic Modernism, finding in I. A. Richards, for instance, but a latter-day Matthew Arnold, Richards's psychological and linguistic sophistications notwithstanding. Eliot subsequently published critiques of Modernism in his *Idea of a Christian Society* (1939) and *Notes towards a Definition of Culture* (1948). But one of the most telling harbingers of the appearance of a new intellectual upon the confused stage of intellectual history was C. S. Lewis's *Abolition of Man* in 1947.

In his small, but highly effective examination of Modernism, Lewis recognizes that ideology's ancestry lies in Renaissance Humanism. As if echoing Pico della Mirandola's assurance to the new Adam which the new Humanism would create that he could "mold and fashion yourself into that form you yourself shall have chosen," Lewis points to present effects of that intent. For "the power of Man to make himself what he pleases means," says Lewis, "the power of some men to make other men what they please." The advocates of this Modernism are the "Innovators" (the Gnostic theorists) and the "Conditioners" (the Gnostic activists) who have brought mankind to the verge of extinction as human by the mid-twentieth century. Man's intended conquest of nature reveals in the end the abolition of man himself, nature's last crumbling frontier under assaulted by Gnostic intellect. An intent to conquest of nature had been born of Pico's dream, and Francis Bacon initiated a program for its realization, the establishment of power over the physical universe in the interest of man's pleasure. Aided by Descartes's dislocation of thought from the complex reality of existence, empiricism increasingly gave rise to a technology which reduced existence itself to the arena of a physics lost to metaphysical perspective upon existence, a reductionism long underway before its traumatic effect called the

Industrial Revolution changed forever the conditions of man's existence in the world. One may follow the gradual recognition of this
change in Humphrey Jennings's anthology, *Pandaemonium: The
Coming of the Machine as Seen by Contemporary Observers, 1660-1886*,
in which the social world as affected by machine technology is increasingly described as Pandaemonium by some observers in opposition to those who yet foretell a new Eden. (Jennings compiles his
anthology from 1937 to his death in 1950, in response to the conditions of war-time England, and though not published till 1985, the
work is contemporary to Lewis's *Abolition of Man*.) Lewis, looking
about him at the end of World War II as a general euphoria enve-
lopes war-weary Europe, observes that the last frontier has
crumbled: man is on the verge of being abolished from nature. Our
growing mysteries of "artificial intelligence" seem to substantiate
Lewis's point.

Lewis came to his position by a journey in some points parallel
to Eliot's, out of the swamps of Modernism, though he navigated
more through analytical criticism than through poetry. His criticism, anchored in literature, began in the 1930s. He published *The
Allegory of Love* in 1936, the same year Arthur O. Lovejoy published
The Great Chain of Being. E. M. W. Tillyard's *The Elizabethan World
Picture* (1943) opened literature to the metaphysical grounds of metaphor that flourished in the sixteenth and seventeenth centuries, before that "dissociation of sensibilities" occurred which attracted
Eliot's attention. And then, along with that flowering of work by
historians and philosophers in the 1950s there was a sudden rush of
concern for the loss of the ground of metaphor in literature. This
exploration of modern literature tended to focus on nineteenth-century Romanticism, and to that extent lacked the intellectual perspective of Lewis or Eliot or Weaver or Voegelin. Still, there was in this
work a growing disquiet over our Modernist dislocation. The attention centered upon the nineteenth-century Romantic's sense of isolation that seemed occasioned largely by the emergence of economic,
and so new social, forces out of the Industrial Revolution. The new
literary concern, then, looked largely at our poetry from Blake to
Eliot, and from Whitman in American Romanticism. The difficulty

of explaining what had occurred in letters since the late eighteenth century was exacerbated by a confusion: our own century's major poets professed and sometimes believed themselves in radical revolt from Romanticism, and so a continuity in Modernism's effect upon letters seemed the more difficult to establish.

It is appropriate to name some of these works of criticism, the titles themselves reflecting on our point: Robert Langbaum's *The Poetry of Experience: The Dramatic Monologue in Modern Literary Tradition* (1957), Frank Kermode's *Romantic Image* (1957); John Bayley's *The Romantic Survival* (1957); M.H. Abrams's *The Mirror and the Lamp: Romantic Theory and the Critical Tradition* (1958). What proved most troublesome to the Romantic poet in the nineteenth century, as these works in their several ways begin to discover, was his loss of authority in his poetry through the loss of image and metaphor as acceptably grounded in reality. His was a struggle to recover reality to intellect's confidence through his words. Not since Dante had the poet—or critic—so inescapably discovered himself lost in the dark wood of the world, and if he found monsters in those woods, his somewhat desperate engagement of them—general pollution of existence, with man himself the victim—made symptom the apparent cause. A present state of being lost in a decayed world becomes the poet's theme—from Blake and Wordsworth to our own latest Modernist poets. It is the concern conspicuously pursued by Yeats and Pound and Eliot and William Carlos Williams and by all this century's principal poets.

VI

By the 1950s, it had become the critic's growing concern as well, which he began to pursue in psychological and philosophical—in economic and social and political—manifestations. And there was even the beginning at last of a new concern for the necessity of a metaphysical dimension to bring all these concerns into focus, lest the nature of Modernism continue unyielding to comprehension through its diversity as specialized science, sharing no common ground save those established by Modernism itself. If Freud can explain everything except Freud, Lewis says, we haven't a significant purchase upon the reality of mind through Freudianism. And the enlargement of critical concern, the growing tendency to recognize the necessity of some metaphysical vision of mind's relation to reality, began to bring the crucial work of those "philosophical" critics of Modernism, emerging in the 1950s, into even the specialized study of literature itself, often to the discomfort of the specialist who must thereby reconsider his narrow ground as an expert in a narrow segment of intellect's address to reality.

The openness to the possibility of a metaphysical ground to intellectual speculation, whether about literature or politics or social phenomena, owes a debt increasingly realized to this revival of intellect by such conservative thinkers as Eliot, Lewis, Weaver, Voegeln, and Strauss, among others. And in doing so, the literary critic begins to understand Wordsworth's concern for whether image is a mirror merely reflecting isolated intellect or a lamp beckoning and leading intellect to a relation with reality. That is the most ancient of philosophical questions, and so inescapably a modern question long deflected from serious engagement by the presumption that intellect is autonomous. From the end of World War II, some poets and critics began to realize that Gerard Manley Hopkins made purchase upon the concern in his *inscape* and *instress*, a beginning which Maritain had already explicated in *Art & Scholasticism* in the 1920s. That work helps recover us from the pretentions of the new aesthetics proposed by Diaghilev which would "sweep away" traditional understandings. Maritain's book has proved influential upon poets from Eliot to O'Connor and continues of central importance.

Surveying the diversity of the conservative analysis of Modernism, especially that of the 1950s, one has the impression of our entering upon a new Scholastic Age, out of the trauma of intellect's recognition of its isolation. There has been an outpouring of both practical and speculative monuments to intellect, more open to the possibility of surprising discovery than is allowed under presumptions of autonomy. And what increasingly emerges from these new stirrings of intellect in pursuit of reality in the post-World War II world is the recovery of a fundamental desire in intellect itself for a spiritual context for its action. The desire is not always (or is only fleetingly) recognized by many who are nevertheless stirred by it. That is why Voegelin suggests that at this juncture of intellect with reality we very much need a new St. Thomas Aquinas to recover us to metaphysical vision. What I suggest is that the needed work is considerably advanced already through Voegelin's work, and through a now considerable library flowing from the new intelligentsia committed to the "permanent things."

Voegelin is himself a central figure to this recovery of vision, his own work having been focused increasingly in its development upon the reality of our experience of existence. In "Immortality: Experience and Symbol" (1967) he cites Eliot's words from *Four Quartets* as symbolizing the nature of that experience: "History is a pattern of timeless Moments" and "the point of intersection of the timeless with time." It is this point of intersection in conscious experience that he designates by the Platonic term *metaxy*, adding that it designates "the In-Between, in the sense of a reality that partakes of both time and eternity and, therefore, does not wholly belong to the one or the other." Lacking an English equivalent, he designates the Platonic *metaxy* as *presence*, the "point of intersection in man's existence" recognized sometimes by a person, sometimes shared by persons in their recognition of it. Consciousness responds to the *flow of presence*, which is the dimension of its existence both in and not in time. It is the recovery of this sense of participation in reality which recognizes reality as larger than temporal reductions, an ancient recognition always as modern as the openness of consciousness in the particular person to the complexity of reality itself at this present moment. The rejection of that openness, in the Voegelinian and Eliotic view alike, results in the intellect's entrapment in itself. In that entrapment, which Voegelin and Maritain and Gilson see occurring as a result of the Renaissance, the faint hope of recovery emerges out of the intellect's rupturing of its own principle of closure by substituting immanence for transcendence.

In his *New Science of Politics*, Voegelin explores the consequences to Western thought of a reduction of complex *presence*, the rejection of transcendence in favor of an immanence whose late manifestation is the intellect isolated from all save its own self-awareness. What occurs, in a famous Voegelinian phrase, is the "immanentization of the Christian Eschaton," leading to a civil theology whereby the particular intellect establishes itself as autonomous. That is the direct means to its assumption of power over being itself. But that program, implicit in Pico's prediction of a new Adam, leads intellect to the terror of the abyss, with nothingness the only alternative to its isolated self-awareness. Such is the circumstance of Eliot's J. Alfred Prufrock, the highly sophisticated intellect "full of high sentence." Still, such a distortion of reality by intellect is the action necessary, Voegelin says, to the "Modern Gnostic." He requires "the nonrecognition of reality [as] a matter of principle." As Gilson pointed out in seminal essays in the 1930s, this principle assures the ascendancy of Cartesian Idealism over Thomistic Realism.

This same point is made, with the satirist's economy, by Swift in his choice of name for the reigning deity of Modernism, Monus, which catches in an allusive way the root meaning of *moment* and *momentum*. *Modus* follows, celebrating the latest, thus giving an ambiance of intellectual fadism. And lurking in its proximity is an echo of a monk as transformed into supermonk by that transmogrification of the Renaissance Man that follows hard upon Swift's century. But Swift's century also gives birth to Descartes's Idealism and to Leibniz's Monadology, preparing a way for the development of alienated consciousness, such pathetic monads as Prufrock.

The progressive immanentization of Western intellect since the Renaissance reaches an initial dead end in nineteenth century mechanistic determinism, an end seemingly certified by the new Darwinian theory, evolution. That dead end denies to intellect its status as the god of being, as the agent of man's becoming whereby he may make of himself whatever he shall choose. And it is from this dead end that Bergson argues a new principle, a "life force," for which the ontological ground proves more problematic than Anselm's—Anselm's long since rejected by the Modernist spirit. Bergson's was an idea nevertheless seized upon in a revolt against the intellectual despair in the face of mechanistic determinism born of Darwinian theory. Mechanistic determinism as an idea was not new, of course, but it seemed to be given credibility by a theory rapidly turning into a pseudo-science, as it were, the science of evolution, which seemed to promise an explanation of all existence.

We might remark here that the soul's immanent desire for some existence other than itself as an object of worship, deflected to center upon the self by Modernism, will by that deflection cause curious effects in the body social. The current fascination with crystals and pyramids stands for a variety of modes of sectarian worship of the self. It is an action of intellect in its gradual decay from thought, made in desperation against the gradual annihilation of the self as the final consequence of Modernist thought, the final abolition of man. Little wonder, then, that in the 1990s we are plagued by a variety of sectarian religions based in Modernist thought, each in quest of a justification of that vital force inescapably recognized as actual by experience. And by *actual* here, we mean *in act*, the undeniable evidence of a "vital" force. For the "self" once spoken of as "soul" knows it exists: that is the necessary ground beneath any doubting of whether it exists or not.

Having lost this common experience, available to common sense, through the machinations of Modernist thought, Modernists sentimentalize the self. It is little wonder, then, that ersatz religions proliferate, becoming more and more *weird*, in the root sense of that term. Thus we become immersed by sentimentality in a new paganism out of Modernist science.

Concerning this reaction against such reductionism, the attempt at recovering life, which at the popular level becomes rather desperate, we may recall Henri Bergson as an important scholastic theologian to our new paganism at the turn of our century. Let us recall some of his words as we explore our concern for science sentimentalized as the new paganism: "[A]n original impetus of life [passes] from one generation of germs through the developed organisms which bridge the interval between the generations. . . . There are no things, there are only actions. . . . God thus defined, has nothing of the already made; He is unceasing life, action, freedom. Creation, so conceived, is not a mystery; we experience it in ourselves when we act freely." *Creative Evolution* (1907); "The universe is a machine for the making of God." *Morality and Religion* (1932).

The Bergsonian idea, so important for recovery from the mechanistic determinism that entrapped nineteenth-century thought, becomes a sentimental crutch by the end of the twentieth century. One sees it nowhere more clearly than in the environmentalism grown out of an increasingly vague attachment to mechanistic principle. It is in that movement called "green," within which there has grown a special species of Manicheanism. For in the old manifestation of Manichean doctrine, nature itself was the evil principle and the existence of the created world to be attributed in one way or another to a dark force. In the new environmental Manicheanism, the dark force, after first having been reconstituted God out of eighteenth-century rationalism, is now reduced beneath nature: I mean man himself. After the supplanting of God by man's own mind, with nature the instrument through which was established the primacy of man's mind, what now envelops is an antagonistic reaction to mind by a new "pagan," the environmentalist, who but reluctantly consents to an identity as "man." Mind requires religious fervor as spark to a combustion of active energy on nature's behalf, but rational mind is rejected in favor of a mysticism only vaguely remembered as an inheritance from empirical science. That is, "scientific" evidence accepted on faith is imbued with mystical authority, seldom rationally tested. Rather, it is knowledge abstracted from being and taken as absolute. In the upshot, what is considered most evil, most to be deplored, is the existence of man himself. One need only listen carefully to the mystical position underlying the typical *Nature* program on public television to realize that the dominant evil, spawned almost inexplicably, is man himself. For how could nature do this to herself?

In these nature programs, one notes the repeated explanation of color on insect wings, or sexual habits of creatures: adaptation is out of an *intent* precedent to the effect. But an intent is never located in an agent. Intent floats free in the argument of the intentionality of species. At best it is anchored in genetic "memory." One has to conclude that such argument as expressed or implied declares intentional purpose in evolution. Intentionality signifies, however, only as some aspect of mind, and the agency of that intent is never addressed. Chesterton, in his works in general, but helpfully in his little book on St. Thomas, addresses the vagueness of this unanchored thought about "creative evolution" which is now pervasive of popular, emotional responses to "nature." He says: "It is typical of [such thinkers] that they will sometimes rather timidly use the word Purpose; but blush at the very mention of the word Person. . . . [W]e do not need anything but our own common sense to tell us that if there has been from the beginning anything that can possibly be called a Purpose, it must reside in something that has the essential elements of a Person. There cannot be an intention hovering in the air all by itself, anymore than a memory that nobody remembers or a joke that nobody has made." That in large part explains why nature personified is so much a necessity to such thinkers.

In recognizing the impossibility of a floating intention, sentimentalists have therefore made nature a substitute "person." It is this person who seems infected by a sort of acne, a disorder to be extirpated, which must be removed if the elected priests of nature, the environmentalists, can do so. That rash on nature's face is man. In those PBS nature programs, widely used in the public schools to educate our young, the metaphysical position implied is the one found in Walt Disney's *Bambi*. Of that subversive film one should note incidentally that the villain is not man transgressing the order of nature as poacher. He is a hunter. The implication to be drawn is that man must at worst be vegetarian, though one wonders whether lettuce may not cry out under vicious chompings. It is quite another matter for the lioness feeding her cubs, for the boa catching the monkey. The concern for balance in nature fails generally to indict man for excess. *That* he is a hunter is sufficient. For all the hard empirical information about nature, the revelations of particular creatures in their habitats gathered through ever more sophisticated technology, the virtues in such discoveries are erosive of our understanding of "nature" when the perspective is so much distorted as to disallow man a position in the ranks of creation according to his nature.

The origin of this species of sentimentality, paraded in art as scientific truth, we find in Darwin. One passage is worth an extensive quotation, from the 1872, sixth edition, of *Origin of Species*. One notes the inversion in Darwin's account of the eye:

> We know that [the telescope] has been perfected by the long-continued efforts of the highest human intellects; and we naturally infer that the eye has been formed by a somewhat analogous process. [One observes the suppression of purposive agent in the passive "has been formed," the agent avoided.] We must suppose that there is a power, represented by natural selection or the survival of the fittest, always intently watching each slight alteration in the transparent layers; and carefully preserving each which, under varied circumstances, in any way or in any degree, tends to procure a distincter image. We must suppose each new state of the instrument to be multiplied by the million; each to be preserved until a better one is produced, and then the old ones to be destroyed. In living bodies, variation will cause the slight alterations, generation will multiply them almost infinitely, and natural selection will pick out with unerring skill each improvement. Let the process go on for millions of years—and during each year on millions of individuals of many kinds; and may we not believe that a living optical instrument might thus be formed as superior to one of glass, as the works of the Creator are to those of man?

The presence in this passage of the "Creator" is a concession typical of the mechanistic thought of the late nineteenth century. For the God recognized here is "natural selection" or the "survival of the fittest," and the process is that descried in the recent evolution of industrial machinery. With the advantage of our hundred years since Darwin's words, we may observe that the analogy Darwin uses is that of attribution, imposed upon nature from art, specifically from mechanical art. By the time of Darwin's words, railroads conveyed three-hundred-and-seven million passengers annually in a wonder of mechanistic order. But what escapes the wonder gives pause, as it did John Ruskin: "Now every fool in Buxton can be at Bakewell in half-an-hour, and every fool in Bakewell at Buxton." Unless Ruskin's "fool" can be translated as the unfittest, one well questions a principle buried in Darwin's words: the principle of self-correcting, self-perpetuating life as machine, whose latest manifestation to us is the current fascination with Artificial Intelligence.

What the environmentalist does, whether intentionally or thoughtlessly, is assume the authority of nature itself, whose agent he claims to be. By suggesting a purpose to be inherent in nature "from the beginning," but attributable to naught else but "Nature," he establishes a pretense of an Absolute Immanence. That is why I have spoken of this as a modern version of paganism. We must nevertheless recognize that, despite the shallowness of pagan thought, it has grown powerful at the end of the twentieth century. Though its power is not justified by the soundness of its vision, it is highly influential. One well notes also that paganism is an intuitive response through a common sense resident in man. That common sense recalls us to stewardship, but when common sense is not supported by thought in a full exploration of the experience of both humanity and creation, it loses the proper orientation of intellect as steward of being—of creation—and becomes highly manipulative and highly susceptible to manipulation by modern Gnostic thought. The ideal implicit in thoughtless environmentalism is nature as an unexplained throb in the void, before which intellect is required to kneel. Intellect may do so for a time, but then appears that director, the Gnostic intellect, who appropriates nature's power for the restructuring of being—a far remove from intellect as steward of being. At the moment, he is present as genetic engineer.

The Bergsonian *élan vital* gave a moment's respite, at least to the poet. Bergson attracted Eliot to Paris. His arguments, taken up by T. E. Hulme (his translator) and Ezra Pound, issued in Imagism. Robert Frost, from "West-Running Brook" on, continues a Bergsonian. But of the attempt by Bergson to enliven an immanence coiled back upon itself, C. S. Lewis remarks, "the Life Force is a sort of tame God," and suggests that it is "the greatest achievement of wishful thinking the world has yet seen." That is the conclusion Eliot comes to, though the idea continues subtly present in our intellectual community, as if in response to a necessity in man's nature to believe in a Paraclete, for whom the *élan vital* seems a temporal substitute. We witness an amalgamation of Darwin and Bergson in the present climate of thought surrounding the latest version of immanence made holy: genetic determinism. "The violent phase of the madness we call modernity," Voegelin told his audience at the Harvard Divinity School on January 14, 1965, "is accompanied throughout by thinkers who, correctly diagnosing its cause, set about to remedy the evil by various attempts at recapturing reality."

Of these, one is Bergson, but for Voegelin less the Bergson of *Creative Evolution* than of that much later work now largely forgotten, *Two Sources of Morality and Religion* (1932). In that late work, Bergson speaks for an openness of intellect to reality which might effect a community, an open society, though as Voegelin points out his "open society" is quite other than Popper's more secular version. Bergson's concept, for Voegelin, allows a recovery of the transcendent—Bergon's *l'ame ourverte* some rescue to the soul (*nous*) as a particular reality, in contrast to that amorphous soul-substitute, the *élan vital*. The later Bergson is finding as best he may an escape from the entrapment of intellect by the idea of immanence, that Modernist dogma which his *Creative Evolution* had seemed to support.

One sees the line of thought Voegelin develops against immanentism reflected in his topical table of contents for *The New Science of Politics*: "Motives and range of Gnostic immanentism . . . from paraclete to superman. . . . from monasticism to scientism. Modern age as a Gnostic symbol. Modern age as Gnostic revolution. . . . Gnosticism as civil theology. . . . Radical immanence of existence. . . . Disease as the nature of man." In this progressive examination, Voegelin discloses the Gnostic's gradual abolition of man, finding the beginnings in the medieval world: "[M]odern

Gnosticism. . . . is accomplished through the assumption of the absolute spirit which in the dialectical unfolding of consciousness proceeds from alienation to consciousness itself." "Itself" is my
self-awareness cut off from all else. This is an initial sense, an initiating strategy, of self-chosen exile, but it is a beginning whose end is
the agony of alienation, the principal literary and philosophical
theme in Western literature since the rise of Renaissance Humanism. In this perspective, we may observe that this strategy, which is
for Lewis and Eliot and many others the gambit represented in the
Fall of Man presented in Genesis, is for the Modernist his own apotheosis as promised by Pico at the outset of Humanism: by a will to
power over being, man makes of himself what he will. But Adam
and Eve's apple, for all its dire effect, seems to have yielded only
ashes when bitten, as has the modern apple of the ego, bringing us in
this century into (as Voegelin says) the "violent phase of madness we
call modernity." Some historians, philosophers, poets, tend to see in
our current dominant religion of secular Gnosticism a second fall of
man. As Eliot puts it in a chorus from *The Rock*, "Something has
happened that has never happened before . . . . /Men have left GOD
not for other gods, they say, but for no god," in this "age which advances progressively backwards." Knowingly or unknowingly—such
is the nature of man himself—his attempt at no-god is by surrepti-
tious substitution of his own self as god. For some god he must have.
And it proves in our day the god that failed—its lesser idols such as
Marxism, Positivism, Fascism, Progressivism, Historicism, and so on
crumbling all about us.

And so conservative critiques of that dissolution point insistently to the engulfing sense of dislocation experienced by the particular intellect: one's sense of having fallen rather than having been
lifted up in the promised apotheosis of man. What is most distress-
ing to the dislocated self is that there is no appeal, within the principles embraced which have led to exile, save to other intellectuals
who are would-be priests of this new construction of being. But
what dawns slowly to the lonely exile is that, long since, reality has
been deconstructed to elemental force indifferent to particular apo-

theosis. Man is no different from a stone in this perspective. And the final indignity to him, the final abolition of man himself, is that even mechanistic existence dissolves into illusion. One is left self-consumed by *angst* or reduced to ironic submissiveness through *ennui*. It is no insignificant point that Baudelaire concentrates his poetic gift upon *ennui* in *The Flowers of Evil*. Baudelaire recognizes a transformation of *acedia*, that old sin of intellectual cowardice, which though reduced by Gnosticism does not thereby disappear, but requires a naming suited to its contemporary manifestation. As *ennui*, that *acedia* is colored by an intellectual sentimentality, a self-pity, leaving its meager rescue that of pathos. For pathos is the condition of intellect uncertain of its ground. When recovered to certainty, its condition is either tragic, as reflected in Dante's *Inferno*, or comic, as reflected in the *Purgatorio* and the *Paradiso*. That is the realization Eliot comes to, in his *Four Quartets*. And that recognition in him is what Voegelin detects and calls attention to, not as orthodox theologian but as philosopher.

These are the gifts to modern man by the Modernist explicator of being, whose explication is a crafty deconstruction: *angst, ennui, alienation*. It is a spiritual state dramatically suspended by Eliot in his early poetry, long before he approached an understanding of its message to him—in "The Love Song of J. Alfred Prufrock," for instance. The Modernist so caught, if he lacks that key whereby to unlock intellect in an openness to being, must daily advance a new "dream-term" to justify the self. Voegelin names some of them: "By Gnostic movements we mean . . . progressivism, positivism, Marxism, psychoanalysis, communism, fascism, and national socialism." Such "coterie passwords," in Weaver's phrase, suggest to the exiled self for a fading moment some possible community of being, and so long as that suggestion is implicit there is a faint hope of a recovery. One thinks at once of Eliot's "conversion," and of Richard Weaver's, or of Whittaker Chambers's. The *persons* turning a key from within Gnosticism's self-imprisonment are so numerous as to constitute a significant chapter in the history of the emergence of the "Conservative Movement" in our day.

VIII

Common sense will in the end recover intellect to reality. That inevitability is widely witnessed by individuals in the final years of our Modernist century, not only in the spectacular collapse of Marxist dreams of Eden in Eastern Europe, but in the stirrings of a new "Moral Majority" of considerable diversity. That diversity is reflected in confusing attempts to articulate a way to recovery, from Fundamentalist reactions to Modernism, largely *ad hoc*, to an emerging community of intellectuals building on the teachings of Voegelin, Weaver, Strauss, Maritain, Gilson, and others. A considerable family within that community develops from Leo Strauss, who writes a version of Swift's *Battle of the Books* in his *Natural Right and History*. Instead of Swift's local deity Monus, Strauss's presiding deity over Modernism is Historicism. He sets "Modern Natural Rights" against the ancient position on the question: Locke, Hobbes, Nietzsche (among others) against Plato, Aristotle, and ancient historians. And he, too, finds a dissociation in philosophy occurring in the eighteenth century, as did Swift and Eliot, Voegelin and Lewis, Maritain and Gilson. Its representative concept for Strauss is that Gnostic address to time past, present, and to come called Historicism.

"Historicism," he says, "appeared as a particular form of positivism, that is, of the school which held that theology and metaphysics had been superseded once and for all by positive science or which identified genuine knowledge of reality with the knowledge supplied by the empirical sciences." (We have discovered the origins of this position much earlier, though a general presumption of autonomous intellectual authority rather surely becomes pervasively decisive in the intellectual West in the eighteenth century.) Strauss demonstrates the self-contradiction in the historicist's position, but he shows how nevertheless it serves the accumulation of Gnostic power, once the divorce of intellect from fundamental philosophical and theological questions occurs. The pragmatic convenience of a false intellectual position is a point made by both Strauss and Voegelin.

As for the contradiction of the historicist's position, "It seems to show that all human thought is dependent on unique historical contexts that are preceded by more or less different contexts and that emerge out of their antecedents in a fundamentally unpredictable way."

The contradiction lies in the new absolutist presumption by Historicism of a predictable control of history through gnosis, a "spiritual" certainty conspicuous to us in the typical Marxist intellectual of this century who posits inexorable history as justifying radical actions against all opposition to the Marxist position. This new faith, however, contradicts its very premise of a dependence upon unique historical contexts in the present moment of intellectual operation which emerges in "a fundamentally unpredictable way." That built-in contradiction is gradually disguised through Hegel, so that the prophecy of a future ideal seems plausible. The consequence of Hegelian thought is nevertheless an inevitable conclusion that all existence is determined, whether by mechanistic nature, that nineteenth century terror to intellect, or by an increasingly little mechanistic universe, Gnostic man, the emergent terror of the twentieth century. The error is, however, a necessary one for Gnostic thought if it is to accumulate power, though the consequences of error is everywhere about us in the chaotic collapse of intellect itself made spectacular in social and political events. Hegel's prediction of "the end of history" one must take ironically in our moment, though seriously advanced recently. What we see, ironically, is the collapse of Hegelean thought in Eastern European Gnostic structures, a collapse within history itself. Not history, but Historicism, has fallen.

Historicism, Strauss remarks, emerged in "the nineteenth century under the protection of the belief that knowledge, or at least divination of the eternal is possible." That is, a "divination of the eternal" called History as that concept has been divorced from metaphysical questions and relegated to principles of mechanistic Newtonian physics, supported not only by Cartesian Idealism but by Kantean thought as well—those two thinkers more supportive of Gnostic thought than diametrically opposed to each other (a point made effectively by Gilson in *Methodical Realism.*) In this intellectual reductionism of being, man is himself moved toward his own abolition, reduced from the complexity of *person* toward the limits of *individual.* Let us consider what Thomas Henry Huxley has to say on the point in his essay "A Liberal Education" (1868).

A man, says Huxley, must be "liberally" trained in his youth so that "his body is the ready servant of his will, and does with ease and pleasure all the work that, as a mechanism, it is capable of." As for intellect as distinct from body, it is "a clear, cold, logical engine, to be turned to any kind of work, and spin the gossamers [as do poets] as well as forge the anchors of the mind [as do scientists]; whose mind is stored with a knowledge of the great and fundamental truths of Nature and the laws of her operation." What is buried in the statement is the question of agency of this necessary turning of the liberally educated man to "work." Implicit are those Voegelinian Gnostic "Directors" and the Lewisonian "Innovators" and "Conditioners." Almost at once such an innovator and conditioner took charge of an academy, and by extension of the American academy in general.

In 1869, Charles W. Eliot inaugurated Huxley's argument as academic policy at Harvard University in the new "elective system," whereby the student becomes a sort of mechanistic intellectual, trained in body and mind to serve the latest science. President Eliot's view of man is to be, in Huxley's words, "as completely as a man can be, in harmony with Nature." So, too, had been the understanding of the ends of liberal education to the medievalist, but with a distinction. By President Eliot's new harmony the new clerk of Harvard is understood as a part of a machine, the universe, however important a part he may be. That, Huxley remarks elsewhere, is "the progress of that fashioning by Nature of a picture of herself, in the mind of man." Mind is nature's receptacle of power, and Huxley finds the fruits of such power collected in chemistry's formulae, in explosives, medicines, and metals, all "begotten by science upon fact" in nature's womb, the human mind. One well recalls here, given Huxley's illustration, that chemistry is that science born directly out of alchemy in the sixteenth and seventeenth centuries, turned to Gnostic alchemy in its operation upon being in the nineteenth.

IX

At this stage of our exploration of Modernism, we are led to consider two versions of Modernism in tandem: one this American version, infused into the academy by President Eliot, the other a continental version growing in the intellectual community of the Church itself. Together they affect our intelligentsia throughout the first half of our century. That continental version, rising in the Roman Church, but particularly through French Catholic thinkers, called itself "Modernism." This Modernism intended to reconcile Roman orthodoxy to both the emerging modern views of philosophy and to recent social and political views grown out of Enlightenment thinking. In these respects it ran parallel to a growing liberal Protestantism, against which Fundamentalism first began to develop in America at the turn of this century. In both was a rejection of Christian orthodoxy in favor of rationalizing Christianity on the evidence of the new sciences, adapting the latest advances in philology to Darwinian thought. Positivism and evolutionism were conspicuous as authorities for this rejection of what was seen as a lingering and outmoded medieval authority. Religion must be reconciled to science, and belief to historical criticism, with religion and belief thus made subordinate. The position argued by Loisy in the late 1890s rejected the supernatural outright, a move awkward to his Christian followers. Still, religion could have meaning only in terms of the immanent, not the transcendent, a climate of thought that made Bergson welcomed as a prophet of the "Life Force."

After Charles W. Eliot succeeded in establishing his elective system, he came, upon his retirement, to advocate a "Religion of the Future" (1909). He spoke to the Harvard Summer School of Theology, seeking converts. (His distant cousin, T. S. Eliot was a resident at Harvard, the year in which he wrote "Prufrock" and began his "Preludes.") The religion President Eliot proposed as emerging "will not be based on authority, either spiritual or temporal," since "the tendency towards liberty is progressive, and among educated men... irresistible." Translated, the only authority is that which is presently exercised by the latest model of the intellectual built to Huxley's specifications. Nor is there to be any "personification of the primitive forces of nature," nature itself as a personification having already successfully established the new intellectual authority. There will be "no worship, express or implied, of dead ancestors, teachers, or rulers," "the primary object will not be the personal welfare or safety of the individual in this world or the other . . . but . . . service to others, and . . . contributions to the common good." This new religion "will not be propitiatory, sacrificial, or expiatory." Nor will it "perpetuate the Hebrew anthropomorphic representations of God." In short, it will reduce man to an enslavement to Gnostic thought, and specifically to the purveyors of that thought who have accrued sufficient power to enforce his consent. This new religion, dare one say it, is most suitable to the emergence in this century of a Hitler or a Stalin. But, less noticed, it is suited also to the suppression of dissent. There has been since President Eliot a very subtle but effective intellectual Inquisition, as anyone knowledgeable about the American academy or centralized government in this century must acknowledge.

Clearly, something like this "Religion of the Future" is necessary to confirm and establish Huxley's and President Eliot's vision of man as mechanism. One is to be "liberally" trained in the academy and go forth as a secular priest in this new religion, so suited to Pico's dream: man thus programmed can be used "to mold and fashion" himself "like a free and sovereign artificer . . . into that form which man himself shall have chosen." One sees the satiric version of that dream in Orwell's *Animal Farm*. Because we seldom grasp the circumstances pressing upon us—the generalized necessity to satiric art—we may not recognize that in perverse and subtle ways we are more like those animals than we suppose. The intellectual address to reality which allowed Stalin to establish his animal farm, however, bears uncomfortable similarities to our own. Solzhenitsyn in his commencement address at Harvard noted the shocking parallels, shocking many in his audience to outrage. By the time of Solzhenitsyn's address, sixty years after President Eliot's proclamation of a new religion, that new religion had so prospered at Harvard and beyond that Solzhenitsyn's demolition of it by incisive compari son to its Eastern version in the Soviet Union upset the American intellectual community, which reacted in shock at this apostate summoning Modernism to the dock.

With such a program as President Eliot's, one has indeed a shocking recognition that Pico's humanist dream of a new Adam leads to a most radical end. Man finds himself almost abolished, the most endangered species of all. But before the sharp reaction to that danger in the second half of our century, there had already occurred a vigorous resistance, appropriately at Harvard itself. Led by Irving Babbitt, George Santayana, and Paul Elmer More, there rose a defense of quite another version of liberal education than Huxley's and President Eliot's. This was largely a defense of literary humanism, and the position must be distinguished in some respects from a subsequently named "Religious Humanism" that grew more directly out of President Eliot's principles. Nevertheless, the two movements are not radically different, as T. S. Eliot (Babbitt's old student) anticipates in his essay "Second Thoughts on Humanism" (1928), just five years before the birth of the movement "Religious Humanism." Babbitt and Santayana protested the extreme emphasis on vocational education which purported to be "liberal education." Their defense was anchored in Renaissance Humanism, and so in that philosophical principle of immanence, in which lay as well the origins of President Eliot's own "Religion of the Future," seen as fundamentally antagonistic by Babbitt, Santayana, and More.

Subsequent to that battle at Harvard in the first decade of our century, a battle progressively lost by the literary humanist and consequently lost in the American academy in general, there appeared a late amalgamation of European Modernism, which Pope Pius x had condemned in 1907. In the 1930s there appeared a movement calling itself "Religious Humanism." It is against this late manifestation of Humanism and its pervasive influence that the Fundamentalist outcry has risen, an outcry too largely lacking the intellectual foundations needed and already supplied by Eliot, Lewis, Voegelin, Strauss, and their peers, yet not appropriated. "Religious Humanism" was founded by left-wing Unitarian ministers in May of 1933, in the depths of the Depression. It requires no god, save the implicit one, man himself. Religion is the "shared quest for the good life." It is a sentimentalized version of President Eliot's program for a religion, and supplied a quasi-religious justification for Modernism as that ideology was establishing a kingdom in our social and political institutions still suffering the post-World War I chaos. It seemed to justify feeling good about man, and so proved somewhat effective in the advancement of New Deal programs devised out of President Eliot's cadre of "liberally educated" Modernists.

Voegelin, observing the emergence of National Socialism in his own Germany, from which he escaped to America just before World War II, and seeing the American version of "national socialism" on his arrival, is prepared to recognize how the New Deal advocates were quick to use Humanism to advantage in establishing Gnosticism as the nation's orthodoxy, subscribed to, by and large, by both political parties. Even Comte, the father of sociology, which is based in positivistic science, had recognized the necessity of a worship of man by man if political power were to be possible. Comptean sociology, then, becomes the scientific theology operative in political and social institutions, which are always promoted in the name of the only holy of holies, humanity. It is only after World War II that there begins to emerge that considerable body of incisive studies of Modernism, initiated by Lewis's *Abolition of Man*. But the most penetrating critique of American intellectual thought in this century is Voegelin's *New Science of Politics*, in which the progress from Eliot's "Religion of the Future" to Roosevelt's "New Deal" is submitted to an incisive critique.

What the emerging studies of Modernism demonstrate—in a multitude of ways whether examining the economic, literary, social, or political structures now operative—is that Modernism is deleterious to persons and institutions alike, through the erosion of mind and spirit, an erosion whose end is "modern" man: that is, man abolished. The Gnostic substitution of human intellect as the object of intellectual fascination turns intellect in upon itself. Intellect becomes its own end. If at first intellect is the object of its own thought, as in Cartesian Idealism, it consequently becomes the only god of thought or of power. That is a shift whereby, as Lewis says, modern man becomes the judge, with God in the dock. There follows not only a dislocation of man as discrete person, a deconstruction of his nature, but the progressive decay of family, community, institutions, and of a congeries of structures of order derived from or recognized as existing independent of human experience. That old condition of intellect in relation to reality is now only residually remembered to our "wretched generation of enlightened men," the poet Eliot declares in The *Rock*: men who "dash to and fro . . . /Familiar with the roads and settled nowhere/Nor does the family even move about together" as did those ancient nomads before the advent of civilization. We have forgotten that "there is no life that is not in community," settled in place, in a communal progress through the world's dark woods by those oriented to the transcendent.

It is to the recovery of that lost heritage of community that such thinkers as we have summoned are devoted. They attempt to rally a remnant, to stir to life residual memory of reality. They would recover to social and religious man the truth in his inescapable experience of reality, as that experience may be supported by witnesses ancient or modern. Their labor is that of prophets, but not of the Modernist variety who dream futures that collapse and so require new dreams even further removed from reality. They are rather prophets in the most dependable of modes and so in the deepest sense always modern: they would recall us here and now to know but forgotten or rejected things. And they do so by putting the new god Modernism in the dock, along with its companion god, Humanism, examining their offspring incisively: Historicism, Positivism, Progressivism, Cartesian Idealism, Communism, Fascism.

In Wandering Mazes Lost

F ORTY YEARS AS STUDENT, then teacher, at the university level, and now a decade as emeritus lecturing widely, what am I to make of my experiences with academe? I have observed and resisted the erosions of traditional liberal arts education, at first intu-itively, only gradually learning the rich tradition under decay. In doing so, I discovered that the enemies of that tradition were not only the increasing clusters of professional schools and institutions about the residual liberal arts colleges of universities. In general, these clustered appendages were openly set upon ends other than those professed by the liberal arts. Less openly, more insidiously, the erosion proved most destructive from within schools and colleges bearing still the old name. Such erosion developed following World War II (though that erosion had been long under way), and with a variety of public justifications.

But that variety of justification now seems to me to have been occasioned by the emergence of a new popular spirit, against which the tradition hardly proved adequate. Fundamentally, the humanis-tic educator found himself increasingly desperate for survival in the post-World War II academy which increasingly consented to a prag-matism demanding conspicuous reward, so that in large part the academy consented to and helped prepare the way for a society now much given to what we hear lamented as our appetite for conspicuous consumption. It became tempting to the humanistic educator to do what he could to gain an advantage in the competition for the increasing largesse of society. But in return for that largesse society expected the academy to supply an immediate return on its "investment." An academician calling such an alliance of intellectual responsibility and appetitive desire in question might be called an "idealist," with a pejorative burden in that term.

And so perhaps by turning to specializations, the humanistic disciplines within liberal arts colleges might be made desirable. Indeed, the less "practical" disciplines might even, if but surreptitiously, be protected, and ancient and honorable responsibilities to intellectual gifts maintained. At least such might be a palatable justification to the "idealist." The society in its new bent, relieved of deprivations and increasingly desiring material advantages to certify social position, could hardly be expected to require philosophers and historians, though in a prospering economy, these might be tolerated yet awhile within the academy. Accountants and social scientists, on the other hand, might be helpful directly. Economic, political, aesthetic philosophers might yet survive. And even the history of ideas or classical culture might prove disciplines in which the love of truth might yet survive. By century's end, however, such justifications now seem to have been a subdued whistling in a growing intellectual dark.

English literature is the example closest to me, given my concern for the literary arts. In order to survive, and perhaps even prosper, English departments began to turn themselves into service departments to the rest of the university. They accepted, and sometimes actively pursued with growing enthusiasm, the special charge to teach business majors business English, or forestry and "education" majors elementary punctuation and grammar, increasingly needed through the neglect of secondary educational institutions. Run-on sentences, sentence fragments, and pronoun reference became specialized concerns in sixth-grade workbooks. My own department, I remember, for years taught a course in "Agricultural English," not having been prescient in divining that "Computer English" was the

more promising. Elementary school concerns became college freshman concerns, while sixth grades in grammar school staged mock
United Nations debates.

By a concession to servicing students in mechanics, the traditional responsibility of liberal arts to humanize intellect—that is, to
perfect discrete intellectual gifts—was increasingly abandoned.
Rigid, scientifically measured maintenance of standards obtained on
freshman themes: run-on sentences cost a student twenty points; a
sentence fragment cost thirty. The procedure systematized "hour"
credits in "basic" courses. At first, while there was still a lingering
respect for "humanities," those courses began to proliferate, as basic
requirements dictated the hours. Larger and larger classes read less
and less the fundamental texts of Western literature and philosophy
and history. Survey courses touching abbreviated texts prospered,
since at least a "smattering" of traditional intellectual history was
still conceded desirable. (Solzhenitsyn, we remember, engages the
"smatterers" as evidencing the intellectual decline of his beloved
Russia in this century, that term applied to Soviet educators bent
upon a parallel destruction of intellectual gifts.)

In our own academies, as the survey courses multiplied, the principle underlying this blossoming was the intellectual weaknesses of
the students. Such weaknesses at century's end have become the determinant of curriculum. Concomitantly, that principle could also
serve the convenience of the increasingly specialized instructor himself. And that tendency soon enough became elevated to graduate
courses. A build-it-yourself undergraduate curriculum careened toward absurdity.

As for the hapless student, funneled in his freshman and sophomore years into the holding patterns of the changed liberal arts programs, he found concessions to his sense of intellectual deracination.
The limited calendar of requirements for the undergraduate degree
(the number of "credit hours" in "basic" courses required before entering upon his "major") might seem formidable. But then there was
a wide range of choices in satisfying the credit hours. For twenty
hours of humanities (four courses at my institution) he could shop
about—Romance language literature in translation, or English lit-

erature, or American, and presently, Eastern literature and culture, or South American, or African. So long as the necessary hours were satisfied. The student might choose from offerings seemingly enlarged every academic year, and that student tended to do so in the randomness of whim. He could shop about for easy courses or easy teachers. To hold the academic line, given the hoard of undergraduates, there developed (for example) departmental multiple choice or fill-in-the-blank final examinations intended to maintain threshold "standards." Or so the argument held.

Our own survey of the history of the decline of "higher education" is spare, but not a caricature, the details of such procedures differing, but the tendency the same among institutions of higher learning. The overwhelming tendency became fragmentation of fragmentations. Exacerbated by the growing internal competition of department with department, or competition within departments— as between the advocates of English literature in contest with advocates of American literature—the possibilities of catering to student whim while maintaining a respectable catalogue were limitless. And taking advantage of student whim has led at last to the present collapse of undergraduate education, in which students dictate what is or is not intellectually acceptable, so that the vague cause of the "politically correct" must measure the acceptable curriculum.

In this "progress" of higher education since World War II, particularly, there has grown within the academy a cynicism toward curricula as irrelevant. The advantage of the AB or BS degree is like the ink stamp on a beef carcass, a factory product of the academic jungle, as some Sinclair Lewis might put it. By the stamp, one is certified for issue into the real market world. Or by that stamp perhaps he is credentialed into that other unreal world, graduate education—unreal world, in that this higher higher education seems so seldom to recover the person in his intellectual deportment as suited to a membership in the community. For in his pursuit of an ever-the-more-refined specialization requiring above all an esoteric sign language to pursuit, the professional graduate student is likely to find himself the more removed from community in which he is properly member.

If this deportment of my own toward the collapsing academy is somewhat caustic, that manner is perhaps in recognition that irony itself proves no longer salutary to the recovery of language—of signs—toward the truth of things. Indeed, the satirist finds himself impoverished by academic reality at our century's end, endangered by cynicism, though cynicism is by now so pervasive within the academy that the idealist turned cynic is not easily sorted out from the self-centered whose *modus vivendi* is cynicism. And thus we reach the final end of Charles W. Eliot's dream of a new intellectual religion. That dream was of the "expert" as an operative cog in society as machine, the ultimate perfection of wayward evolutionism engaged and controlled by intellect. Through programmed courses, defined in the manufacture of intellect as serving the current demands of society itself, individuals were turned to pragmatic service, through patterns centralized and in the control of the joint establishments of society, the state, and the academy,

One finds Charles W. Eliot's dream in his *Educational Reform* (1898), but the intention is clearer in his address at retirement. In 1869, as a new nation is rising out of the recent terrors of war and the wide destruction of a part of the nation, Eliot anticipates an intellectual "aristocracy which excels in many sports, carries off the honors and prizes of the learned professions, and bears itself with distinction in all fields of intellectual labor and combat." And after looking back upon his own achievements in educational reform, he then looks forward as a John the Baptist anticipating "The Religion of the Future."

In the direction of education in its reform under Eliot's auspices, there lay inevitably a shifting from a responsibility of humanizing intellect. The concern became for a technological, a "grammatical" education in isolated specialties whose end was a "common good" as defined gnostically. Intellect as autonomous, in reconstituting society, must abandon tradition itself, and it must above all deny that orthodoxy which holds that truth is independent of gnostic intellect. The new "grammar" of higher education must, as quickly as possible, abandon the traditional perceptions of human nature, whereby the person is intellectual soul incarnate, whose limits are engaged through formal education underlying the traditional version of liberal arts training. That old perspective was of a tripartite attempt at intellectual unity—a perfection of limited intellectual gifts—involving *grammar, logic,* and *rhetoric.*

We have come a long way in abandoning that old vision of the manner and ends of higher education, only to find ourselves to have regressed, to be the more lost in dark intellectual woods, and the symptoms of that losing of the way appear sharply evident as beams of light—the truth of reality itself—occasionally pierce that darkness. And among those symptoms we discover that not only English departments in higher education but other "departments" engage in particular, isolating "grammars" to establish specializations toward intellectual survival in the dissolving academy. There have appeared not only English 101, but as well Sociology 101 and Philosophy 101 and Economics 101, with but a residue of the old concern for the unity of intellect in its perfections of peculiar, "personal" gifts.

The dislocation of intellectual responsibility, justified by increasing enrollment (presented at once as a burden upon the institution and as proof of its worth), exacerbated the lowering of academic standards and led a spiraling down of intellectual integrity. The university thus burgeoned in measurable ways: the number of faculty (with terminal degrees certifying intellectual authority, in my own neighborhood an authority relative to the geographical distance from my institution of the awarding institutions) and the number of students, graduate and undergraduate, from which followed the ranking for public relations purposes of the institution in respect to legislative grants and research grants from federal agencies and from foundations. (I remember the wave of public relations advertising within our state when our institution was ranked among the "top fifty" institutions of higher education as measured by money spent.) There followed forthwith an increasing bane upon higher education, the concern for the number of publications the faculty could claim, proof positive of their intellectual vitality.

In a market responsive to such concerns journals proliferated and university presses multiplied, increasingly imitating the commercial publishers, having established themselves as necessary to "scholarly" work for which there was no commercial demand. Along the way, a

refinement of prestige, so that in guidelines for promotion committees some journals were marked with an asterisk to signify them as
more significant, relieving such committees of personal judgment.
Thus a "scientific" dimension was implied.

The danger of the entrenched clique protecting its territory from
intrusive threats is everywhere present. Any active faculty professor
of the past quarter century can supply his own illustration to the
point. An instance of my own: recently an editor involved in university publications told me (sadly) that I might well be aware that the
"S" word and the "C" word in a writer's position made for difficulties
with a publication board—the "S" word, "Southern," the "C" word,
"Christian." Sufficiently sophisticated in such matters, one knows
that all depends upon whether the writer assumes the politically correct deportment to the concepts behind those words.

How else shall we measure? Let us count another way or two.
The number of professional organizations in which one holds membership; the number of professional conferences attended and (with
asterisk for committee) the number of papers given at such; and the
number of elected offices held in the professional organization.
Again, my argument lies not with such participation, necessarily, but
with the emphasis on the measure of number, whose ill effect was (as
with publishing lest one perish) a multiplying of conferences and
sections of specialized papers under the organizations umbrella.
What the sophisticated faculty thus involved are likely to know,
however, is that the most significant accomplishment of such conferences was the informal, unlisted, engagement in intellectual community as quite separate from the formal, programmed, meetings. I
suspect this generally true, but it is rather certainly true of those professional gatherings of the "humanities" such as occurred in the 1950s
and into the 1960s within the operations of the MLA and SAMLA and
the like.

Out of a complex of numbers emerged, increasingly, the local
prestige of chaired positions, celebrated as of striking advantage to
students, graduate and undergraduate, in having "name" experts in
residence. In the event, many such "names" were less and less sitting
in their chairs or standing before classes, the "perks" of such chairs

increasingly a release from teaching responsibilities and a budget allowing travel and secretarial help personal to the chair. No wonder that such names (certainly some of them) were more and more on the road in pursuit of higher and higher chairs. The sum of such dislocation of intellectual responsibilities at the local level was the deracination of faculty. I recall my own institution's president praising his own accomplishments: his faculty at that point, he said with pride, was predominantly made up of degreed faculty who had been at the institution *less than ten years.*

Meanwhile, back in the trenches of English 101, I became increasingly aware of a new symptom of the decay of higher education. Presently, the faculties of philosophy or history or biology began to turn to the faculties of English departments for advice on where to place a comma, or begged a judgment as to whether a group of words constituted a sentence—a lingering concern with their professional papers destined to peer review within increasingly isolated specializations. As for the English departments, the drift in literature was away from the relevance of philosophy and history to the imaginative witness in literature, though it became increasingly of interest when the latest of science could be imported to literary analysis. That is what happened, for instance when Freudianism became a substitute science and philosophy and theology in relation to the literary text. And even Heisenberg's "uncertainty principle" had its isolated literary moment.

Such were my observations of decay of higher education underway immediately after World War II, to which concern I began to speak out in the 1950s and 1960s, and have continued to do so ever since—these essays evidence of that attempt. For what concerned me was the accelerating decay of higher education, in consequence of an abandonment of intellectual integrity. There arose a pursuit of pragmatic advantage, even through the liberal arts, still generally assumed central to the concern of higher education. Of course, not realized in the first half of our century was the insidious dislocation of the liberal arts to those specialized concerns effected by Charles W. Eliot as President of Harvard. Thereafter, though gradually, the liberal arts were reordered to serve specializations through his "elective" system of undergraduate education. At the more popular level, by mid-century and in the wake of excited educational expansions of higher education after World War II, the concern for "communication" became dominant, overriding the more fundamental concern for the truth of what was being "communicated," the old responsibility of the liberal arts. Thus what was required as common to a body of students was correct grammar and punctuation, as now a facility in electronic communications techniques is the program of necessity to any higher education. A student's facility with computer equipment is now considered a species of grammar, and some considerable attempt is made to "equip" the student with its fundamentals at the grammar school level.

As for the concern for "grammar" as the basis of higher education itself in the post-World War II world, common sense recognized the virtue of that elementary necessity, though reason did not sufficiently raise the question why such grammar was not the responsibility of grammar schools. And even should one raise such a question the answer was already at hand. Look at the composition of a university freshman! Clearly the necessity was to teach that student sixth-grade proficiencies. The dumbing down of curricula through the dumbing down of texts was underway, the flood leveling to an egalitarian plane of intellect—the new "intellectual playing field." If the flood waters were not so deep, their very horizontal broadness seemed justification enough of the public pumping of resources into the rapidly growing marsh. In the appeals by higher education for more and more waters to wash the educationally unwashed, the intermediaries were the politically appointed governing bodies of institutions (as a general rule) working in concert with legislative committees—representatives of the electorate. These were the pervasive regents and governors and legislators crying the pressing needs, money the matter of communicational concern.

I remember a conversation with our local legislator, an old political pro on such a legislative committee concerned with the attrition rate at our university. We were in my old study above Hurt's Sundries in Crawford, he having offices near me. Mine was a huge, empty room save for a card table with plywood extension to a window sill and a clutter of books and papers. He drew up the other chair to where I sat at my old Remington, took an envelope, and drew a rectangle on it. That was the University, he said. At this end enter x number of students, but at this end, four years later, there exits only—30 percent of the total, 40 percent? I don't remember the precise data. What I remember is his argument that a university is, after all, a species of factory. (He was himself a graduate in law from that university.) Something was wrong with such a system—so little return on such large capital investment And indeed something was wrong. Much was wrong, and of such a complexity of wrongness as to make it difficult to "communicate" with such an elected official, whose concern for his alma mater was a genuine one. How could one make him see that his sentimental attachment to his "alma mater" bore implications that a university is more than a factory, or ought to be, or used to be, or might even be once again?

Meanwhile, if privately consenting to forensic explorations of that alma mater in respect to its mechanical dimension as a machine—a factory—there was yet a necessity for a quite different public address. On either hand, the rhetorical address implied residual recognitions of that through which rhetorical power is possible: on the one hand, the university as a factory, but on the other the university as alma mater, an appeal particularly viable in relation to athletic programs. And by a playing of one false attributive poetry against the other, as if a balance in the truth, the principle educators in the public eye—the administrators of the humming factories—gained purchase in the public sector upon and through its mediators. What it gained was the mother's milk of alma maters, transfused from public funds.

And so there arose an elaborate public relations apparatus in the university devoted to showering the constituencies of the academy with persuasive, often graphic (in several colors) rhetorical defenses of higher education. They promised a diversity of goods and services filling the "felt" needs of the general public in the moment, whatever the moment. The spectacle of this public relations assault was (and is) a curious anomaly. For on the one hand there is the self-elevation and self-congratulation by the academy of itself as servant to community, but on the other is its fear of starvation from public largesse should its stewardship be too closely examined. By our century's end, however, even the public sector has become aware of the disparity between the promises and the actuality of the education the public's sons and daughters were receiving in the academy. Academic decline has become increasingly a scandal to the public patrons of higher education, even if they could only see the problem by analogy of the university as factory.

And so we have reached a crisis, at the close of our century, in which an erosive pragmatism serving inherent selfishness has led to intellectual anarchy on our academic reservations. On those reservations, where the academician and student alike are separated from the larger supporting body of community, restless natives grow more restless. Students and faculty agitate for intellectual anarchy in the name of "multiculturalism" and attempt to establish by fiat a letter of the law replacing community manners as those manners are properly dependent upon intellectual integrity: the letter of the law called the "politically correct." It is in witnessing to the necessity of a recovery of intellectual integrity as fundamental academic concern, in the interest of restoration of community itself, that these essays have been written, early and late.

Indeed, it might be said that the concern all along has been to recover our understanding of the nature of liberal arts as "higher education" from that transferred Hesienberg uncertainty in which the only principle is the isolated, separated, alienated intellect. How else may it see itself, so conditioned, except as a small closed world, one such as T. S. Eliot recognized as he turned poet in his attempt to escape the Modernist cul de sac? In his first moment, he could only respond with sardonic irony, wiping a hand across the mouth and laughing at the futile prospect of community, seeing the "worlds" of isolated persons as isolated "like ancient women/Gathering fuel in vacant lots," refugees surviving minimally, no longer persons as *homo viator.* (Eliot's poem, prophetic in its imagery of the "inner city" was written in 1910-11). Out of that awakening, for Eliot, follows a long and difficult journey, until he arrives (as he says in his last important poem) at the place from which he set out and sees that place with understanding for the first time. My hope is that, through these es-says, a reader will experience such a journey, as I believe myself to have experienced that journey properly common to us, whereby we recover somewhat a vision of ourselves. We cannot live as lost hol-low men, with a "Headpiece filled with straw," wandering a land-scape of broken columns in vacant lots. What one desires and hopes for is a recovery of the *person* as member in that *body* called commu-nity. But that recovery is heavily dependent upon our seeing again, and understanding for the first time, that as intellectual soul incar-nate, it is ordinate intellect that effects the integrity of person and in turn the integrity of persons, that body in communion with reality called "community."

Index

A Note on the Author

Marion Montgomery, scholar, critic, and award-winning poet and novelist, is one of America's preeminent men of letters. From 1954 until 1987 he taught English literature at the University of Georgia and became an authority on Eliot and the Southern Agrarians. A prolific author, he has published twenty books—including a monumental three-volume cultural critique, *The Prophetic Poet and the Spirit of the Age*—and some 250 articles. His work appears frequently in *First Things*, *Crisis*, *Modern Age*, and a host of other journals. A frequent campus lecturer, Mr. Montgomery lives and writes in Crawford, Georgia.

This book was designed and set into type
by Mitchell S. Muncy,
with cover art by Stephen J. Ott,
and printed and bound
by Thomson-Shore, Inc.,
Dexter, Michigan.

The text face is Caslon,
designed by Carol Twombly,
based on faces cut by William Caslon, London, in the 1730s
and issued in digital form by Adobe Systems,
Mountain View, California, in 1989.

The paper is acid-free and is of archival quality.

17